Williams College

Phi Beta Kappa, Gamma of Massachusetts, Williams College : charter, register of officers and members, constitution, united chapters, etc.

Williams College

Phi Beta Kappa, Gamma of Massachusetts, Williams College : charter, register of officers and members, constitution, united chapters, etc.

ISBN/EAN: 9783741151255

Manufactured in Europe, USA, Canada, Australia, Japa

Cover: Foto ©ninafisch / pixelio.de

Manufactured and distributed by brebook publishing software (www.brebook.com)

Williams College

**Phi Beta Kappa, Gamma of Massachusetts, Williams College :
charter, register of officers and members, constitution, united
chapters, etc.**

PHI BETA KAPPA,

GAMMA OF MASSACHUSETTS,

WILLIAMS COLLEGE.

Charter, Register of Officers and Members, Constitution, United Chapters, etc.

COMPILED BY

E. B. PARSONS,

CLASS OF '59.

SYRACUSE, N. Y.:
HALL & LYON, STATIONERS, PRINTERS AND BOOK BINDERS.
1887.

"More than a hundred years ago, in 1776, Thomas Jefferson organized the Phi Beta Kappa Society in William and Mary's College, Virginia. It was probably based upon the philosophic clubs which were then common among the collegiate students of France and the Continent." Hon. Stewart L. Woodford, *Oration before the New York Delta, 1896.*

"Phi Beta Kappa would be glad to hang Mr. Jefferson's portrait in its hall, but unfortunately there is not a shadow of a line of evidence to show that Mr. Jefferson had anything to do with it." Rev. Edward Everett Hale, *Article in the Atlantic Monthly, July, 1879.*

Introductory Note.

The original chapter, founded at the College of William and Mary in 1776, granted charters to the Alpha of Connecticut at Yale, Nov. 13, 1780 and to the Alpha of Massachusetts at Harvard about the same time. These Alphas, the original Alpha of Virginia having become extinct, established the Alpha of New Hampshire at Dartmouth in 1787 and from that time other charters have been granted.

As time went on the Society came near being what Mr. Hale calls it in that magazine article,—"A Fossil from the Tertiary",—when the Harvard chapter at its Centennial and largely by the personal force of Mr. Hale himself quickened new interest in the Fraternity by proposing a union of the chapters. This was effected and the delegates who met at Saratoga the first week of September, 1883 constituted the First National Council. The number of chapters now enrolled is twenty-two. The council meets every three years. Prof. William D. Whitney, '45 is a member of the Senate and Rev. E. B. Parsons, '39, represented Williams College in the Council of 1886.

A provisional society was formed at Williams July 12, 1864, recognition was at once secured from the Alpha of Massachusetts and the Charter was presented by Hon. William Everett, July 30, 1867. By vote of the Society, August 1, 1864, the "Honor Men" of all preceding classes were made members of the Fraternity. Some other graduates of recognized scholarship were also elected. A Catalogue was published in 1868.

At the annual meeting in 1886 a committee was appointed to consider any change that should be made in the Constitution of the Society. The Chairman of that committee, Rev. A. C. Sewall, '67, gave careful attention to the matter and at the annual meeting of 1887 presented a report that was unanimously adopted and the result of which is given in this pamphlet. Meanwhile another member of the committee obtained by correspondence the preference of the Society as to the form of the Catalogue. The Catalogue was then ordered by the Society, June 29, 1887, Judge J. M. Barker, '60, in the chair.

Here are the names of a little more than six hundred of the twenty-nine hundred and seventy-five Alumni of Williams College.

As to the value of such a Catalogue. Perhaps it will encourage in good scholarship those now in College. Perhaps it will have some suggestions in the pending College issue between brain and brawn. Perhaps it will help our youth realize that it pays to study faithfully and master thoroughly the foundation studies. No one will claim that all the rich fruitage of Alma Mater's service in the world is visible in this quarter-section, but any one looking over these pages intelligently will see that good work in College gives fair assurance of the same in after life.

The compiler wishes to acknowledge the kindness of all who have helped him so generously. The abbreviated sketches of deceased members have been gathered from all available sources. The sketches of living members have been obtained as far as possible from the men themselves. It has been difficult to discriminate between books and pamphlets. It is hoped that what is given will indicate correctly the line of a man's literary work. It is too much to expect that entire accuracy has been obtained. Those who notice mistakes of any kind will please send word to

REV. E. D. PARSONS,

Baldwinsville, Onondaga Co., N. Y.

Officers.

PRESIDENTS.

1864-1876.	Hon. Emory Washburn, LL. D.,	Class of 1817.
1877-1886.	Prof. William Dwight Whitney, LL. D.,	" 1845.
1886-1887.	Hon. Stephen Johnson Field, LL. D.,	" 1837.
1887——.	Hon. Francis Henshaw Dewey, LL. D.,	" 1840.

VICE-PRESIDENTS.

1864-1867.	Prof. John Tatlock, LL. D.,	Class of 1838.
1868-1869.	Hon. Joseph White, LL. D.,	" 1838.
1870-1876.	Prof. William Dwight Whitney, LL. D.,	" 1845.
1877-1883.	Rev. Peter Miles Snyder,	' 1878.
1884-1885.	Hon. James Madison Barker,	" 1860.
1886-1887.	Hon. David Ames Wells, LL. D.,	' 1847.
1887——.	Prof. Luther Dana Woodbridge, M. D.,	" 1873.

SECRETARIES.

1864-1867.	Rev. Nathaniel Herrick Griffin, D. D.,	Class of 1834.
1868-1869.	William T. R. Marvin, M. A.,	" 1834.
1870-1883.	Prof. Arthur Latham Perry, LL. D.,	" 1852.
1884——.	Harlan Hoge Ballard, M. A.,	" 1874.

TREASURERS.

1864-1867.	Hon. Joseph White. LL. D.,	Class of 1836.
1868-1869.	Prof. Arthur Latham Perry. LL. D.,	" 1852.
1870-1881.	Prof. Charles Franklin Gilson, M. A.,	" 1853.
1881-1885.	Charles Marsh. M. A.,	" 1855.
1886——.	George Franklin Mills, M. A.,	" 1882.

ORATORS AND POETS.

1865.	Pres. Thomas Hill, DD., LL. D.,	Orator.
1865.	Edward W. D. Canning. M. A.,	Poet.
1866.	Rev. Thomas March Clark, D. D., LL. D.,	Orator.
1867.	Pres. Julius Hawley Seelye, D. D., LL. D.,	Orator.

RECORDING SECRETARIES.

Spoor '65, Myers '66, Günster '67, Woodward '69, Powell '69, Judson '70, McLean '71, Eaton '72, Birge '73, Watson '74, Locke '75, Reute '76, Ogden '77, Gross '8, Fiske '79, Hale '80, Bassett '81, Matz '82, Pratt '83, Bicknell '84, Cobb '85, Kilbon '86, Clarke '87.

Charter.

Charter Members.

Members.

1797.

Asa Burbank.

Physician. b. Wn. Ma. 177?. T. Salutatory, Ttd. W. C. 1796-1800. M. A. s. Med. Wn. 1801-2 p. Med. Lanesboro, 1806-09. Prof. Mat. Med. and Obst. Berk. Med. Sch., 1825-6. M. D. same 1828. p. Med. Albany, N. Y., 1805-06. M. R. S. 1st Pres. Alumni. d. Wn. 1848.

Homer Towner.

Physician. b. N. Fairfield, Ct., 1771. L. French o. s. Med. Wn. 1801-2 p. Med. Vt. 1808-12; Ohio, 1812-17. d. Ohio, 1817.

1799.

Egbert Ten Eyck.

Lawyer. b. Bern. Co., N. Y., Apr. 18, 1779. Pres. L. Salutatory. s. Law, Albany, 1806-8 mem. Assembly 1813-18; Speaker, 1818. mem. Const. Conv., 1821. M. C. 1823-5. Judge Jeff. Co. Court. d. Watertown. Apr. 11, 1844.

1802.

Henry Halsey Childe.

Physician. b. Pittsfield, Ms., June 7, 1783. L., M. A. s. and p. Med. at home. Organized Berk. Med. Sch. Sept. 1822. M. D. same, 1823. Prof. Theor. and Prac. Med. same, 1822-62. Lect. Med. Bow'doin, &c.; Woodstock, Vt.; Columbus, O. Ma. H. of R., 1816, 1827. mem. Const. Conv., 1821. Senator, 1837. Lieut. Gov. Ms., 1843. Dem. Cong. Ct., Pittsfield, 1850-64. Pres. Berk. Bib. Soc., 1862-4. M. M. S. d. house of son-in-law, Boston, Mar. 24, 1868.

1803.

Calvin Briggs.

Physician. b. Cummington, Ms., May 10, 1776. T. Salutatory, M. A. M. D. Harv., 1808. M. M. S. p. Med. Lancaster, 1808-?; Marblehead. 1810-38. d. there, 1858.

1805.

Israel Williams.

Lawyer. Pres. L. Salutatory. s. Law, Wash. Co., N. Y. M. A. p. Law, Greenwich, 1807-30; Albany. 1830-40. d. Apr. 28, 1840.

1806.

Samuel Rossiter Betts.

Lawyer. b. Richmond, Ms., June 8, 1787. l. Lenox. T. s. Law, Hudson, N. Y., 1808-9 Sullivan Co., 1810-13. Army, 1813-4. M. C., 1815. Judge U. S. Dist. Court, S. N. Y., 1827-68. LL. D., W. C., 1830. m. dau. of Judge Dewey, Wn. 1818. d. N. Haven, Ct., Nov. 3, 1868.

Chester Dewey.

Clergyman. b. Sheffield, Ms., Oct. 25, 1784. Pres. L. s. Theol. Stockbridge, 1806-8. Tut. W. C. 1808-10. M. A. also Yale, 1808. Prof. Math. and Nat. Phil. W. C., 1810-27. Prof. Chem., Nat. His. and Nat. Phil. Berk. Med. Sch., 1822—M. D., Yale, 1825. Prin. Sch., Pittsfield, 1827-36; Rochester, 1836-50. Prof. Nat. Sci. Univ. Rochester, 1850—D. D., Union, 1838. LL. D., Williams, 1850. A. A. S. A. P. S. d. Rochester, Dec. 15, 1867.

Elizur Goodrich.

Lawyer. b. N. Haven, Ct., 1788. T. Salutatory. s. and p. Law. Hartford. smts. H. of R. Ct. m. dau. Gen. Champion. d. Hartford. Nov. 8, 1808.

Theodore North.

Lawyer. b. Goshen, Ct., 1780. T. Valedictory. M. A. s. and p. Law, Chenango Co., N. Y. d. Elmira, 1848.

1807.

John Bascom.

Clergyman. b. Chester, Ms., Dec. 29, 1794. T. Salutatory. A. T. S., 1809-11. Ord. Jan., 1814. Pas. Presb., Smithfield, Pa., 1814-5; Geneva, N. Y., 1815-38. m. Laura Woodbridge, Glastenbury, Ct., Sept. 3, 1810. d. Geneva, Mar. 3, 1889.

Abel Cutler.

Clergyman. b. Sudbury, Ms., Feb. 14, 1781. T. Valedictory. A. T. S., 1807-10. R. M., Russell's Mills, N. Y., 1810-5. Ord. Oct. 24, 1816. Pas. Congr., Yarmouth, N. S., 1816-32. rem. Northampton, Ms., 1849-39. d. there Feb. 27, 1869.

John Nelson.

Clergyman. b. Hopkinton, Ms., 1786. f. Worcester. Tut. W. C., 1808-10. M. A. s. Theol. Worcester. Ord. Leicester, Mar. 4, 1812. Pas. Cong. there, 1812-71. pub. "Evening," "Gatherings from a Pastor's Drawer." Trustee W. C., 1808-33. D. D., W. C., 1843. m. Zibiah Bigelow, May 4, 1812. d. Leicester, Dec. 6, 1871.

Richard Salter Storrs.

Clergyman. b. Longmeadow, Ms., Feb. 6, 1787. f. W. Haven. Ct. A. T. S., 1807-10. M. A., also Yale, 1803. Ord. Braintree, Ms., July 3, 1811. Pas. Cong. there, 1811-73. D. D., W. C. and A. C., 1838. m. thrice; one son, Rev. Dr. Storrs, of Brooklyn. d. Braintree, Aug. 11, 1873.

1808.

Joseph Boles.

Lawyer. b. Blandford, Ms., Oct. 2, 1782. Salutatory. M. A. s. and p. Law, Salem and Union Village, N. Y., 1811-50. Judge Court Com. Pleas, Wash. Co., N. Y. Eld. Ref. Ch. m. Anna Eights, Albany, Oct. 16, 1813. d. Union Village, Feb. 11, 1868.

Gordon Hall.

Missionary. b. Tolland, Ms., Apr. 8, 1784. Valedictory. A. T. S., 1811. M. A. Ord. Salem, Feb. 6, 1812. For. M. Bombay, 1816-26. m. Margaret Lewis, Bombay, Dec. 19, 1816. d. of cholera on a missionary tour, Mar. 20, 1826.

Francis Le Barron Robbins.

Clergyman. b. Norfolk, Ct., 1787. Prec. L. Greenfi o. s Theol. Worcester and Lee, Ms. M. A., H. M., N. H. and Vt., 1811-6. Ord Apr. 24, 1816. Pas Cong. Enfield, Ct., 1816-50. m. Priscilla Alden, 1817 (d. 1840). m. Hannah Cook, Danvers, Ms., Jan. 1, 1848. d. Enfield, Ct., Apr. 6, 1850.

1809.

Josiah Clark.

Clergyman. b. Northampton, Ms., 1788. T. Salutatory. Prin. Acad. Leicester, 1809-16. M. A. Ord. Rutland, Vt., June 2, 1818. m. Asenath Edwards, Northampton. d. 1846.

Samuel Austin Talcott.

Lawyer. b. Hartford, Ct., Dec. 31, 1789. L. Valedictory. s. Law, Whitesboro, N. Y. Att. Gen. N. Y., 1820-6. m. Rachel Skinner. m. Mary K. Stanley. d. New York, Mar. 19, 1852.

1810.

Justin Edwards.

Clergyman. b. Westhampton, Ms., Apr. 25, 1787. Valedictory. A. T. S., 1811. Ord. Dec. 2, 1812. Pas. Cong. Andover, 1812-77; Boston, 1828-9. Sec. Am. Temp. Soc., 1829-36. Pres. A. T. S., 1836-42. Sec. Am and For. Sab. Union, 1842-9. res. Andover, 1849-53. D. D., Yale, 1827. d. Bath Alum Spa., Va., July 24, 1853.

Lorrin Chittenden Hatch.

Clergyman. b. Granville, Ms., Mar. 14, 1789. T. Salutatory. A. T. S., 1811. d. 1812.

Daniel Kellogg.

Lawyer. b. Amherst, Ms., Feb. 10, 1791. L. s. Law, Newfane, Vt. p. Law, Rockingham, 1818-65; Brattleboro, 1865-73. U. S. Dist. Art. Vt., 1835-41. Pres. Const. Conv., 1843. Vt. H. of R., 1845. Judge Sup. Court. Vt., 1845-56. Pres. Elector, 1864. Vt. Senate, 1865-6. LL. D., Univ. Vt., 1855. m. Miranda Aikin, St. Albans, 1847. d. Brattleboro, May 10, 1875.

1811.

Charles Augustus Dewey.

Lawyer. b. Wm., Ms., Mar. 18, 1788, (son of Hon. Daniel Dewey, Judge Sup. Court, Ms., and Treas. W. C., 1793-1811). Prec. L. a. Law with his father. M. A. p Law, Wo., 1811-30; Northampton, 1830-30. Dist. Att. W. Ms., 1830-?. Judge Sup. Court. Ms., 1837-66. Trustee W. C., 1841-66. LL. D., Harv., 1850. m. Frances A. Henshaw, May 18, 1810, (d. 1831). m. Caroline H. Clinton, July 18, 1834. (d. 1854). d. Northampton, Aug. 28, 1866.

Herman Halsey,   East Wilson, Niagara Co., N. Y.

Clergyman. b. Bridgehampton, N. Y., July 18, 1788. Logian, Salutatory, A. T. S., 1814-3. Ord. May 15, 1816, H. M. Ky. and (N., 1816 N. Pas. Presb. Boyne, N. Y., 1819-31; Cambria, 1831-5; Niagara Falls, 1830-39; East Wilson, 1849-. m. Sophia Woodworth, Bridgehampton, June 15, 1820; seven c.

Cyrus Yale.

Clergyman. b. Lee, Ms., May 17, 1798. T. Valedictory. Ord. Oct. 18, 1814. Pas. Cong., N. Hartford, Ct., 1814-34, 1836-34; Ware, Ms., 1834-7. Adelphic Un. o., 1827. m. Amanda Bradley, Lee, Nov. 9, 1838. d. N. Hartford, May 21, 1854.

1812.

Alonzo Christopher Paige.

Lawyer. b. Schaghticoke, N. Y., July 31, 1797. Prec. L. Salutatory. a. Law, Schenectady; Admitted, 1879. M. A. also Union. 1816. p. Law. 1819-69. Reporter Court Chancery, 1849-48. mem. Assembly, 1889-81. N. Y. Senate, 1850-3. Judge Sup. Court. N. Y., 1847-51, 55-57. mem. Const. Conv., 1867. LL. D., W. C., 1860. Annual o., 1832. Eld. Pres. Ch. m. Harriet Mumford. July 11, 1838; six c. d. Schenectady, Mar. 31, 1868.

John Woods.

Clergyman. b. Fitzwilliam, N. H., T. Valedictory. a. Theol. Kindge, 1816-8, M. A. Dart., 1816. Pas. Cong., Warren. 1814-66; Newport, 1844-51; Fitzwilliam, 1851-61. d. there, 1854.

1813.

Elisha Dow Barrett.

Clergyman and Physician. b. Montgomery, Jan. 19, 1790. T. Salutatory. a. and p. Med. W. Va., 1814-45. a. Theol., 1845-6. Pas. Glade Silver, Pa., 1836-40; Leatherwood, 1841-9. p. Med. Granville, O., 1850-9. Ind. Agt., Yankton Dak., 1861-3. res. Assumption, Ill., 1863-78; Kedalia, Mo., 1878-80. m. thrice; sixteen c. d. Sedalia, Nov. 6, 1880.

Reynolds Bascom.

Clergyman. b. Chester, Ms., 1790. T. Valedictory. Tut. W. C., 1813-7. M. A. A. T. S., 1816-8. Ord. Jan. 8, 1817. Chy. M. Charleston, S. C., 1831-8. Prin. Acad. and Pas. Presb. Camden, 1846-7. d. there, Oct. 6, 1847.

William Cullen Bryant.

Poet, Editor, Lawyer. b. Cummington, Ms., Nov. 6, 1794. Wrote "Thanatopsis," 1816. a. and p. Law, Plainfield and Gt. Barrington, 1815-25. M. A., 1819, also Columbia, 1827. Phi Beta Kappa Poem, "The Ages," Harv., 1821. Ed. N. F. Review, 1825; N. Y. Evening Post, 1826-78; pub. several Vols. Travels; many editions Poems; trans. "Iliad," 1870; "Odyssey," 1871. LL. D., Union, 1831, also N. Jersey, 1873. L. H. D., Univ. State N. Y., 1870. A. A. S., Pres. Elector, N. Y., 1867. M. H. S., N. Y. m. Fanny Fairchild, Gt. Barrington, 1821 (d. 1866). Pres. Alumni, W. C., 1869. d. New York, June 12, 1878.

Orville Dewey.

Clergyman. b. Sheffield, Ms., Mar. 28, 1794. Prec. L. Valedictory. A T. S., 1816-8. Ord. Dec. 17, 1822. Pas. Unit., N. Bedford, 1823-33; New York, 1835-18; Boston, 1857-61. D. D., Harv., 1839. pub. "Problems of Human Destiny," "The Old World and the New," and many sermons. m. Louisa Farnham, Boston, Dec. 30, 1820. d. Sheffield, Mar. 21, 1882.

Caleb Rice.

Lawyer. b Conway, Ma. Apr. 4, 1788. f Westfield. Prea. L. Salutatory. a. and p Law. Westfield and W. Springfield, 1815-31. Sheriff Hamp. Co., 1831-51. rea Springfield, 1844-78; 1st Mayor same, 1852-3; Prea. and Treas. Ma. Life Ins. Co., 1851-78. m. Marietta Parsons Stebbins, July 16, 1828. d. Mar. 1, 1873.

1815.

Epaphras Clark.

Lawyer. b. Westhampton, Ma. June 29, 1790. T. Valedictory. a and p. Law. W. Springfield, 1815-7; Granby, 1817-30; S. Hadley, 1830-3; Enfield, 1844-63. d. 1863.

Franklin Sherrill.

Teacher. b Richmond, Ma., Aug. 2, 1795. Prea. L. Salutatory. A. T. S., 1815-8. M. A. Tut. Middlebury. Prin. Westfield Acad. Tea. Madison, N. Y. d there, 1850.

1816.

Flavel Stebbins Gaylord.

Clergyman. b. Hartland, Ct., Aug. 62, 1795. L. Salutatory. A. T. S., 1816-80. Ord. Nov. 6, 1818. H. M., Ohio, 1826-4; Pas., Sparta, N. Y., 1845-8; Gorham, 1850-56. Prin. Acad., Prattsburgh, 1856-67. Pas., Naples, 1847-52. Hopewell, 1854-60. d. Feb. 8, 1868.

Joseph Bachellor Goddard.

Clergyman. b. Pelham, Ma. Aug. 17, 1790. L. Greek o. e. Theol., Northbridge. Pas. Londonderry, N. H.; Pitcairn, N. Y. m. Lucy Lincoln, Sept. 3, 1865. d. Pitcairn, 1842.

Jonas King.

Missionary. b. Hawley, Ma., July 80, 1792. T. Philosophical o. A. T. S., 1818-2. Ord. Charleston, S. C., Dec. 17, 1819. F. M. Jerusalem, 1819-2. Prof. Orient. Lit., Amherst, 1822-3. F. M., Greece, 1826-63. D. D., N. Jersey, 1862. pub. four Vols. d. Athens, Greece, May 22, 1869.

Stephen Taylor.

Clergyman. b. Tyringham, Ma., Feb. 20, 1795. f Lenox. Prea. L. Valedictory. Tut. W. C., 1817-9. M. A. Tea., Boydtown, Va., 1829-42. A. T. S., 1822. Ord., 1844. Pas., Richmond-Va., 1840-45, 1847-53. Prof. Excl. His. U. T. S., Va., 1843-5. Pas. Abingtton, 1855-62; Petersburg, 1848-7. D. D., Emory and Henry, 1847. d. Richmond. Mar. 4, 1856.

1817.

Henry Walker Bishop.

Lawyer. b. Richmond, Ma. Apr. 12, 1798. f. Lenox. Prea. L. Valedictory. M. A. a. and p. Law. Richmond and Lenox, 1820-6. Register Probate, 1835-51. Judge Court Comn. Pleas, 1851—. Trustee, W. C., 1847-70. LL. D., W. C., 1865. m. Sarah Bulkley, Wn., 1846. d. Lenox, Apr. 18, 1871.

William Eastman.

Clergyman. b. Granby, Ma., Jan. 4, 1796. Prea. L. Greek o. P. T. S., 1820. Tra. Ga. H. M., Ky. Tea. Orid, N. Y.; Newton, Mich. d. there, Feb. 16, 1853.

Medad Pomeroy.

Clergyman. b. Southampton, Ma. Apr. 4, 1792. T. Phil. o. Tea. Aurora, N. Y., 1817-9. a Theol., Auburn. Pas. Preab., Cayuga Bridge, 1821-83; Elbridge, 1833-80; Cayuga, 1840-54; Wellsburg, 1854-6; Ithaco, 1856-61. m. Lilly Maxwell, Owasco, May 5, 1819. rea. Auburn. 1861-7. d. there, 1867.

Emory Washburn.

Lawyer. b. Leicester, Ma., Feb. 14, 1800. T. Salutatory. a. Law with Judge Dewey (W. C., 1811). M. A. p. Law, Leicester, 1821-9; Worcester, 1829-30. Ma. H. of R., 1848, 1827, 1869, 1876; Senate, 1841-2. Judge Court Com. Pleas, 1848-7. Governor Ma., 1854. Lect. and Prof. Law Harv., 1856-76. LL. D., W. C. and Harv., 1854. A. A. S. Hair Bd. Ed., 1866-70. M. H. S. Trustee W. C., 1843-51. Prea. Phi Beta Kappa, 1854-76. pub. "His. Leicester," "Sketches Ma. Jud. His," "Law of Easements," "Law of Real Property." m. Marianne Giles, Walpole, N. H., Nov. 2, 1830; three c. d. Cambridge, Ma., Mar. 18, 1877.

1818.

Homer Bartlett.

Lawyer. b. Granby, Ma., July 19, 1793. f. Westfield. L. a Law with Hon. Daniel Noble (W., C., 1793). Cash. Bank, Ware, 1834-36. Agt. Manf., 1836-7. Lowell, 1837-40; Boston, 1840-74. Ma. H. of R. 1833. Trustee W. C., 1834-40. m. Mary Starkweather, Wn., 1840. m. Mrs. Louisa Hubbell, Albany, N. Y. d. Boston. Mar. 30, 1874.

George Wyllys Benedict.

Teacher and Editor. b. Stamford, Ct., Jan. 11, 1796. T. Phil. o. Tut. W. C., 1819-22. M. A. Prof., Math. Nat. Phil., Chem., also Sec. and Treas., Univ. Vt., 1825-47. Ed. Free Press, Burlington, 1847-26. VI. Senate, 1864-5. LL. D., Univ. Vt., 1857. m. Eliza Dewey, 1826. m. Mrs. Elvira Kellogg. d. Burlington, Sept. 24, 1871.

William Augustus Porter.

Clergyman. b. Spencertown, N. Y., Oct. 8, 1798. T. Valedictory. Tut. W. C., 1819-21. P. T. S., 1823-4; A. T., K., 1824-5. X. A. o. Prof Gr. and Lat., Mor., Phil. and Phet., Univ. Vt., 1826-30. m. Mary Noble, Wn., 1828. d. there. Apr. 30, 1830.

Royal Wells Smith.

Clergyman. b. Rowe, Ma., 1790. T. Greek o. d. Harv. Div. Sch., Sept. 8, 1821.

John Whiton.

Clergyman. b. Stockbridge, Ma., Feb. 14, 1794. f. Lenox. Prea. L. Haldeatory. A. T. S., 1820-1. Ord. Salem, Nov. 2, 1822. City M., 1822-5; Pas. Granville, N. Y., 1826-9; Salem, 1830-6; Enfield, Ma., 1837-41; Amherst, 1841-2; W. Stockbridge, 1842-49; Wolcott, N. Y., 1849-62. Trustee W. C., 1832-3. d. Wolcott. Nov. 25, 1864.

1819.

John Clark Brigham.

Clergyman. b. N. Marlboro, Ma., Feb. 69, 1794. T. Salutatory. A. T. S., 1819-22. M. A. Bro. Agt M Am., 1822-6. Ord. Oct. 10, 1822. Cor. Sec. Am. Bib. Soc., 1827-62. D. D., Jefferson. d. Brooklyn, N. Y., Aug. 10, 1862.

Gerard Hallock.

Editor. b. Plainfield, Ma., Mar. 8, 1800. T. Greek o. M. A. Ed. Telegraph, Recorder, Boston, 1824-8; Journal of Commerce, New York, 1828-41. d. Jan. 4, 1866.

William Allen Hallock.

Clergyman. b. Plainfield, Ma., June 2, 1794. T. Valedictory. A. T. S., 1819-22. M. A. Ord. Oct. 2, 1822. Rev. Am. Tr. Soc., 1825-80. D. D. Rutgers, 1850. pub. Life "Harlan Page." "The Venerable Mayhew," "Moses Hallock," "Justin Edwards," and several Tracts. m. Fanny Leffingwell Lathrop, Norwich, Ct., Sept. 1, 1833 (d. 1867). m. Mrs. Mary A. Lathrop, Rowe, Ma., Nov. 19, 1848. d. New York. Oct. 2, 1880.

William Richards.

Clergyman. b. Plainfield, Ma., Aug. 22, 1793. L. Phil. o. A. T. S., 1819-22. M. A. Ord. N. Haven, Ct., Sept. 12, 1822. F. M. Haw. Islands, 1822-38. Rec. State. Amb. and Min., Haw. K., 1834-47. m. Clarissa Lyman, Northampton. Oct. 28, 1822. d. Honolulu, Dec. 7, 1847.

1820.

Charles Baker.

Lawyer. b. Conway, Ma., 1798. T. Valedictory. M. A. s. and p. Law, Wa. Killed by lightning. Conway, May 28, 1822.

Judah Ely.

Clergyman. b. Sharon, Ct., 1794. T. Phil. o. A. T. S., 1823. H. M., Isle of Shoals. d. England, 1841.

Elijah Thayer.

Physician. b. Buckland, Ma., 1794. T. Greek o. d. 1836.

Alvan Wheeler.

Physician. b N, Marlboro, Ma., Nov. 30, 1797. T. Salutatory, Tut. W. C., 1821-4. M. A. M. D. Berk. Med. Sch., 1824, p. Med. Paterson, N. J., and (N. Barrington Ma., 1824-28. Far. Binghamton, N. Y., 1825-66. m. Harriet Buckley, Wa. d. Houston, Del., Oct. 16, 1869.

1821.

Erastus Cornelius Benedict.

Lawyer. b. Branford, Ct., Mar. 19, 1802. T. Tut. W. C., 1804. M. A. s. and p. Law. New York, 1824-60. New York Bd., Ed., 1850-63; Regent, 1855-80; Chancellor, 1873-67, mem. Assembly, 1858, 1861; Renair, 1873. Ll. D., Rutgers, 1863. M. H. H. Trustee W. C., 1855-80, Alumni o., 1849. Donor Prizes W. C. Ed. Ref. Ch. pub. "American Admiralty," "Run Through Europe," "Medieval Hymns." d. New York, Oct. 22, 1840.

Emerson Davis.

Clergyman. b. Ware, Ma., July 15, 1798. Prea. L. Valedictory. Prin. Acad., Westfield. 1821-2, 1825-30, Tut. W. C., 1822-3. M. A. s. Theol., Wa. D. D., Harv., 1845. Trustee W. C., 1835-66; V. Prea. W. C., 7839-86. Pas. Westfield, 1836-62. d. there, June 8, 1866.

Lucius Field.

Clergyman. b. Northfield, Ma., Aug. 21, 1798. L. Salutatory. Tut. A. C., 1822. M. A. A. T. S., 1825. Ord. Jan. 18, 1826. Pas. Tyringham, 1826-2. d. Northfield, June 1, 1864.

William Cullen Kittredge.

Lawyer. b. Dalton, Ma., Feb. 23, 1801. T. p. Law. Rutland, Vt., 1824-60. Vt. H. of R., eight yrs.; Speaker, two yrs.; Senate, two yrs.; Judge Co. Court, six yrs.; Lieut. Gov., one yr. Thrice m. d. Rutland, Vt., June 11, 1869.

Henry Lyman Sabin.

Physician. b. Wn., Ma. May 19, 1801. f. Lenox. L. M. D. Berk. Sch., 1822. p. Med., Chatham, N. Y., 1824-8; Wa., Ma., 1829-44. Ma. Senate, 1857. M. H. S. Trustee W. C., 1829-41. Prea. Wn. Cong. Ch., 1824-41. m. Lucy Whitman; m. Abby Benjamin; five c. d. Wa., Feb. 24, 1864.

1822.

Parsons Cooke.

Clergyman and Editor. b. Hadley, Ma., Feb. 18, 1801. T. Greek o. a. Theol. Wn. M. A. Pas. Ware, 1826-35; Lynn, 1836-64. Ed. Puritan Recorder. D. D., Lafayette, 1849. W. C., 1862. m. Hannah Markweather, Wa. m. dau. Rev. Dr. Woodbridge. d. Lynn, Feb. 16, 1864.

Joseph Hyde.

Lawyer. b. Lee, Ma., (son of Rev. Dr. Alvan Hyde) Sept. 8, 1879. f. Lenox. L. Salutatory. Tut. W. C. 1824-5. M. A. s. and p. Law. Catskill, 1827; New York, 1828-31. Agt. and Asst. Treas. Am. Bib. Soc., New York, 1831-46. Ed. Madison Sq. Presb. Ch. Tea. Sheffield, Ma., 1848-78. m. Catherine M. McEwen, New York, July 30, 1831; seven c. Phi Beta Kappa sons '56 and '60, grandson '87. d. Stamford, Ct., July 29, 1879.

Chalres Alfred Lee.

Physician. b. Salisbury, Ct., Mar. 3, 1801. f. Lenox. L. Phil. o. M. A. M. D. Berk. Med. Sch., 1825. N. Disp. New York, 1828-30. Prof. Mat. Med. Geo. Med. Coll., also Univ. City N. Y., also Univ., Buffalo; Prof. Med. Jur. Univ., City N. Y. pub. "Physiology," etc. m. Hester A. Mildeberger, New York, 1826 d. Peekskill, Feb. 14, 1872.

Jonathan Edwards Woodbridge.

Clergyman. b. Worthington, Ma., June 14, 1801. T. Valedictory. Tut. W. C., 1826-6. M. A. Law, 1829-8. P. T. S., 1831-1. Ord. May 24, 1835. Pas. Worcester, 1835-8; Ware 1838-49. Assoc. Ed. Puritan Recorder, 1849-55. Tea. Auburndale 1855-64. m. Catherine Markweather, Wa. Nov., 1884. m. Lydia F. Poole, Boston, Sep. 22, 1850. d. Hartford, Ct., Nov. 16, 1877.

1823.

Elisha Hunt Allen.

Lawyer. b. N. Salem, Me., Jan. [illegible] 1804. L. Salutatory. s. and p. Law. Burlington and Brattleboro, Vt. Bangor, Me. [illegible], Me. H. of R. five terms; speaker of same. M. C., 1849. p. Law, Boston, 1847-8. Consul Haw Is., 1849. Chief Just. Sup. Court Haw Is., twenty yrs. Min. Finance and Amb. Haw. Kingdom 1870-69. LL. D., Colby, 1869. m. Sarah E. Fessenden 1847 (d. 1845). m. Mary H. Hobbs, 1857, five c. d. Washington, D. C., at Pres. Reception, Jan. 1, 1883.

Thomas Pierson Allen.

Merchant and Teacher. b. Hinsdale, Me., 1875. L. Valedictory. Charleston, S. C., 1848-61, m. Sarah P. Bell, 1884; two sons. d. Greenville, Oct. 1887.

Ebenezer P. Niles.

Teacher. b. W. Stockbridge, Ma., 1797. T. Greek o. Camden, S. C., 1848-[?]. d. there 1857.

Royal Loomis Porter.

Editor. b. Wn., Ma., Feb. 24, 1801. T. Phil. o. Ed. Traveller, Boston, 1840, Ma. H. of R. m. Sarah A. Pratt, June, 1831. d. Charleston, S. C., June 9, 1844.

1824.

Henry Davis.

Lawyer. b. N. Haven, Ct., Feb. 14, 1805. L. Salutatory. A. T. S., 1827. M. R., also Hamilton. Ord. June 8, 1835. Law. Utica, and Syracuse, N. Y., 1849-54. m. Emily Turner, Huntsville, Ala., Jan., 1834. d. Austria, Sept., 1844.

William Hervey.

Clergyman. b. Kingsbury, N. Y., Jan. 22, 1793. T. Phil. o. Tut. W. C., 1825-6. M. A. P. T. S., 1826-7. Ord. Sep. 24, 1830. m. Elizabeth Smith, Hadley, Ma., June 20, 1830. P. M. India, 1830-2. d. May 14, 1832.

Mark Hopkins.

President Williams College. b. Stockbridge, MA., Feb. 4, 1802. T. Valedictory. Tut. W. C., 1825-7. M. A. M. D., Berk. Med. rich., 1829. Prof. Mor. Phil. and Rhet. W. C., 1830-61; President, 1836-72 ; Prof. Mor. and Intel. Phil., 1836-87 ; Prof. Theology, 1858-87. Trustee W. C., 1830-87. A. A. S. Pres. A. B. C. F. M., 1857-87. D. D. Dart., 1837, also Harv., 1841. LL. D. Univ. State N. Y., 1857. pub. "Lectures on the Evidences of Christianity," 1846 ; "Miscellaneous Essays and Discourses," 1847 ; "Lectures on Moral Science," 1862 ; "Baccalaureate Sermons," 1862 ; "Law of Love, Love as a Law," 1869 ; "An Outline Study of Man," 1873 ; "Strength and Beauty," 1874 ; "The Scriptural Idea of Man," 1883, and many addresses and articles. m. Mary Hubbell, Wn., Dec. 25, 1832; four W. C. sons, '58, '66, '68, '71. d. June 17, 1887.

Charles George Judd.

Lawyer. b. Wn. Ma., Oct. 14, 1802. T. Greek o. s. Law, Ithaca, N. Y., 1831-7. M. A. p. Law. Havana, 1838-51 ; Penn Yan, 1851-66. Dist. Att. Yates Co., 1836-41. Ed. Presb. Ch., 1863-66. m. Amelia H. Goodrich, Pittsfield, Ma., Feb. 22, 1832. d. Penn Yan, N. Y., Dec. 1, 1866.

1825.

Alonzo Calkins.

Physician. b. Waterford, Ct., Nov. 27, 1804. I. N. London. T. Greek o. Tut. W. C., 1834-6. M. A. M. D. Coll. Phys. and Surg. N. Y., 1841. p. Med. Ala. and Ga., 1841-8 ; Brooklyn, N. Y., 1848. pub. "Opium and the Opium Appetite." d. Hammondsport, N. Y., Mar. 3, 1878.

David Dudley Field,   ) Broadway, New York City.

Lawyer. b. Haddam, Ct., Feb. 18, 1805. L. s. Law, Albany and New York. Admitted 1828. p. Law, New York, 1830-80. M. A., 1828. LL. D., W. C., 1855. Code Com. N. Y., 1857. mem. Institute Int'l Law, also Assn. Ref. and Codif. Law of Nations. M. C., 1876. pub. "Sketches over the Sea," 1833. "Reform of the Judiciary," 1846. "Codes of Civil and Criminal Procedure," 1850. "Outlines of an International Code," 1872. "Speeches, Arguments and Misc. Papers," two Vols., 1884. Alumni o., 1851. Endowed Professorship W. C. Indlt Observatory, etc. m. Jane L. Hopkins (d. 1855). m. Mrs. Harriet Davidson (d. 1864). m. Mrs. Mary E. Carr; three c. ; Phi Beta Kappa son, '30.

David Addison Noble,

Lawyer. b. Wm. Ms., Nov. 9, 1802. T. Salutatory. p. Law, Albany. Hudson, New York, 1830-33. Monroe, Mich., 1837-70 ; Mayor, 1849 ; Mich. H. of R., 1845 ; M. C., 1838. m. Sarah A. Shaw, Leansboro, Ms., 1833 ; three c. d. Monroe, Oct. 13, 1871.

Norman Spencer Sprague.

Lawyer. b. W. Poultney, Vt. L. Valedictory. Probably killed with Fanning's troops in Texas, 1836.

Lyman Thompson.

Teacher. b. Pownal, Vt., Apr. 7, 1808. T. Phil. o. Tea. Red Hook, N. Y., 1827-34, Prattsbill, 1834-40, N. Adams, Ms., 1848, Port Chester, N. Y., 1851-57. m. Tryphosa M. Parker, Pownal, Vt., Apr. 18, 1836. d. Port Chester, N. Y., Sep. 6, 1857.

1826.

Levi Fisk Claflin,   South Toledo, Ohio.

Teacher and Manufacturer. b. Westhampton, Ms., July 31, 1801. f. Andover. T. Salutatory. M. A. Tea. Pittsfield, 7 yrs; Bridgeton. N. J., 7 yrs; Steubenville and Dayton, O., 6 yrs. Paper Manf. Dayton and S. Toledo since. m. Elizabeth P. Dickinson, Pittsfield, Ms., Apr. 15, 1831 (d. 1857); m. Martha Cushman, Middlesex, Vt., Feb. 25, 1879; three sons. Dea. and Eld. in Church.

Albert Hopkins.

Teacher. b. Stockbridge, Ms., July 14, 1807. L. Phil. o. Tea. W. C., 1827-9. M. A. Prof. Math. and Nat. Phil. W. C., 1829-38; Prof. Nat. Phil. and Astro., 1838-68; Prof. Astro., 1868-72. Built first Astro. Obs. in this country, 1835. A. A. S. LL. D., Jefferson, 1859. Noon Prayer Meeting. W. C., 1858-72. Ord. Dec. 23, 1869; Pas. White Oaks. m. Louisa Payson, Portland, Me., Aug. 25, 1841, (d. 1860). m. Elizabeth Kilby, Dec. 30, 1862. d. Wm., May 24, 1872.

William Hyde,   Ware, Hampshire Co., Mass.

Teacher, Lawyer, Banker. b. Lee, Ms. (son of Rev. Dr. Alvan Hyde) Aug. 16, 1808. f. home. Lenox and Hadley. L. Tea. Catskill, N. Y., 1826-7. M. A. s. Law. Lee, 1827; Springfield, 1829-30; Admitted Nov., 1831; p. Law, Springfield, 1830-1. Cash. and Pres. Bank, Ware, Senate, Ms., 1851. Trustee, W. C., 1859-77, Williston Sem., 1859-80, A. T. S., 1858-4; Overseer A. C., 1848-59. Corp. Mem. A. B. C. F. M., since 1852. pub. "History of Ware," 1847. m. Harriet Newell Sage, Blandford, Ms., July 4, 1838; three c., son W. C., '76. dea. Cong. Ch., 1847-84.

John Morgan.

Teacher and Clergyman. b. Cork, Ireland, Nov., 1802. L. Valedictory. Tea. New York and Law. Theol. Sem., 1824-34. Prof. Bib. Lit. Oberlin, 1835-81, also Hebrew, 1846-72. Ord. 1837. D. D. W. C., 1857. pub. "The Gift of the Holy Ghost," "Holiness Acceptable to God," "Christ's Missionary Charge." m. Mary A. Dewey, 1829 (d. 1830). m. Sophia Dewey, 1831 (d. 1862). m. Elizabeth M. Leonard, 1836 (d. 1873). Two c. d. Oberlin, Sep. 27, 1884.

William Codner White.

Clergyman. b. Sandisfield, Ms., 1802. L. Greek o. P. T. S., 1829-6. Ord. Feb. 18, 1832. Pas. Presb. Orange, N. J., 1833-55. d. there Feb. 7, 1858.

1827.

Joseph Anderson.

Farmer. b. Shelburne, Ms., Dec. 4, 1795. f. Deerfield. T. Phil. o. Tea. N. Salem and Deerfield, 1827. Pas. Univ. Ch. and Farmer, Shelburne. Pres. Co. Agrl. Soc. m. Dolly A. Lyman, 1830. m. Thankful E. Stevens, 1841; three c. d. Shelburne, Feb. 17, 1868.

James Morrison Arnell.

Clergyman. b. Goshen, N. Y., Sep. 23, 1808. Pres. L. Greek o. H. M. Ala. Pas. Presb. Ashwood, Tenn., 1833-50. Wife and five c. d. Mar. 4, 1850.

James Ballard.

Clergyman. b. Charlemont, Ma., Apr. 27, 1806. Pres. L. Salutatory. M. A. Tea. Heath. 1827-9; Bennington, Vt., 1829-37. Pas. Cong. Grand Rapids, Mich., 1838-46. Far. and Tea. 1848. m. Emeline Blaisdell, Agr. 68, 1831; three c. d. Grand Rapids, Jan. 7, 1894.

Nathan Brown.

Missionary. b. N. Ipswich, N. H., June 22, 1807. T. Valedictory. Tea. and Ed., Brandon, Vt., 1827-31. M. A. s. Theol. Newton, Ms., 1831-2. F. M. India, 1832-55. Ed. Am. Baptist, 1856-71. F. M. Japan, 1872-86. Wrote "Missionary Call," 1827. Trans. Bible and Hymns. Pres. Am. Philol. Soc. D. D., W. C., 1854. m. Elizabeth Ballard, 1830. d. Japan, Jan. 1, 1886.

Mason Noble.

Clergyman. b. Wm., Ma., Mar. 19, 1809. T. P. T. R., 1829-2. Tut. W. C., 1829-31. Ord. Feb. 15, 1832. Pas. Presb. Washington, D. C., 1832-3. New York, 1839-50. Baltimore, 1850-1; Tea. Washington, 1851-3. Chap. U. S. N., 1854-73; Pas. Presb., Washington, 1870-81. D. D., W. C., 1868. m. Anne C. Pleasants, Harrodsburg, Ky., four sons W. C., '55, '62, '65, '66. pub. many sermons. d. Washington. Oct. 24, 1881.

1828.

Alonzo Clark.

Physician. b. Chester, Ms., Mar. 1, 1807. T. M. A. also Dart.. 1844. M. D. Coll. Phys. and Surg., N. Y., 1835. also Berk. Med. Sch., 1843. Prof. Anat. and Patho. Univ., City N. Y. Prof. Path. and Prac. Med. Colum., also Dean and Pres. Med. Fac. same. Pres. N. Y. N. Y. mem. Acad. Sci. N. Y., and Acad. Med. Pres. Coll. Phys. and Surg., N. Y. LL. D., Univ., Vt., 1884. d. Sep. 13, 1887.

Henry Richard Hoisington.

Clergyman. b. Vergennes, Vt., Aug. 23, 1801. T. Greek o. Auh T. R., 1828-31. M. A. Ord. Aug. 30, 1831. Pas. Presb., Aurora, N. Y., 1831-3. F. M. and Pres. Batt. Coll. Ceylon, 1833-50. Pas. Cong. Wn., 1854-6. Centre Brook, Ct., 1857-8. pub. "The Oriental Astronomer." 1848. m. Nancy Lyman, Chester, Ms., Sep. 31, 1831; six c. d. Centre Brook, May 16, 1858.

Fordyce Mitchell Hubbard,   Raleigh, N. C.

Clergyman and Teacher. b. Cummington, Ma., Jan. 15, 1809. I. Hadley, Prva. L. Phil o. Tut. W. C., 1830-1. M. A. Prof. Lat. Lang. and Lit. Univ., N. C., 1840-68. Tea. St. John's Sch., Manlius, N. Y., 18 yrs. Rector, Newbern, N. C. 5 yrs.; Raleigh since 1880. pub. "Life of Gov. Davie." D. D., Trinity and Colum., 1860. m. Martha Henshaw Bates, Northampton, Ms., May, 1832; two c.

Edward Lasell.

Teacher. b. Schoharie, N. Y., Jan. 21, 1809. T. Valedictory. Tut. W. C., 1830-33. M. A. Prof. Chem. W. C., 1833-54. Founded Lasell Sem. m. Ruth Whitman, Wn. d. 1852.

William Pitt Palmer.

Pres. Ins. Co. b. Lee, Ms., Feb. 22, 1805. Pres. L. Law. Med. Tea., 1829-34. Ins., 1834-54. pub. Poems. m. Clara Gardner, Fishkill, N. Y., 1832; six c. d. Brooklyn, May 2, 1884.

Joseph Lyman Partridge,   Brooklyn, N. Y.

Teacher. b. Hatfield, Ms., June 7, 1804. I. Hadley, Pres. L. Salutatory. Tut. W. C., 1832-4. M. A. A. T. R., 1834. Tea. Leicester, 1834-42. Assoc. Ed. Puritan Recorder, 1848-54. Justice of Peace 14 years. Mer. New York, 1855-7. Supt. Schs., Lawrence, Ms., 1858-61. Collec. Int. Rev., 1864-73. Treas. Manf. Co., 1873-4. res. Brooklyn since 1879. m. Zibiah Nelson Willson, Leicester, Ms., Aug. 9, 1837; three sons, .

1829.

Simeon Howard Calhoun.

Missionary. b. Boston, Ms., Aug. 15, 1804. T. Tea. Springfield, 1829-32. Tut. W. C., 1833-4. M. A. Ord. Oct., 1836. Agt. Am. Bib. Soc., Turkey, 1837-44. Mis. A, B C F M., 1844-75. D. D., W. C., 1864. m. Emily P. Reynolds, Sep. 19, 1849; five c. d. Buffalo, N. Y., Dec. 14, 1876.

William Hicks.

Teacher. b. Bennington, Vt. T. Valedictory. d. 1832.

Sardis Brewster Morley,   Pittsfield, Mass.

Clergyman. b. Otis, Ma., Sep. 17, 1804. f. Stockbridge. T. Phil. o. Tra. Winsted, Ct., 1867-8). M. A.. W. C. and Yale. Y. T. R., 1833-4. Tea. Springfield, Ma., 1834. Pas. Bloomfield and Attleboro, 1844. Mis. Am. Tr. Soc., 1867-8. rea. W. Hartford, 1869-50. Pas. Attleboro, 1851-7. rea. Wo. 1857-68.; Andover, 1868-7; Pittsfield since 1867. m. Anne Clarissa Treat, Hartford, Ct., 1834; four c., two Phi Beta Kappa sons, W. C. '60, '82.

Samuel Irenaeus Prime,

Editor and Clergyman. b. Ballston, N. Y., Nov. 4, 1812. T. Greek o. P. T. R., 1832. Ord June 4, 1835. Pas. Presb., Ballston, 1835-6; Matteawan, 1837-40. Rec. Am. Bb. Soc., 1840. Ed. Presbyterian, 1840-50. Ed. N. Y. Observer, 1842-85. D. D., Hamp. Hidney, 1864. Trustee W. C., 1865-83. pub. "The Old White Meeting House," 1845. "Life in New York," 1845. "Death of Little Children," 1850. "Travels in Europe and the East," 1855. "The Bible in the Levant," 1859. "Power of Prayer," 1859, "Letters from Switzerland," 1860. "Memoirs of Rev. Nicholas Murray," 1856." "Five Years of Prayer." 1864. "Fifteen Years of Prayer." 1872. "The Alhambra and the Kremlin." 1873. "Under the Trees." 1874. "Life of S. F. B. Morse," 1874. "Irenaeus' Letters," and many other volumes. m. Elizabeth Thornton Kerneys. m. Eunice Le Mot Williams, Ballston, N. Y. Four c. d. on summer trip, Manchester, Vt., July 18, 1885.

George Ashley Williams,

Student. b. Salem, N. Y. Prea. L. ap. Salutatory. d. before Commencement, 1869.

Jacob Merritt Howard.   1830.

Lawyer. b. Shaftsbury, Vt., July 10, 1805. T. s. and p. Law, Detroit, Mich., 1832-71. Mich. H. of R., 1838. M. C., 1843. Att. Gen. Mich., 1854-60. U. S. Senate, 1862-71. LL. D., W. C., 1865. pub. "Secret Memoirs of Empress Josephine," 1841. m. Catherine A. Shaw, Ware, Ma., Oct. 8, 1835; seven c. d. Detroit, Apr. 8, 1871.

Eli Thornton Mack.

Teacher. b. Granville. N. Y., May 18, 1808. l. Prea. Phil. o. Tut. W. C. 1833-4. M. A. Tra. Granville, 1834-50; N. Brunswick, N. J., 1851-5; Guilford. Ct., 1855-9; N. Haven, 1859-62; Flatbush, N. Y., 1863-74. m. Abbie M. Savage, Salem, N. Y., May 18, 1844; three c. res. Brooklyn, 1874-6. d. there Feb. 2, 1880.

Benjamin Robbins Sheldon,   Rockford, Ill.

Lawyer. b. Randsfield, Ma., Apr. 15. 1812. f. Stockbridge and Lenox. T. Salutatory. s. Law, Yale. p. Law, Pittsfield, Ma., 1840-3; Galena and Rockford, Ill. since 1844. Judge Circ. Court, Ill., 1864. Judge Sup. Court, Ill., 1870. Chief Justice same. LL. D., W. C., 1877.

David Newton Sheldon,   Waterville, Me.

Clergyman. b. Suffield, Ct., June 28, 1807. f. Westfield. Prea. L. Valedictory. s. Theol. Newton, 1832-5. M. A. Mis. A. B. F. M., Paris, 1835-9. Pas. Bapt., Halifax, N. S., 1841; Waterville, Me., 1843-53. Prea. Colby Univ., 1843-53. Pas. Roth, Mr., 1853-67; Waterville, since 1866. D. D., Brown Univ., 1867. pub. "Sin and Redemption," 1856. m. Rachel M. Ripley, Chelsea, Ma., Oct. 10, 1835; nine c.

Westerlo Woodworth,

Lawyer. b. Albany, N. Y., 1812. T. 1st Eng. o. s. Law, Yale. M. A. p. Law, Albany. d. New York, 1849.

Alfred Henry Corning.   1831.

Lawyer. b. Troy, N. Y., Mar. 11, 1811. T. Valedictory. s. Law, Hudson and New York; Admitted 1834; p. Law, New York, 1834-77. d. there Mar. 2, 1877.

George Hale,   4524 Paul St., Frankford, Philadelphia.

Clergyman. b. Catskill, N. Y., June 8, 1812. T. Salutatory. Tra. S. Hadley, 1831-2. Tut. W. C., 1834-6. M. A. P. T. R., 1836. Ord Feb. 7, 1839. Pas. Presb., Frankington, N. J., 1839-52. Sec. Bd. Rel. Dis. Mis., 1852-66. mem. Bds. Pub. and Ed. Trustee (Gen. Assem., Trustee and Sec., P. T. R. D. D., Lafayette, 1862. pub. "Year Century Sermon," 1862, "Sketch of the Kirkpatricks," 1867, "His. Hopewell Church," 1878. m. Eliza Rebecca Ingham, New Hope, Pa., June 22, 1843; six c., two W. C. sons, '66 and '74.

Aaron Hicks Hand.

Clergyman. b. Albany, N. Y., Dec. 11, 1811. Prea L. P. T. N., 1827. M. A. Ord. Apr. 11, 1841. Pas Marietta, Ga., 1839-41; Berwick, Pa., 1843-5; Greenwich, N. Y., 1851-70; Palisades, 1871-9. D. D., Lafayette, 1887; Trustee same. m. Elizabeth C. Boswell, Norwich, Ct., Aug. 10, 1843; also c. res. Easton, Pa., 1879-80. d. there Mar. 8, 1880.

Caleb Perkins Seymour.

Teacher. b. Granby, Ct., June 8, 1878. f. Leonr. Prea L. Phil. o. Auh. T. 8., 1885. Tea Miss., Tenn., Ill., found dead in a deserted house, Sedalia, Mo., Sept. 25, 1872.

William Stuart.

Lawyer and Editor. b. Binghamton, N. Y., Dec. 23, 1810. T. 1st Eng. o. s. Law, Yale. M. A. Ed. Americus. Chicago, 1839; P. M. Chicago, 1841-3. Ed. Republican, Binghamton, 1844; P. M. there 1861-4. m. Eliza G. Backus, New York, Aug. 20, 1835. d. Binghamton, 1870.

1832.

Thomas Dutton.

Clergyman. b. Guilford, Ct., March 8, 1812. L. Phil. o. Tut. W. C., 1836-7. Y. T. 8. Ord. Apr. 11, 1847. Pas. Meriden, Ill., 1847-50. N. Guilford, Ct., 1855-9. Ashford, 1859-66. m. Sarah M. Whiting, Nov. 17, 1849. res. Durant, Ia., 1868-80. d. there Mar. 4, 1890.

Jonathan Edwards Field.

Lawyer. b. Haddam, Ct., July 11, 1813. T. Salutatory. s. Law, New York. p. Law. Ann Arbor, Mich., 1834-9; Stockbridge, Ma., 1839-68. Ms. Senate, 1854, 1863; Pres same, three times. m. Mary A. Stuart, 1835 (d. 1859). m. Mrs. Ruldah F. Pomeroy, 1860. d. Stockbridge, Apr. 23, 1876.

George Clinton Gibbs.

Lawyer. b. Orid, N. Y., Mar. 8, 1811. Pres L. 1st Eng. o. s and p. Law. Marshall Mich., 1835-58. N. Y. Assembly, Judge Super. Court. Cal. m. Elmina Raley, Ludl, N. Y., Nov. 8, 1835; seven c. res. San Gabriel, Cal., 1879-83. d. there Dec. 31, 1883.

Nelson Elwood Spencer.

Clergyman. b. Ogden, N. Y., 1811. Pres L. Valedictory. Tea. Palmyra, 1844-5. M A. Prof. Kenyon; Ord. Epis. d. 1857.

1833.

Samuel Buel,   Gen. Theol. Sem., W. 20th St., New York.

Clergyman and Teacher. b. Troy, N. Y., June 11, 1815. Pres L. Valedictory. Tut. Kenyon, 1838-41. s. Theol. Sem., Va. M. A. Ord., 1847. Rector, Marshall, Mich., 1847-9; Minersville, Pa., 1849-51; Cumberland, Md., 1851-7; Poughkeepsie, N. Y., 1847-66. Prof. Eccl. His. and Div., Fairbault, Minn., 1866-71. Prof. Sys. Div. and Dogm. Theol. New York, 1871. D. D., Colum., 1864. N. T. D., Gen. Theol. Sem., 1885. pub. "Reply to Whately on Kingdom of Christ," 1844, "Eucharistic Presence, Sacrifice and Adoration," 1874, "Academic Lectures," 2 Vols. (Ms.) m. Jane E. Wilcox, Fairfax Co., Va., June 11, 1868; four c.

Jonas Denton,   Cuba, Crawford Co., Mo.

Clergyman. b. Chester, N. Y., Aug. 11, 1807. T. Salutatory. P. T. N., 1833-4. Ord. Nov., 1839. Pas Presb., Chippewa, O., 1839-47; Canal Fulton, 1847-56; Flanders, 1856-9. Ma. Pa and Mich., 1859-67. Greenwood, Mich., 1867-72. res. Cuba, Mo., since 1873. m. Frances W. Liddel, Menalham, N. J., July 16, 1838; four c.

Willis Lord,   Chatfield, Fillmore Co., Minn.

Clergyman and Teacher. b. Bridgeport, Ct., Sep. 15, 1810. f. Wilson, Ct. Pres T. 1st Eng. o. M. A. P. T. N., 1839. Ord. Aug., 1834. Pas Providence, R. I., 1849-40; Philadelphia, Pa., 1840-50; Cincinnati, O., 1850-4; Brooklyn, N. Y., 1855-9; Chicago, Ill., 1859-70; Denver, Col., 1870-5; Columbus, O., 1876-9. res Chatfield, Minn. Stated Clk, Gen. Assembly, O. S., 1848-50. D. D., Lafayette, 1847; Ll. D., Univ. Wooster, 1878. Prof. Theol. Sem. Chi.; Prof. Bib. and Eccl His.; Prof. Did. and Pol. Theol. Presb. Sem., N. W. Pres. Univ., Wooster. pub. "Men and Scenes before the Flood, 1861, "Christian Theology," 1874, "The Glorious Appearing," 1877. m. Hannah W. Boughton, Danbury, Ct., June, 1834; seven c.

Martin Ingham Townsend,   Troy, N. Y.

Lawyer. b. Hancock, Ma., Feb. 6, 1810. f. Wn. Prea L. Phil. o. M. A. Law, Troy, N. Y., since 1838. Dist. Att Rens. Co., 1841-5. mem. Congd. Conv., 1867. M. C., 1874-9. U. S. Att. N. Dist. N. Y., 1879-88. Regent Univ. State N. Y. Orator W. C. Alumni. 1869. LL. D. W. C., 1888. m. Louisa R. Kellogg, Wo., May 10, 1838; one dau. wife Prof. Nason, R. P. L.

1834.

Edward W. B. Canning,   Stockbridge, Mass.

Teacher. b. (till) Ma., Nov. 8, 1818. f. at home. Prea L. Sigma Phi. Rhet. Prize, 1831. 1st Eng. o. Tra. Wheeling, W. Va., 1835-40; Stockbridge, Ma., 1840-55; Mass. H of R., 1858, 1859; Com. Rev. Stat. Dep. Col. Customs, Boston, 1861-5; Rep. Nav. Officer, N. Y., 1875-7. M. A. W. C., also Yale, 1852. Phi Beta Kappa Poet, 1865. pub. Poems. Mag. Articles. Lectures, etc. m. Eliene J. Catlin, N. Marlboro, Aug. 22, 1857, (d. Sep. 20, 1840). m. Catharine Peet, same place, Nov. 30, 1843.

Azariah Sylvester Clark.

Lawyer. b. Canaan, N. Y., Dec. 11, 1818. f. Lemon, Ma., and Winsted, Ct. Kappa Alpha. L. Salutatory. a Law, Troy. d. Canaan, May 12, 1857.

Wells Colton.

Lawyer. b. Lenox, Ma., Mar. 4, 1812. f. Lenox. Prea L. Phil. o. a Law, New York, 1834-7. p. Law, Bloomington, Ill., 1837-45; th. Louis, Mo., 1848-9. Accidentally killed at a fire there May 25, 1849.

James Dixon.

Lawyer. b. Enfield, Ct., Aug. 5, 1814. f. Ellington. Prea T. Class Poet. K. A. Master's o. Law, Enfield and Hartford. Ct. H. of R., 1837. M. C., 1845-9. U. S. Senate, 1857-69. LL. D., Trinity, 1863. m. Elizabeth Cogswell, E. Windsor, Oct. 1, 1840; four c. d. Hartford, Mar. 27, 1873.

Nathaniel Herrick Griffin.

Clergyman and Teacher. b. Southampton. N. Y., Dec. 24, 1814. f. Bridgehampton. Prea L. X. A. P. T. S., 1834. Tut. W. C., 1836-7. M. A. Pas. Westhampton, N. Y., 1837-9; Franklin, 1839-4. Ord. June 27, 1838. Install. 1839-41. Asst. Prof. W. C., 1841-3. Tra. Brooklyn, 1843-5. Prof. Lat. and Gr. Lang. W. C., 1845-55; Prof. Gr. Lang. and J.R., 1855-7. Tra. Wn., 1857-68. Libr. W. C., 1858-78. D. D., Lafayette 1867. Rec. Alumni. 1878; Orator, 1854. Cor. Sec. Phi Beta Kappa, 1861-7. m. Hannah F. Buddey, Wn., Aug. 39, 1860; four c. three sons W. C., '88, '90, '73. d. Wn., Oct. 16, 1878.

John Hall.

Teacher. b. Halifax, N., Aug. 8, 1810. T. Valedictory. Tra. Red Hook, N. Y., 1834-5. d. Nov. 5, 1835.

Alexander Hyde,

Teacher and Farmer. b. Lee, Ma., Sep. 29, 1814. (son of Rev. Dr. Alvan Hyde). f. Lenox. K. A. Prea T. Jun. Ex., 1833; Ad Un. Ex., 1834. Tra. Pittsfield, 1834-4. M. A. Law, 1842-64. Agr. Ed. Berkshire Co. Engle; Lee Gleaner, 1856-7. mem. Mass. Bd. Agr. Lowell Lect., 1850. Prea Berk. Hts., Soc., 1859. Prea Alumni W. C. Dea. Cong. Ch. Mass. H. of R., 1840-1. d. Boston, Jan. 11, 1891. m. Cornelia Hull, N. Marlboro, Oct. 1, 1839; nine c.

1835.

James Homer Ellis.

Student. b. N. Salem, Mass., Feb. 11, 1810. f. at home. K. A. Prea T. Ad Un. Ex. 1833. Salutatory. d. Wn., Sep. 11, 1835.

Jesse Olds Norton.

Lawyer. b. Bennington, Vt., Dec. 18, 1812. K. A. Prea T. Law, Joliet, Ill., 1840. Probate Judge, 1846. mem. Const. Conv., 1848. Ill. H. of R., 1850. M. C., 1851-7, 1863-5. U. S. Dist. Att. No. Ill., 1868-9. m. P. A. Sheldon, Dec. 22, 1867. Elder Presb. Ch., Chicago. d. there Aug. 3, 1875.

Abraham Baldwin Olin.

Lawyer. b. Shaftsbury. Vt., Sep. 21, 1808. Prea L. Law, Troy. N. Y., 1840-48, (with Hon. Joseph White, '28, 1841-8). Recorder, 1844-8. M. C., 1856-60. Judge Sup. Court, D. C., 1863-79. LL. D., W. C., 1868. m. Mary Danforth, Wn., Dec., 1834. d. Four Corners, Md., July 7, 1879.

George Sheldon.

Clergyman. b Northampton, Ms., Oct. 4, 1812. T. Phil. o. A. T. S., 1839. Tra. Orangeburg, N. C., 1837-40. Ord. June 12, 1841. Pas. St. George's Parish, 1841-4. Died Supt Am. Bib. Soc., Princeton, N. J., 1844-51. D. D. Jefferson, 1862. N. J. His. Soc. pub. "History Dorchester Colony," 1854. "Memoir Rev. Dr. R. K. Rogers, 1879. m. Martha Lyman, Northampton, Ms., Sep. 1\, 1839; six c. d. Princeton, N. J., June 16, 1893.

Samuel Corylus Wilcox.

Clergyman. b. Sandisfield, Ms., Dec. 21, 1802. f. Lenox. T. 1st Eng. o. Tra. Lenox, 1836-7. Anh. T. S., 1837-40. Ord. May 25, 1842. Owego Presb., 1841-7; Williamsburg, Mass., 1847-9; Owego Cong., 1849-53. m. Mary S. Darling, Dec. 1, 1846; four c. d. Owego, N. Y., Mar. 20, 1864.

Charles Ashley Williams.

Clergyman. b. Salem, N. Y. Sep. 20, 1814. Pres. L. K. A. Valedictory. Tra. Ala., 1837-. Pas. W. Gloucester, Ms., 1842-4; Mo. Ottawa, Ill., 1850-51. Tra. Galena, 1852-; Keokuk, Ia., 1853-55; Chaplain. U. S., 1861-4. Pas. Rockford, Ill., 1865-8. Tra. Geneva, Wis., 1870-3. pub. "The Age Temptations," 1879; " Alike and Perfect," 1885; "Romanism in Art;" Christ Our Model." m. Susan F. Hawkes, Galena, Ill., May 1, 1838. d. Geneva, Wis., Aug. 18, 1878.

1836.

Samuel Knox,   506 Olive Street, St. Louis, Mo.

Lawyer. b. Blanford, Ms., Mar. 15, 1815. f. Monson. T. Sigma Phi a. Law, Springfield and Harvard. p. Law, St. Louis, Mo., since 1838. City Counsellor, 1845. M. C., 1864. m. Mary Kerr, St. Louis, Mar. 19, 1845 (d. 1863); als c.

John Tatlock.

Teacher. b. Island of Anghers, Dec. 4, 1808. f. Hunter, N. Y. K. A. Jan. Ex., 1831; Ad. Un. Ex., 1834, 1835. Pres. T. Valedictory. Tut. W. C., 1835-6. Tra. Math. W. C., 1836-47; Prof. Lat. and Gr. Lang. W. C., 1845-6; Libr. W. C., 1845-56; Prof. Em., 1857-68. Ord. Cong. Oct. 14, 1856. Law, Pittsfield, 1859-66. Ll. D. West Res., 1857. V. Pres. Phi Beta Kappa, 1860-4. m. Sarah M. Benjamin, Wa., July 19, 1842. d. Pittsfield Feb. 19, 1886.

Bushnell White.

Lawyer. b. Buckland, Ms., Nov. 4, 1813. Sigma Phi. Pres. L. Phil. o. Law, Cleveland, 1835-40. City Att. 1841. U. S. Dist. Att., 1844. 1848. U. S. Commissioner, 1858-63. m. Northford, Ct., 1844. Elizabeth B. Clarke; two c. d. Cleveland. Apr. 45, 1883.

Joseph White,   Williamstown, Mass.

Lawyer. b. Charlemont, Ms., Nov. 19, 1811. f. Bennington, Vt. K. A. Moonlight, 1835; Jun. Ex., 1835; Ad Un. Ex., 1835. Pres. T. 1st Eng. o. Tut. W. C., 1836-40. Master's o., 1839. M. A. College o., 1839, 1841. Law, Troy, N. Y., 1857-9, 1841-4. Manager Manf. Co., Lowell, Ms., 1846-57. Mass. Senate, 1857; Bank Commissioner, 1858-60; Alumni o., 1864. Sec. Mass. Board Ed., 1861-78. Ll. D., Yale, 1878. Mass. H. of R. 1873. Treas. Phi Beta Kappa, 1864. Trustee W. C. since 1856. Treasurer W. C., 1859-80. Pres. North Berk. Conf. Cong. Ch., 1877. m. Hannah Danforth, Williamstown, 1841.

Walter Wright.

Lawyer. b. Sheffield, Ms. May 21, 1812. f. Wa. K. A. Jun. Ex., 1835. L. Salutatory. a. Law, Troy and Chicago, 1838-9. Ed. Tribune, Chicago. d. there Oct. 45, 1876.

1837.

Israel Ward Andrews,   Marietta, Ohio.

College President. b. Danbury, Ct., Jan. 3, 1815. f. privately. Sigma Phi. Pres. L. Phil. o. Tra. Lev. Ms., 1837-8. Tut. Marietta Coll., Ct., 1838-9; Prof. Math. and Nat. Phil., same, 1839-55; Pres. and Prof. Mor. and Men. Phil. and Polit. Econ., same, 1855-85; Ex. Pres. and Prof. Polit. Phil., same, since 1885. M. A., W. C. in course; Marietta, 1841. D. D., W. C., 1856. Ll. D., Iowa, 1874; Wabash, 1876. Corp. Mem. A. B. C. F. M. since 1867. mem. His. Soc. N. H. pub. "Inaugural Address," 1855; "A Beginner," 1862; "Phi Beta Kappa Oration," 1880; "Manual of the Constitution of the U. S.," 1874, (25,000 copies sold); "Historical Sketch Marietta College," 1876; "Fiftieth Anniversary," 1885, and many sermons and lectures. m. Sarah H. Clark, Danbury, Ct., Aug. 5, 1838, (d. 1840.) m. Marianna B. Clark, Danbury. Aug. 24, 1843; four c., none living.

Jonathan Henry Ferris.

Lawyer. b. Peekskill, N. Y., May 5, 1809. Sigma Phi. L. Salutatory. Law, Peekskill and Haverstraw, N. Y., 1837-78. d. June 2, 1852.

Stephen Johnson Field,   Supreme Court. Washington, D. C.

Lawyer and Judge. b. Haddam, Ct., Nov. 4, 1816. res. Stockbridge, Ma., 1819-29; Smyrna, Turkey and Athens, Greece, 1829-32. Delta Upsilon. T. Valedictory. Law, New York, 1839-48. Europe, 1848-9. California, Dec., 1849; First Alcalde, Marysville, Cal., Jan., 1850; Cal. Legislature, 1851; Asso. Judge Sup. Court, Cal., 1857-9; Chief Justice, same, 1859-63. Justice Supreme Court U. S. since 1863. LL. D., W. C., 1884. pub many legal opinions, etc. m. June 2, 1859. Hon Virginia Swearingen, San Francisco, Cal., where he resides when not at Washington.

Samuel Goode Jones.

Civil Engineer. b. Petersburg, Va., 1817. Sigma Phi. Pres I. 1st Eng. o. Civil Eng., Va., Ga., Ala., 1837-78. R. R. Pres. Treas. Univ., South Newmarne, Tenn., 1878-9. d. Winchester, Oct. 4, 1886.

1838.

William Bross,   Pres. Tribune Co., Chicago, Ill.

Editor and Publisher. b. Montague, near Port Jervis, N. J., Nov. 4, 1813. f. Milford, Pa., and Sussex Co., N. J. Delta Upsilon. Pres. T. Oration, 1838. Tre. Ridgebury, N. Y. and Chester, Pa., 1838-34. Chicago since 1848. Editor and Publisher Prairie Herald, Democratic Press, Tribune. Lieut. Governor, Illinois, 1865-9. H. A. Williams. Mem. Chicago H. S. Trustee L. F. Univ. W. C. Alumni Orator, 1869. pub. "History of Chicago," 1876. "Tom Quick," 1882. mem. Presb. Church. m. Mary J. Jansen, Ridgeway, N. Y., 1839; eight c., four boys and four girls, only one dau. living.

James Dennison Colt.

Lawyer. b. Pittsfield, Ma., Oct. 8, 1819. Kappa Alpha. Monslight, 1838. Junior Ex., 1837. Pres. L. Oration, 1838. Prof. Med. Juris. Berk. Med. Sch., 1850-2. Law. Pittsfield, 1843 ml. Mass. H. of R., 1853, 1854. Judge Mass. Supreme Court, 1863-6. 1868-81. Trustee W. C., 1863-81. LL. D., W. C., 1871. m. Elizabeth Gilbert, Gilbertsville, N. Y., June 10, 1857; am c. d. Pittsfield, Aug. 2, 1881.

Thomas Amory Hall.

Clergyman. b. Hawley, Ma., Sep. 2, 1812. Delta Upsilon. Pres. L. Salutatory. Tre. Worthington, Ma., 1834-7. a. Theol., same place. Ord. June 19, 1841. Pas. Dalton, 1841-7. Tre Lee, 1848-54. Pas. Otis, 1856-64. Chap. U. S. C. I., 1864-5. Pas. Monterey, 1865-71. m. Mary Strong, Northampton, Aug. 5, 1840. d. Monterey, Sep. 17, 1871.

Rowland Sears Howes.

Teacher. b. Hawley, Ma., Nov. 25, 1818. f. Bennington, Vt. Delta Upsilon. L. Phil. o. Tre. Shelburne Falls, Ma. and Troy, N. Y., 1838-90; Staten Island, 1844-57; Wilkesbarre, Pa., 1858-64. M. A. m. Harriet Cook, Ashfield, Ma., Aug. 19, 1841. d. Rome, Pa., July 11, 1887.

John Isham,   41 Crew St., Atlanta, Ga.

Teacher. b. Bennington, Vt. Sigma Phi. T. 1st Eng. o., 1836. Tre. N. C., 1846-7; Columbus, Ga., 1847-57; Atlanta, since 1868.

John Wells.

Lawyer. b. Rowe, Ma., Feb 17, 1819. Kappa Alpha. T. Ad. Ub. Ex., 1837. Valedictory. a. Law, Greenfield and Harv. Law Sch. Admitted 1841. Master's Oration. p Law, Chicopee, 1841-66. Mass. H. of R. four terms. Judge Mass. Supreme Court, 1866-75. LL. D., W. C., 1870. W. C Alumni Orator, 1869. m. Sophia Dwight, Boston, May 15, 1850; two c. d. Salem, Nov. 24, 1875.

1839.

Alvan Severance Anderson.

Lawyer. b. Shelburne, Ma. Sigma Phi. Pres. L. Phil. o. Tre. Shelburne Falls, Law, Greenfield. d. Aug. 1, 1841.

George Kerr.

Clergyman and Teacher. b. Carrickfergus, Ireland, Dec. 18, 1818. Delta Upsilon. Pres L. Valedictory. U. T. N., 1840-8. Ord., 1843. Pas. (Somerville, N. Y., 1843-8. Tea. Franklin, 1848-60. Prof. Math. N. Y. Agr. Coll., 1861. Tea. Watertown, 1862-5. Ll. D. Ham. C., 1862. Tea. Cooperstown, 1863-7. d. there, Mar. 2, 1897. m. Lucy Hamilton, Schoharie, N. Y., 1845: eight c.

Nathaniel Lasell.

Clergyman. b. Schoharie, N. Y., Feb. 4, 1818. Delta Upsilon. T. Salutatory. Auh. T. S., 1841-5. Ord., May 15, 1846. Pas. W. Stockbridge, Ma., 1850-3; Amesbury, 1858-6; Exeter, N. H., 1858-60; Salisbury, Ma., 1850-4; Brentwood, N. H. 1865-9; W. Newbury, Ma., 1869-73; Malapolmit, 1873-8. m. Mrs. Susan Shaw Todd Winkley, June 20, 1854. d. Amesbury, Feb. 4, 1890.

William Porter,   Prof. Latin, Beloit College, Beloit, Wis.

Teacher and Clergyman. b. Lee, Ma., Jan. 10, 1810. f. Hadley and Lenox. Kappa Alpha. L. Monolight, 1837. Latin o. Jun. Ex., 1838. Oration, 1839. A. T. S., 1840-1. Ord. Cong., Aug. 43, 1847. Travel Ga and Fla., 1847-9. Tea. Marietta, O., 1849-4; Prof. Math., Beloit, Wis., 1852-6; Prof. Latin, same, since 1856. Europe, 1873-4. M. A. and D. D., (1868.) Williams. m. Ellen G. Chapin, Beloit, July 18, 1854; four c.

Isaac Vanderpoel.

Lawyer. b. Kinderhook, N. Y., May 7, 1810. Sigma Phi. L. 1st Prg. o. Law, Albany. City Att. Adj. Gen. State N. Y. m. Susan Foster, Cohoes, May 14, 1870. d. Albany, Dec. 6, 1879.

1840.

James Watson Brown,   Framingham, Mass.

Teacher. b. Framingham, Ma., Apr. 19, 1818. f. Phillips Acad., Exeter, N. H. Delta Upsilon. Pres L. 1st Eng. o. Tea. Pawtucket, R. I., 1838; Stowe, Ma., 1840; Framingham, 1842-50. M. A., Williams. M. D. Univ., Pa., 1851. Mass H. of R., 1858, 1861. Dep Collector Int Rev., 1862-70. Supt. Schools, Framingham, seven years. School Com. fourteen years. Justice of Peace, 1862-62. Rep. Co. Agr. Soc., seventeen years. Chairman of Selectmen, five years. Rep. Warden Epis. Ch., since 1867. m. Mary Jane Brower, Framingham, Apr. 14, 1841; five c., one living. Winter home, Bergen Point, N. J.

Francis Henshaw Dewey,   Worcester, Mass.

Lawyer. b. Williamstown, Ma., July 19, 1821. f. Northampton, Pittsfield and Amherst. Kappa Alpha. Jun Ex., 1839. Adel Uo. Ex., 1839. Pres L. Oration, 1840. Master's Oration, 1843. M. A. 3 Law, Yale and Harvard Admitted, 1843. p. Law, Worcester, 1843-69. Judge Mass. Superior Court, 1869-81. mem. Mass. Senate, 1858, 1859. mem. Am. Antiq. Soc., 1868. LL. D. W. C., 1872. Trustee W. C., since 1869. President Phi Beta Kappa Society. m. Frances A. Clarke, Northampton, Nov. 8, 1846 (d. Mar. 18, 1851.) m. Sarah E. Tufts, Boston, Apr. 89, 1858; eight c., three W. C. sons. 76, 78, 79.

Charles Hawley.

Clergyman. b. Catskill, N. Y., Aug. 19, 1819. Delta Upsilon. Pres T. Valedictory. U. T. S., 1841-4. Ord. Presb., Jan. 89, 1845. Pas. N. Rochelle, N. Y., 1845-4; Lyons, 1845-57; Auburn, 1857-91. D. D., Ham. C., 1861. Pres. Cayuga Co. His. Soc. pub. "Jesuit Missions," 1878; "Early Chapters of Cayuga History," 1879, and many historical papers. Trustee Auburn T. S., 1876-91. m. Mary Hubbell, Lyons, Sep. 10, 1850; three c. d. Auburn, Nov. 89, 1885.

John Adam Walker.

Lawyer. b. Lenox, Ma., Jan. 7, 1821. Kappa Alpha. Pres T. Jun. Ex., 1839. Adel Uo. Ex., 1839. Phil. o., 1840, and Master, o., 1843. M. A. A. T. S., 1843-5. U. T. S., 1845-6; Tut. W. C., 1844-5. Law, Lenox, 1848-50; Pittsfield, 1850-64. Mass. H. of R., 1859. m. Margaret Sayre, Boston, Oct. 14, 1847; three c. d. May 68, 1864.

Charles Worthington.

Lawyer. b. Lenox, Ma., Feb. 28, 1822. Kappa Alpha. Jun Ex., 1839. Adel Uo. Ex., 1839. L. Salutatory. Law, Boston. d. Stockbridge, May 29, 1847.

1841.

Timothy Childs.

Physician. b. Pittsfield, Ma., Dec. 1, 1822. L. Salutatory. M. A. M. D., Berk. Med. sch., 1844. Prof. Anat. and Phys., same. Prof. Surg. Bellevue Med. Coll. and Bowdoin. M. M. S. Surgeon Mex. War. d. Norwich, Ct., Sep. 8, 1853.

Melzer Montague.

Clergyman and Teacher. b. Westhampton, Ma., May 5, 1818. Kappa Alpha. Adel. Ub. Fx., 1840. Pres. T. Phil. o., 1841. grad. Theol Inst., (Ct., 1844. Ord. Cong., Oct. 28, 1844. Past. Fort Atkinson. Wis., 1844-58. Tra. Milton, Beloit. Ripon, 1858-7; Allen's Grove, 1858-70; Co. Supt. Schools, 1870-2. m. Mary Hale, May 51, 1845. Thrown from sleigh and d. Elkhorn, Dec. 81, 1872.

Thomas Thornton Read.

Merchant. b. Troy, N. Y., Dec. 8, 1822. Kappa Alpha. T. Greek o., 1841. Business in New York. Travel in Europe. d. Dec. 20, 1874.

Samuel Goode Wheeler,   22 Pine Street, New York City.

Lawyer. b. Providence, R. I., Mar. 80, 1821. f. with Dea. Foote, Wa. L. Valedictory. Law, New York. Donor W. C. m. Anita Carolina Crabbe, Paksillas, Island of Cuba, May, 1856; five c.

Russell M. Wright,   Castleton, Vt.

Teacher. b. Easthampton, Ma., Dec. 17, 1815. f. Acad., Leicester. Delta Upsilon. L. 1st Eng o., 1841. Tra. Cambridge, N. Y., 1841-2. a. Theol Inst., (Ct. 1842-3. M. A. Tra. Williston Seminary, 1845-7, 1848-49; Washington, Ga., 1849-51; Athens, 1853-53. m. Caroline A. Branch, Washington, Ga., Dec. 16, 1854; two c.

1842.

Addison Ballard,   Prof. Lafayette College. Easton, Pa.

Teacher and Clergyman. b. Framingham, Ma., Oct. 18, 1822. f. Framingham, Ma., and Brimington, Vt. Delta Upsilon. Moonlight, 1850. Pres. L. Valedictory. Prin. Hopkins Acad., Hadley, 1842-3; Tut. W. C., 1843-4; Tra. Grant Rapids, Mich., 1845-6; Prof. Lat. and Math., Ohio Univ., 1847-54; Prof. Rhet., W. C., 1854-3; Prof. Astro., Math. and Nat. Phil., Marietta, 1855-7. Pas. Cong. Ch., Wn., 1857-63; Death in Cong., 1858-73. Prof. Ch. Gr. and Lat., Lafayette, 1874-9; Prof. Mor., Phil. and Rhet., Lafayette, since 1879. M. A. and D. D. (1857), Williams. m. Julia Perkins Pratt, Athens, O., Aug. 7, 1861.

George Patrick Briggs.

Lawyer and Farmer. b. S. Adams, Ma., Mar. 4, 1821. f. Lenox. Kappa Alpha. L. Jun. Ex., 1841. First Eng. o., 1848, 1J, B, Harv., 1846. M. A. Law, Boston and Lowell, 1846-51. Law. and Farm, Pittsfield, 1851-52. Europe, 1867. m. Cornelia Cushing, Cleveland, O., Aug. 4, 1856, (d. 1858). m. Mrs. Sarah E. Leland, Detroit, Mich., Oct. 6, 1873. d. Mar. 85, 1882.

William Henry Edwards,   Coalburgh, Kanawha Co., W. Va.

Lawyer. b. Hunter, N. Y., Mar. 15, 1822. Social Fraternity. L. Phil o., 1841. Tra. Hampton and Princeton, N. J., 1842-4. Law, New York. Business, Amazon Region, S. A., 1846. Admitted to the Bar, 1847. England, 1848; New York, 1849-51; England, 1852-3; New York, 1853-9; Newburgh, 1859-68; Coalburgh, since 1868. pub. "Voyage up the River Amazon," 1847; "Butterflies of North America," 1868-1882, (Mo). m. Katharine C. Tappan, Belleville, N. J., May 20, 1850.

Leland Fairbanks, Jr.,   245 Broadway, New York City.

Lawyer. b. Wardsboro, Vt., Sep. 9, 1820. f. Troy. Sigma Phi. L. Salutatory. Law, Troy, 1852-55; New York City, since 1856. Secretary and Counsel, Valentine & Co. Pres. International Bank Note Co. m. Rebecca J. Valentine. St. Paul's Church. Boston, Dec. 17, 1855; two c., one living.

Eli Andrews Hubbard,   Hatfield, Hampshire Co., Mass.

Teacher. b. Hinsdale, Ms., Dec. 11, 1814. f. Shelburne Falls and Cummington. Delta Upsilon. Moonlight, 1899. Jan. Ex., 1840. Prea. L. Oration, 1842. Tea. Worthington, 1843-4. Tut. W. C., 1844-1. M A. Lev, 1845-7; Northampton, 1847-8; Easthampton, 1849-54, 1857-60; Fitchburg, 1854-57, 1873-5; Springfield, 1855-73; 1875-83; Hatfield, since 1883. Supt of Schools. Agent Mass Board of Ed. mem. Mass. H. of R., 1872. Pres. Elector, 1884. m. Frances Durkin, Worthington, Aug. 19, 1844; two c., dau. from Vassar, and W. C., 77.

George Washington Pleasants,   Rock Island, Ill.

Lawyer. b. Harrodsburg, Ky., Nov. 24, 1820. f. Washington, D. C. L. Oration, 1842. Law, New York, 1842-9. M A. Wn., 1849-51. Washington, 1851-3. Rock Island, since 1853. Judge Sixth Jud. Dist., Ill., 1867, re-elected 1873, 1879, 1885, and assigned to duty as one of the Appellate Court, 1877. mem. Const. Conv., 1861. m. Sarah T. Bulkley, New York City, Jan. 24, 1850; four c.

Oliver Warner.

Secretary Mass. b. Northampton, Ms., Apr. 17, 1818. Delta Upsilon. 7. Oration, 1842. x. Theol. Gilmanton, N. H. Pas. Cong. Chesterfield. Ms., 1845-7. Easterns. Northampton. Mass. H. of R., two terms. State Senate two terms. Secretary. Mass., 1857-75. Librarian, Mass., 1875-7. Twice married. d. Lynn, Sep. 16, 1885.

1843.

Reuben Patrick Boise,   Salem, Marion Co., Oregon.

Lawyer. b. Blandford, Ms., June 9, 1819. f. Granville. Delta Upsilon. 7. Oration, 1843. Law, Chicopee Falls, 1845-50. Pros Att. Or. Ter., 1850-3. mem. Or. Legislature, 1853-7. mem. Const. Conv., 1857. Chief Justice Or. Supreme Court. 1864-6. Judge Third Jud. Dist. since 1868. LL. D. Pacific Univ., 1887. m. Ellen F. Lyon, San Francisco, Cal., 1861, (d. 1883), m. Emily A. Pratt, Webster, Ms., 1887; five c.

Abraham Gosman,   Lawrenceville, Mercer Co., N. J.

Clergyman. b. Danby, N. Y. July 23, 1819. f. Ithaca. Delta Upsilon. Pres. L. 1st Eng. o. P T. S., 1844-7; Inst. P. T. S., 1850-1; Ord. Presb. May 22, 1851; Pas. Lawrenceville since 1851. D D., New Jersey, 1872. Trustee P. T. S. since 1868. Director P. T. S. since 1878. Pres. Board of Directors. pub. "Alexander's History of the Israelitish People. Samuel to Babylonish Captivity." 1884. Genesis in Lange's Com., chap. 14-37; Numbers chap. 20-34, 34-35; Deuteronomy. Princeton Review. "Newman's Hebrew Commonwealth," 1850; "Pearson on Infallibity," 1864. m. Lettia H. Naman, Oct. 22, 1852; seven c., five living.

Henry Brown Hosford,   North Platte, Lincoln Co., Neb.

Teacher and Clergyman. b. Wn., Ms., Dec. 17, 1817. f. Wn. and Leonx. Delta Upsilon. Pres. L. Valedictory. Prin. Hopkins Acad., Hadley, 1843-4. Tut. W. C., 1844-8. M A. Pas. Jordan, N. Y., 1848-50; Sunderland, Ms., 1850-3. Prof. Men. Phil. and Rhet. West. Res., 1853-61. Prin Fem. Sem., Hudson, O. Hospital Visitor U. S San. Com., 1863-5. res. Hudson, O., 1854-84; North Platte, Neb., since 1884. m. Mary E. Plant, New Hartford, N. Y., Sep. 3, 1850; seven c.

Addison Henry Laflin.

Manufacturer. b. Lee, Ms., Oct. 24, 1823. 7. Salutatory. Paper Manf., Hardwick, Ms., and Herkimer, N Y., 1844-57. N. Y. Senate. 1857-9. M. C., three terms, 1865-70. Naval Officer, N. Y., 1871-7. m. dau. Judge Hall, Syracuse, N. Y., 1854; two c. d. Pittsfield, Ms., Sep. 24, 1878.

Seth Smith Mellen,   Livingston, Sumter Co., Ala.

Teacher and Merchant. b. Brookfield, Ms., Feb. 7, 1821. f. Wilbraham. Kappa Alpha. Moonlight. 1843. L. Phil. o. 1843. Longstreet Ga., eleven years; Dakota, Miss., fifteen; Mt. Sterling, Ala., eleven; Tuskaloosa, three; Livingston, four. Co. Supt. Schools. LL. D. Univ. Ala., 1872. m. Martha H. Crocker, Marion, Ga., June 23, 1851, (d. July 27, 1855). m. Susan H. Bush. Westfield, Ms., Aug. 24, 1856; seven c., two living.

1844.

Samuel Wells Bowerman,   Pittsfield, Mass.

Lawyer. b. North Adams, Ms., May 8, 1820. Sigma Phi. L. Oration, 1844. s. Law, North Adams. p Law, North Adams, 1847-57; Pittsfield, since 1857. Mass. Senate, 1856, 1857, 1858. Mass. H. of R., 1868. m. Ann Eliza Smith, South Adams, 1849. (d. 1859.)

Henry Shaw Briggs.

Lawyer. b. Lanesboro, Ma., Aug. 1, 1824. Chi Psi. T. Oration, 1844. s. Law, Harvard and Pittsfield, 1844-5, Admitted 1846. p. Law, Pittsfield. M. A., Mass, H. of R., 1858. Enlisted June 19, 1861. Brig. Gen., July 17, 1862. Mass. Auditor, 1865-8. Judge Dist. Court, 1869-78. U. S. Custom House Appraiser, 1874-82. m. K. Tatnall, Aug. 4, 1848, (d. 1848); [cour c. d. Pittsfield, dep. 22, 1887.

Joseph Henry Budd,   Stockton, San Joaquin Co., Cal.

Lawyer. b. Pleasant Valley, N. Y., Jan. 18, 1822. f. Acad. New Philz. Kappa Alpha. Jun. Ex., 1842. Adel. Un. Ex., 1842. Pres. L. 1st Eng. o., 1841. a. Law, Poughkeepsie. p. Law, Janesville, Wis., 1849-57; Stockton, Cal., since 1858. m. Lucinda M. Ash, Janesville, June, 1849; two c.

Charles Demond,   Pension Office, Washington, D. C.

Lawyer. b. Ware. Ma., Sep. 22, 1823. f. Ware. Delta Upsilon. T. Phil. o., 1844. s. Law, Harvard. Admitted, Dec. 27, 1844. Boston, 1845-80; Washington, since 1881. mem. Mass. H. of R., four years. Boston City Gov't., 1852-3. school Board, fifteen years. U. S. Civ. Com. Pres. Y. M. C. A. W. C. Alumni Orator, 1865. m. Ada B. Campbell, Washington, D. C., Nov. 18, 1856; two c., W. C. are 53.

Theron Holbrook Hawkes,   Springfield, Mass.

Clergyman and Teacher. b. Charlemont, Ma., Oct. 24, 1820. f. Buckland. Delta Upsilon. Pres. T. Valedictory. U. T. S., 1849-53. Inst. U. T. S., 1852-4; H. T. S., 1854-3. Ord. Cong., Mar. 7, 1855. Pas. W. Springfield, 1855-61; Cleveland, O., 1861-8; Marietta, 1869-88. rec. Northampton, Ma., 1866-4. Tea. N. C. W., Springfield, since 1844. D. D. Williams, 1864. Trustee Mt. Holyoke Sem., West, Rev and Marietta. m. Mary O. Hundly, New York, June 5, 1855; five c.

Charles Spafford Spencer.

Lawyer. b. Ithaca, N. Y., Feb. 13, 1828. f. Cazenovia. Sigma Phi. T. Salutatory. s. Law, Ithaca; Admitted, 1847; p. Law, Ithaca. 1847-50; New York City, 1850-67. mem. N. Y. Assembly, 1858, 1864. Col. 5th Reg., N. G. S. N. Y., ten years. m. Orlia A. Loomis, Auburn, Aug. 16, 1849. d. New York City, Aug. 11, 1867.

Marshall Wilcox,   Pittsfield, Mass.

Lawyer. b. Stockbridge, Ma., Mar. 19, 1821. f. Lenox. Kappa Alpha. Jun. Ex., 1842. L. Oration, 1844. s. and p. Law, Oba, 1844-52; Admitted, 1847; Lee, 1853-71; Pittsfield, since 1871. Mass. H. of R., 1868. Mass. Senate, 1868. m. Nannie F. Bradley, Detroit, Mich., Jan. 7, 1857; one son.

1845.

Charles Jewett Collins,   161 Madison Ave., New York City.

Clergyman and Teacher. b. Wilkesbarre, Pa., June 22, 1828. f. Lancaster, 1837-41. Kappa Alpha. Adel. Un. Ex., 1844. Jun. Ex., 1844. Prex. L. Oration, 1845. Tea. Wilkesbarre, 1845-6; Alexandria, Va., 1847-8. Tut. W. C., 1849-50. M. A. U. T. S., 1850-1; P. T. S., 1851-4. Ord. Presb., Dec. 81, 1866. Pas. Danville, Pa. 1858-68. Supt. Schools, Wilkesbarre, 1868-74. Prep. Sch., Princeton, N J., 1874-80; Tea. Rye, N. Y., 1880-4; New York, since 1884. m. Annie Ranklin, New York, June 15, 1856, (d. May 19, 1884; four c.

Charles Augustus Davison,   71 Wall St., New York City.

Lawyer. b. Saratoga Springs, N. Y., May 27, 1825. f. under Rev. Dr. Chester. Sigma Phi. Jun. Ex., 1844. Pres. f.; Adel. Un. Ex., 1845. Philosophical o., 1845. Master's Oration, 1848; M. A., Williams. Law. New York City, since 1848. mem. N. Y. His. Soc., Nat. His. Soc., Amer. Geog. Soc., Board of Managers Am. Bib. Soc. Trustee W. C., since 1877. Elder Presb. Church. m. Mary E. Vermilye, New York, June 6, 1850; two c., son W. C., 74.

Samuel McClellan.

Merchant. b. Wheeling, W. Va., Mar. 3, 1825. f. under Cumming, '34. Sigma Phi. L. Jun. Ex., 1844. Salutatory, Business, Wheeling, 1845-78. M. A., W. C., 1868. Mayor, Wheeling, 1869. d. there, Dec. 22, 1873.

Stephen Chester Strong, South Natick, Middlesex Co., Mass.

Clergyman. b. Northampton, Ma., Jan. 22, 1824. f. Leicester. Sigma Phi. Pres. T. Moonlight. 1842; Jun. Ex., 1844; First English Oration, 1845. U. T. S., 1848. Ord. Apr 12, 1854. Tea. Flushing, N. Y., 1848-52. Pas. Southampton, Ms. 1854-9; Gorham, Me., 1849-8; South Natick, Ma., 1869-71. res. South Natick. m. Myra Peters Brown, Pittsfield, Ma., July 21, 1852.

William Dwight Whitney,   New Haven, Conn.

Teacher. b. Northampton, Ma., Feb. 9, 1827. f. in public schools. Sigma Phi. L. Jun. Ex., 1844. Valedictory. Clerk in Bank, Northampton, 1845-9. U. S (Geol. Surv., 1849, a Yale, 1849-50, Europe, 1850-4 Prof. Yale, since 1854. pub. "Atharva-Veda," text, 1856; Index Verborum, 1881; "Surya-Siddhanta, (Hindu Astronomy), 1860; "Atharva-Veda Pratiçakhya," and "Taittiriya Pratiçakhya." (Vedic grammars), 1862 and 1871; "Sanskrit Grammar," 1879; Sanskrit Roots, Verb-Forms and Derivatives, 1885; "Language and the Study of Language," 1867; "Life and Growth of Language," 1875; "Oriental and Linguistic Studies," 3 vols., 1873, 1874; "Essentials of English Grammar," 1877; "German Grammar," 1869, smaller, 1885; "German Reader," 1870; "German Dictionary," 1877; "French Grammar," 1886. M. A. also Yale, 1865. LL. D., 1869, also William and Mary, 1869, also Harvard, 1876. J. U. D., St. Andrews, Scotland, 1874. Ph. D., Breslau Univ., 1861. L. H. D., Columbia, 1887. Pres. Oriental Soc.; Hon. mem. Asiatic Soc. Ot. Br and L. Or. Soc.'s. Germany, Italy, Bengal, Japan, Peking. First Pres. Am. Philol. Assoc'n, 1869. Hon. mem. Philol. Soc., London. Lit. Soc's, Leyden, Upsala and Helsingfors; Acad's, Dublin, Turin, Rome, Lincei, St. Petersburg and Berlin; (corresp't.) Inst. de France; For. Knight of Prussian Order, "Pour le Merite" for Sci. and Arts, (taking the place of Thomas Carlyle.) m. Elizabeth Wooster Baldwin, New Haven, Aug 27, 1856; six c. Europe, 1856-7, 1875, 1878-9. "Forty Years' Record, Class of 1845," 1885. Pres. Phi Beta Kappa, W. C., 1870-1: National Council, 1886-88.

1846.

John Fowler Allen.

Teacher. b. Sandisfield, Ma., May 25, 1844. f. Lev. Kappa Alpha. Jun. Ex., 1845. T. in Eng. o., 1846. Tea. Orange C. H., Va., 1849-56; Prof. Few. Coll. Eufaula, Ala., 1856-60; Prof. Math and Nat Sci., Marion, Ala, 1867-70. m. Eliza F. Atkins, Orange C. H., Va., Aug., 1857; two c. d. there, May 19, 1874.

Allyn Stanley Kellogg,   58 Niles St., Hartford, Conn.

Clergyman. b. Vernon, Conn., Oct. 15, 1824. f. privately and H. S. Vernon. Delta Upsilon. L. Full o., 1848. Y. T. S., 1850. Preaching, 1851-7. Literary work since 1858. res. Vernon, Conn., 1858-74; Hartford, since 1874. mem. H. S. (Con. pub. "Memorials of Elder John White and his Descendants," 1860. m. Maria L. Avery, Auburn, N. Y., May 15, 1854; two c. one living.

Josiah Griswold McClellan,   Hopkinsville. Ky.

Lawyer. b. Wheeling, W. Va., Oct. 14, 1844. Sigma Phi. Pres. L. Valedictory. Law. M. Louis, Mo., and Hopkinsville, Ky.

Charles Stebbins Sylvester, Feeding Hills, Hampden Co., Mass.

Clergyman. b. Wa., Ma., Aug. 14, 1822. f. Wa. L. Salutatory. And. T. S., 1849-9; H. T. S., 1854. Ord. Presb., Oct., 1855, Lyons, N. Y., 1849-54; Spencertown, 1857-60; Cranockie, 1865-4; Richmond, Ma., 1865-6; Feeding Hills, 1869-79. res. Hartford, Conn., 1879-84. Compiler of English and Chinese Dict. and Heb. Books. m. Harriet Arms, Conway, Ma., May 15, 1857. (d. 1865.) m. Julia Ann Sykes, Clarkston, Mich., May 11, 1871.

1847.

Freeman Josiah Bumstead.

Physician. b. Boston, Ma., Apr. 21, 1826. Sigma Phi. Nat. His. o., 1847. M. A.   M. D. Harv., 1851. Colum., 1855. Prof. Coll. Phys. and Surg. New York, 1868-74. LL. D., W. C.; 1875. Trans. "Hunter-Ricord Treatise." "Pathology and Treatment." "Cullerier's Atlas," 1868. m. Mary Josephine White, Boston, 1851; two c.; Phi Beta Kappa soc. 'W. d. Nov. 27, 1879.

Samuel Partridge Ely,   Cleveland, Ohio.

Civil Engineer. b. Rochester, N. Y., Oct. 14, 1827. Kappa Alpha. T. Mathematical o., 1847. Master's o., 1850. Building R. R.'s and working mines, Marquette, Mich., 1867-75; Colorado, 1876; Utah, Cal., Arizona, 1877-82. res. Cleveland, O., since 1884. Mayor of Marquette. m. Harriet H. Greenough, Cambridge, Mass., Aug. 4, 1852. (d. 1873); five c.

Henry Fowler.

Clergyman. b. Stockbridge, Ms., Oct. 17, 1824. T. Oration, 1845. Journalist, 1847-53. Prof. Polit. Econ. Univ. Roch., 1854-61. Pas. Presb. Auburn, 1859-72. pub. "The American Pulpit." Chap. 19th, N. Y. Vols. m. Elizabeth H. Dewey, Rochester, 1856; three c. d. Aug. 4, 1872.

Isaac Newton Lincoln.

Teacher and Clergyman. b. Plainfield, Ms., Aug. 16, 1815. Delta Upsilon. Pres. L. Classical o., 1842. Theol. Inst., (Gem., 1845). Tra. Hinsdale, 1849-51. Ord., 1854. Prof. Lat. and Fr. Lang., W. C., 1854-62. m. Lucy C. Phillips, Windsor, Ms., 1851 d, Sep. 5, 1862.

Thomas Mather North,   120 Broadway, New York City.

Lawyer. b. Ellington, Conn., Aug. 14, 1823. Sigma Phi. L. Historical o., 1847. Admitted to the Bar, 1847. Law. New York City, since 1847. m. Mary A. Wayland, Saratoga Springs, Apr. 16, 1849; two c.

John Lemuel Thomas Phillips.

Teacher. b. Windsor, Ms., Mar. 16, 1827. Delta Upsilon. Pres. T. Valedictory. Tra. Ropetertown, N. Y., 1847-9; W. Fem., Easthampton, Ms., 1849-52. A. T. K., 1854. Prof. Greek, W. C., 1857-69. res. Halliston, N. Y., 1869-77. Elder Presb. Ch. Librarian, W. C., 1857-62. d, Apr. 4, 1879.

Charles Burt Sheldon,   Pomona, Los Angeles Co., Cal.

Clergyman. b. Wm., Ms., Dec. 18, 1821. f. Stockbridge. Delta Upsilon. L. Phil. o., 1847. s. Theol. West. Res. T. S., Hudson, O., 1847-50. Pas. Republic, O., 1850-5; Farmbidw, Minn., 1855-63; Pomona, Cal., since 1864. mem. Minn. Cong. Conv., 1854 m. Mary K. Prentice, New York, May 12, 1847; eleven c., seven living.

Samuel Bridges Sheldon.

Teacher. b. Lenoxboro, Ms., Apr. 10, 1824. f. Stockbridge. Delta Upsilon. Salutatory. Tra. Cambridge, N. Y., 1854. d. Stockbridge, Apr. 12, 1849.

David Ames Wells,   Norwich, Conn.

Author, Editor, Scientist. b. Springfield, Ms., June 17, 1827. Delta Upsilon. T. Oration, 1847. Lawrence Sci. Sch., Harv. Univ., 1851. Asst Ed. Republican, 1845. Tra. Groton, 1850. Prof. Register Sci. Sch., Harv. Univ., 1851-2. Chemist, Boston, 1853-4. Ed. Annual of Scientific Discovery, 1850-65. Ed. Prun. Farm Journal, 1855 Publisher. etc. P. Putnam & Co., 1854. U. S. Rev. Commissioner, 1865. Special Com. of Revenue, 1865-70. Chairman Bd. Tax Com., N. Y., 1871-3. Director Erie R. R., 1878-9. mem. U. S. Bd. N. Y. Arbitration, 1878-82. pub. "Sketches of Williams College, 1847; " Annual of Scientific Discovery," 16 vols., 1850-65; "Things not Generally Known," 1857; "Year Book of Agriculture," 1856; "Knowledge is Power," 1856; "Familiar Science," 1856; "Science of Common Things," 1857; "Natural Philosophy," 1857; "Chemistry," 1858; "Geology," 1861; "Our Burden and Our Strength;" "Report U. S. Revenue Commission," 1866; Eight "Special" Reports, same, 1866; Four "Reports U. S. Special Com. of Revenue," 1867-70; "Report of N. Y. State Bd. Com. to review Tax Laws," 1871; Second Report, same, 1872; "The Recent Financial, Industrial and Commercial Experiences of the U. S.," 1872; "The Creed of Free Trade," 1875; "Robinson Crusoe's Money," 1876; Tax, N. Y Report, 1878; "Our Merchant Marine," 1880; "Practical Economics," 1885; "A Study of Mexico," 1887; "The Economic Disturbances since 1873," 1887. President Am. Social Sci. Assoc., 1875-6; West Point Visitors, 1876; New London Hist. Soc., 1880-1; Am. Free Trade League since 1881. Hon. member Cobden Club; Am. Geog. Soc.; Hist. Soc., Penn. and N. Y.; Boston Nat. His. Soc.; London Math. Soc., etc. M. A. W. C., 1854; B. S., Harv., 1850; M. D., Berk. Med. Sch., 1854; LL D., W. C., 1851; D. C. L., Oxford Univ., 1874. Cor. Mem. Institute of France, taking the seat of John Stuart Mill. m. Mary N. Dwight; m. Ellen A. Dwight; one son.

1848.

Henry Hill Anderson,   35 Wall St., New York City.

Lawyer. b. Boston, Ms., Nov. 9, 1827. f. P. A. Andover. Sigma Phi. T. Oration, 1848. Law. New York, since 1851. M. A., Williams. mem. Epis. Ch. m. Sarah B. Burrall, Lakeville, Ct., Dec. 88, 1851; four c.

Paul Ansel Chadbourne.

President Williams College. b. North Berwick, Me., Oct. 21, 1823. f. P. A. Keeter, N. H. Kappa Alpha. l. Jun. Ex., 1847. Valedictory. Tea. Freehold, N. J., 1848-9. Tut. W. C., 1849-51. M. A. Theol. Inst., Conn. 1851. Prof. Chem., W. C., 1853-8; Prof. Botany, 1868-9; Prof. Nat. His., 1849-67. Pres. Mass. Agr. Coll. 1867. Pres. Wisconsin Univ., 1866. Pres. Williams College, 1872-81. pub. "Relations of Natural History to Intellect, Taste, Wealth and Religion," 1869; "Natural Theology," 1867; "Instinct in Animals and Men," 1872; "Hope of the Righteous," 1877; The Public service of N. Y. State, 8 vols.; Natural Religion, 1878, and many addresses. mem. Mass. Senate, 1865, 1866. Pres. Elector, 1861. M. D. Berk. Med. Sch., 1850; LL. D., Williams, 1868; D. D., Amherst, 1873. Trustee, W. C., 1874-81. m. Elizabeth S. Page, Exeter, N. H., Oct. 9, 1850; three c. d. New York City, Feb. 23, 1883.

James Dickson Clark.

Lawyer and Teacher. b. Northampton, Ms., Nov. 12, 1825. Kappa Alpha. l. Latin, Jun. Ex., 1847. Classical., 1848. s. Law, New York and Cambridge, 1848-51. M. A. Admitted, 1851. p. Law, Brooklyn and New York, 1851-3. Tea. Brooklyn, 1853-61. Business, New York, 1864-73. pub. "The Biographical Record of the Kappa Alpha Society of Williams College," 1864. d. Brooklyn, N. Y., June 2, 1892.

Charles Seely Dunning.

Clergyman. b. Wallkill, N. Y., Jan. 21, 1827. Delta Upsilon. Pres. L. Historical o., 1846. U. T. S., 1849-52. Ord. Presb., Nov. 8, 1856. Tut. U. T. S., 1856-7. Pas. Franklin, N. Y., 1849-51; Honesdale, Pa., 1861-63; Kingston. 1864-4. D. D. Lafayette, 1871. m. Maria White, New York, Nov. 4, 1857; four c. d. Metuchen, S. J., June 1, 1895.

Samuel Tobey Field.   Shelburne Falls, Mass.

Lawyer. b. Hawley, Ms. Apr. 20, 1825. f. Zachmanjesse. Delta Upsilon T. Math. o., 1846. s. Law, New Haven Law School. Tea. Freehold, N. J., 1848-51. Law, Shelburne Falls, since 1852. School Com., 1855-6. Mass. H. of R., 1855-56. Dist. Att., 1864-8. m. Sarah H. Lamson; m. Susan E. Smith; seven c.

John Gibson McMynn,   Racine, Wis.

Teacher. b. Palatine Bridge, N. Y., July 9, 1824. f. Union Village and N. Granville. Delta Upsilon. Pres. L. Moonlight. 1846. Jun. Ex., 1847. Oration, 1848. s. Law. Prin. H. S. Kenosha, five yrs.; Europe, one yr.; Prin. H. S. Racine, seven yrs.; Union Army, two yrs.; Agt. Bd. Regents Normal Sch., one yr.; State Supt. Public Instruction, Wis. four yrs.; Sec. Throwing Machine Manf. Co., six yrs. Prin. McMynn Acad. seven yrs. M. A. Williams City Supt. Sch., Racine; Prin. Wis. Normal Sch., Winona, Minn.; Pres. and Sec. Board Regents, Wis. Univ.; Supt. Indian Affairs, Wash. Ter.; Pres. State Tea. Assoc.; Major, Lieut. Col., and Col. 10th Wis. Infantry. mem. His. Soc.; U. S. Loyal Legion. pub. School Reports, etc. m. Marion P. Clarke, Racine, Aug. 1, 1860; four c. res. Racine, thirty-four yrs. (Finally now at Madison, educating the children.)

Daniel Ephraim Safford,   Hamilton, Essex Co., Mass.

Lawyer. b. Hamilton, Ms., Feb. 5, 1823. f. P. A. Andover. Kappa Alpha. Pres. L. Jun. Ex., 1847. Phil. o., 1848. Master's o., 1851. Harv. Law Sch., 1849-50; LL. B., Harv., 1870. Law officer at Salem, Mass. H. of R., 1861; Senate, 1871-4. m. Mary E. Smith, Ipswich, Dec. 7, 1854; three c.

Theodore Strong.

Student. b. Northampton, Ms., June 19, 1823. T. Salutatory. d. Aug. 21, 1845.

1849.

John Bascom,   Williamstown, Mass.

Teacher, Clergyman, Author. b. Genoa, N. Y., May 1, 1827. f. Flower. Beta Theta Pi. T. Phil o., 1849 Anh. T. S., 1852-3 Tut. W. C., 1853-4. M. A. A. T. S., 1854-6. Prof. Rhet. W. C., 1855-74. Ord. Pownal, Vt. Dec. 15, 1850. Pas. North Pownal, 1854-61. President Univ. Wis., 1874-87. pub. "Political Economy," 1859; "Aesthetics," 1862; "Philosophy of Rhetoric," 1865; "Science of Mind," 1869; "Science, Philosophy and Religion," 1871; "Philosophy of English Literature," 1874; "Philosophy of Religion," 1876; "Growth and Grades of Intelligence," 1878; "Ethics," 1879; "Natural Theology," 1880; "Words of Christ," 1884; "Problems in Philosophy," 1885; "Sociology," 1887. LL. D., Amherst, 1873. D. D., Iowa, 1873. m. Abbie Burt, Gt. Barrington, Dec. 9, 1856. (d. 1858). m. Emma Curtis, Sheffield, Jan. 8, 1868.

Edward Griffin Beckwith,   **Honolulu, Hawaiian Islands.**

Clergyman and Teacher. b. Gt. Barrington, Ma., Nov. 14, 1826. Delta Upsilon. Pres. L. Valedictory. Tra. Mass., 1850-1. Prin. Royal Sch., Honolulu, 1951-4. Pres. Oahu Coll., 1854-9. Sacramento, Cal., 1859-62. A. T. K., 1861-2. Ord. Cong., Feb. 8, 1853. Pas., San Francisco, Cal., 1863-9; Waterbury, Conn., 1869-81; San Francisco, 1881-7; Pas. Foreign Ch., Honolulu, since Oct., 1887. D. D., Williams, 1874. m. Carrie P. Armstrong. Honolulu, 1854; four c., one living.

Fisher Ames Boise.

District. b. Blandford, Ma., July 17, 1804. Delta Upsilon. T. Math o., 1825. d. Westfield, 1882.

Robert Russell Booth,   **7 West Sixteenth St., New York City.**

Clergyman. b. New York City, May 18, 1830. f. Univ. Gram. Sch., New York. Kappa Alpha. T. Oration, 1849. Auh. T. K., 1849-52. M. A. Ord., Nov., 1853. Pas. Troy, N. Y., 1853-8; Stamford, Ct., 1858-61; Mercer St. Ch., New York, 1861-70; Univ. Place Ch., New York, 1870-83. Rutgers Ch., New York, since 1884. Trustee W. C., since 1884. Director U. T. K. since 1861. Director P. T. K. D. D., Univ. City N. Y., 1865. pub. Pamphlets, Magazine Articles, etc. m. Emma Louise Lathrop, Auburn, N. Y., Oct. 25, 1856; two c.

Isaac Gray Ogden,   **Conklin, Broome Co., N. Y.**

Clergyman. b. Binghamton, N. Y., Nov. 27, 1827. Delta Upsilon. Pres. L. Historical o., 1849. M. A. Tut. Lafayette Coll., 1854-5. Tra. Sand Lake, N. Y., 1855-8. A. T. K., 1854. Ord. Presb., Jan. 25, 1856. Pas. Portville, N. Y., 1856-61; Almond, 1865-71. Tra. East Greenbush, 1872-6. Pas. Hunkirk's Bridge, 1876-81; Marvah, 1881-5; Conklin, since 1885. m. E. K. Huntington, Aug. 1, 1851; four c.

Charles Seymour Robinson,   **57 East 54th St., New York City.**

Clergyman. b. Bennington, Vt., Mar. 31, 1821. f. Union Acad., Bennington. Chi Psi. Beta Theta Pi. T. Jan. Ex., 1847. Poem, 1849. Master's o., 1852. Tra., 1849-52. U. T. K., 1852-3. P. T. K., 1853-3. Ord., June 18, 1855. Pas. Troy, N. Y., 1855-60; Brooklyn, 1860-8; Am. Chapel, Paris, 1868-71; New York City, since 1871. pub. "Songs of the Church," 1862; "Songs for the Sanctuary," 1865; "Short Studies for Sunday School Teachers," 1868; "Bethel and Penuel," 1873; "Church Work," 1873; "Psalms and Hymns," 1875; "Calvary Songs for Sunday Schools," 1875; Ed. Illus. Christian Weekly, 1876-7; "Spiritual Songs for Church and Choir," 1878; "Studies in the New Testament," 1880; "Spiritual Songs for Sunday Schools," 1881; "Studies of Neglected Texts," 1883; "Laudes Domini," 1884; "Sermons in Songs," 1886; "Sabbath Evening Sermons," 1886; "The Pharaohs of the Bondage and the Exodus," 1887, and several others. D. D., Hamilton, 1868. LL. D., Lafayette, 1886. m. Harriet M. Church, Troy, N. Y., Nov. 4, 1855; one daughter.

Newton Henry Rosseter.

Student. b. Gt. Barrington, Ma., Oct. 24, 1830. Delta Upsilon. L. Salutatory. A. T. K., 1851-3. d. Gt. Barrington, Dec. 20, 1853.

Milton Burrall Whitney,   **Westfield, Mass.**

Lawyer. b. Granville, Ma., Oct. 5, 1828. Delta Upsilon. L. Classical o., 1849. Tra., 1849-51. Law, Admitted June, 1854; Westfield, since 1851. Trial Justice, 1854-88. Ram. Senate, 1885, 1886. Pres. Elector, 1884.

1850.

Peter Mason Bartlett,   **Maryville, Tenn.**

Clergyman and Teacher. b. Salisbury, Ct., Feb. 6, 1820. f. Oberlin, O. Delta Upsilon. Pres J. Metaphysical and Salutatory. U. T. K. 1850-3. Ord. Cong., Aug., 1853. Agt. A. T. K., 1853-4. Pas. Presb., Circleville O., 1854-7; Lansingburgh, N. Y., 1858-60; Flushing, 1860-4; Chaplain, U. S. Army, 1864-5; Pas. Windsor Locks, Ct., 1866-9. Prof. Rev. and Mor. Sci. and Didac. Theol., and President Maryville College, Tennessee, 1869-87. M. A., Williams. D. D., Dartmouth, 1872. m. Florence M. Abbe, Clove Spring, Ga., Apr. 25, 1873; two c.

John Bassett Chapin, Penn. Hospital, West Philadelphia, Pa.

Physician. b. New York City, Dec. 4, 1829. f. Hudson, O. Chi Psi. L. Oration, 1850. grad. Jeff. Med. Coll., 1853. Resident Phys. N. Y. Hosp., 1854-9; Brigham Hall, Canandaigua, 1859-9; Phys. and Supt. William Asylum, 1869-84; Phys. in Chief, Penn. Hosp. Insane, Phila., since 1884. M. D., Jefferson, 1853. Permanent mem. N. Y. State Med. Soc.; Fellow College of Physicians Phila. pub. "Care, Treatment and Provision for the Insane," and similar treatises. m. Harriet E. Preston, Philadelphia, Mar. 18, 1858; four c.

Charles Chauncey Dwight, — Auburn. N. Y.

Lawyer. b. Richmond, Ma., Sep. 13, 1809. f Ithaca, N. Y. Chi Psi. Pres. T. Jus Ex., 1849. Albany Law School; Admitted, 1854. Auburn, since 1854. Judge Cayuga Co., 1856. U. S. Army, 1861-5; (Vd. 16th N. Y., 1862-3, mem. Const Conv., N. Y., 1867-8. Judge N. Y. Supreme Court since 1868. LL. D., Williams, 1874. Trustee Aub. T. S., since 1871; Cornell Univ.; Albany Univ ; Wells College. Pres. W. C. Alumni, 1884. m. Emma Munro, Camillus. N. Y., July 30, 1834.

Dudley Field.

Lawyer. b. New York City, Nov. 28, 1831. Kappa Alpha. T. Jun. Ex , 1849. Phil. o., 1850 Foreign Travel, 1851-2. Law with his father, (W C., 1855), New York, 1853-60. m. Laura J. Belden, New York, Jan. 13, 1861; two c. d. Stockbridge, Mass., Aug. 10, 1860.

William Edward Merriman, — Somerville, Mass.

Clergyman. b. Hinsdale, Ma., Oct. 20, 1825. f. Burr Sem., Manchester, Vt. Delta Upsilon. Pres. L. Ethical n . 1850. U. T. S., 1851-4; Ord. Jan. 13, 1857. Tea., 1859-1. M. A. Pas. Batavia, Ill., 1851-60; Green Bay, Wis., 1861-3; Pres. Ripon, Wis., College, 1863-70; Pas. Somerville, Ms., 1864-?. D. D. Williams, 1874. Pres. W. C. Alumni, 1884. m. Anne Lockwood, Batavia, Ill., July 1, 1857; four c.

William Stark.

Lawyer. b. Manchester, Vt., July, 1828. Sigma Phi. L. Salutatory. Law, New York and Nashua, 1856-?; Manchester, Vt., 1857-70. McLean Asylum, Somerville, Ms., 1870-3. d. there, Oct. 20, 1872.

John Bagg Taylor, — Treasury Dept., Washington, D. C.

Civil Engineer. b. West Springfield, Ma. Sep. 25, 1828. f. Westfield and Easthampton. Beta Theta Pi. T. Maid o., 1850. Tea. Riga, N. Y., 1850-1. M A. Civil Eng., B and N Y. R. R., 1851-3; P. and K. H. R., 1854-5; Pri. Ass. Eng., A. and G. W. R. R., 1855-60. Treas. Dept., Washington, D. C., since 1862.

William Ripley Tompkins, — Wrentham, Norfolk Co., Mass.

Clergyman. b. Madison, N. Y., Mar 10, 1828. Pres. T. Natural History o., 1850. A T. S., 1853-6; Ord. Oct. 9, 1856. M. A. Pas. New England Ch., Brooklyn, 1856-61; Wrentham, Mass., since 1861. Mass. H. of R., 1877, 1880.

Theodore Frelinghuysen Van Vechten.

Student b. Bloomingburg, N. Y., Mar. 14, 1829. Delta Upsilon. Pres. T. Valedictory. d. New York, June 10, 1852.

1851.

Leonard Bronk.

Lawyer. b. Coxsackie, N. Y., Oct. 21, 1831. Kappa Alpha. I. Jun. Ex., 1850. Historical o., 1851. LL. B. Alb. Univ., 1853. Fla., 1853-1. d. Coxsackie, July 28, 1854.

George Ellery Clarke, — Nat. Bank, Falmouth, Mass.

Teacher. b. Needham, Ma., Oct. 20, 1828. f. P. A. Andover. Alpha Delta Phi. L. Ethical o., 1851. Prin. Lawrence Acad., Falmouth, 1851-54. M. A. Clerk U S. Light House Dept., Boston, 1854-73. Cashier Nat. Bank, Falmouth, since 1873. m. Achsah Shiverick, Falmouth, Nov. 25, 1858; one c.

Charles Augustus Dewey, — Milford, Worcester Co., Mass.

Lawyer. b. Northampton, Ma., Dec. 29, 1830. f. W. S. Easthampton. Kappa Alpha. T. Jun. Ex., 1850. Salutatory. a Law, Cambridge and New York. M. A. p. Law. New York, 1854-6; Davenport, Ia., 1858-9; Milford, Mass., since 1859. Judge Police Court, 1864-71. Judge Dist. Court, since 1871. m. Marietta N. Thayer, Milford, Mar. 18, 1865; one daughter.

William Goodell, — 1418 Spruce St., Philadelphia, Pa.

Physician. b. Island of Malta, Oct. 17, 1829. f. Constantinople. Kappa Alpha. L. Greek o., Jun. Ex., 1850. Nat. His o., 1851. M A. N. D , Jeff Med Coll., 1854. p Med., Constantinople, 1854-60; Westchester, Pa., 1860-4; Philadelphia, since 1864. Prof. Gynecology, Univ., Pa., since 1873. Fellow, College of Physicians, Phila. Hon. mem. Med. Soc., London, Constantinople, Edinburgh, etc. pub. "Lessons in Gynecology," 1878. m. Caroline D. Bell, Smyrna, Turkey, Sep. 4, 1857; five c.

Everard Kempshall,   Elizabeth, N. J.

Clergyman, b. Rochester, N. Y., Aug 9, 1831. Chi Psi. T. Oration, 1851. P. T. K., 1851-3. Ord Presb., Jan. 16, 1856. Pas. Buffalo, N. Y., 1856-7; Rochester, 1857-9, Batavia, 1864-61; Elizabeth. N. J., since 1861. D. D., W. C. and N. J., 1870. Director P. T. S. since 1879.

George Mooar,   Oakland, Cal.

Clergyman. b. Andover. Ms., May 27, 1830 f. P. A. Andover. Alpha Delta Phi. Pres. L. Mills Theol. L. N. H. Monalighs, 1851 Valedictory. A. T. K., 1853-5; Ord. Oct 10, 1855 M. A. Pas. No. Ch., Andover, 1855-61; Oakland, Cal., since 1861. Prof. Sys. Theol and Ch. His. Pacific Theol. Sem., since 1874. Assoc. Ed. Pacific since 1873. D. D., Williams, 1875. pub "Manual South Ch., Andover," 1859; "Prominent Characteristics of the Congregational Churches," 1868; "Hand Book, Cong. Churches, Cal.," 1863, 71, 73, 76, 87. m. Sarah Ann Comstock. Crestrebrook, Ct., Oct. 5, 1853; four c.

Charles Newman.

Clergyman. b. Keremont. Ms., Apr. 9, 1829. Alpha Delta Phi. L. Phil. o, 1851, A. T. K., 1851-7; Ord., May 18, 1856, Pas. Torringford, Ct., 1856-58; New Lebanon, N. Y., 1859; Laurebon, Ms., 1861-73. d. West Stockbridge Centre, May 30, 1873.

James White,   Williamstown, Mass.

Treasurer Williams College. b. Hinsdale, Ms., July 9, 1829. f. W. R. Easthampton. Delta Psillon. Pres. I. Classical o, 1851. Tra. W. N. Easthampton, 1851-3. M. A. A T. K., 1855 f; Merchant, Boston, 1855-65; Treasurer Williams College since 1865. member Mass. H. of R., 1866-7; Mass. Senate, 1878-9. Trustee W. C. since 1881. Deacon Central Cong. Ch., Boston, since 1868. m. Harriet Cornelia Kittredge. Hinsdale, Mass., Jan. 62, 1856; two c.

1852.

John Woodbridge Dickinson,   State House, Boston, Mass.

Teacher. b Chester. Ms. f. Easthampton and No. Williamstown. Alpha Delta Phi. T. Classical o, 1852. Tea. Normal School, Westfield, 1856-6; Principal of same, 1856-77. Secretary Board of Education, Mass Home at Newton since 1877. Trustee W. C, since 1878. M. A., Williams. pub. "Reports of Mass. Schools," ten vols. m. Abraine G. Parsons, Yarmouth, Me., 1857; two c.

Charles March Freeman.

Lawyer. h Glen's Falls. N. Y., Aug. 15, 1828. Kappa Alpha. T. Greek o. Jun. Ex., 1851. Redeuridegical o., 1854. s. Law, Troy and Harvard; p. Law. New York, 1854-61. U. S. Army, 1861-5; Captain. res. Oakwood Farm, near Troy, 1865-82. d. there, Mar. 80, 1882.

Edward Warner French.

Clergyman. h. Barre, Vt., Aug. 69, 1829. T. Salutatory. U. T. S., 1854. Ord. Presb., Jan. 15, 1857. M. A. Pas. Bergen. Jersey City, N. J., 1856-80. D. D., Williams, 1878. m. Kate A. Merrifield, May 89, 1857, (d. 1890). m. Julia N. Dey, Aug. 80, 1859; six c. d. Feb. 4, 1890.

Henry Martyn Hazeltine,   Monroe, Fairfield Co., Conn.

Clergyman. b. Jamestown, N. Y., Aug. 59, 1831. Alpha Delta Phi. T. Phil. o, 1852. U. T. S., 1854-7; Ord., Jan. 20, 1859. Pas. Sherman, N. Y., 1859-60; Perry, 1869-70; Henrietta, 1870-1; No. Salem, 1874-6; W. Stockbridge, Ms., 1876-80; Monroe, Conn., since 1881. m. Fannie Hallock, Amherst, Ms., Oct. 7, 1857; two dau.

Charles Henry Holmes.

Teacher. b. Union Village, N. Y., Nov 12, 1828. Pres. L. Ethical o., 1852. d. at home, May 16, 1854.

Horace Judson Hunt.

Lawyer. b. New Salem, Ms., Dec. 15, 1827. Pres. L. Math. o., 1852. s. Law, Pittsfield. d. at home, 1854.

Charles McEwen Hyde,   Honolulu, Hawaiian Islands.

Clergyman. b. (son of Joseph Hyde, 1822,) New York City, June 8, 1832. Pres. L. Valedictory. U. T. S., 1834. Tut. Sheffield, Ma., 1854-8. M. A. P. T. S., 1868-60. Ord. Cong., Aug. 19, 1861. Pas. Onsboro, Ct., 1863-1; Brimfield, Ma., 1865-70; Haverhill, 1870-5; For. Mis. Honolulu, since 1877. Pres. North Pacific Theol. Inst. D. D., W. C., 1882. pub "History of Brimfield," 1876; "History of Law," 1877. m Mary T. Knight. Brimfield, Ct., Oct. 10, 1865; two sons, one Phi Beta Kappa, '87.

Arthur Latham Perry,   Williamstown, Mass.

Teacher and Author. b Lyme, N. H., Feb. 6, 1830. f. Thetford, Vt., Alpha Delta Phi. Pres. L. Metaphysical o., 1852. Tea. Washington, D C., 1853. Tut W. C., 1854-1. M. A. Prof. History, Polit. Econ. and Ger. Lang., W. C., 1854-68. Prof. History and Polit. Econ., W. C., since 1868. Univ. of Heidelberg, 1881. LL. D., Union, 1871. D. D., Dartm., 1883. M. H. S. Pres. Berkshire H. S., since 1868. pub, "Political Economy," 1866, (18th ed., 1883;) "Introduction, Political Economy," 1877, (3rd ed., 1883.) Secretary W. C. Alumni. Secretary and Treasurer Phi Beta Kappa. m. Mary Brown Smedley, Williamstown, Mass., Aug. 7, 1856; six c., Phi Beta Kappa, '81.

Stephen Clapp Pixley,   Lindley, South Africa.

Missionary. b. Plainfield, Ms., June 22, 1853. Delta Upsilon. L. Missionary o., 1852. Theol. Inst., Ct., 1853. Missionary A. B. C. F. M., since 1853. Ord., Sep. 20, 1853. pub. Zulu Bible, 1881-3. m. Louisa Healy, Northampton, Oct. 18, 1853.

Lewellyn Pratt,   62 Niles St., Hartford, Conn.

Teacher and Clergyman. b. Saybrook, Conn., Aug. 8, 1831. f. Essex. Delta Upsilon. L. Moonlight. Jun. Ex., 1851. Oration, 1852. Tea. D. and D. Inst., Philadelphia, 1864-5, 1865-65; Business, 1865-9; Prof. National College, D. and D., Washington, D. C., 1853-9; Prof. Latin, Knox College, 1869-71. a. Tered under Rev. Dr. Barnes in Philadelphia. Pas. North Adams, Mass., 1871-4. Prof. Rhetoric, W. C., 1853-81; Prof. Practical Theology, H. T. S., since 1881. pub. newspaper and magazine articles. M. A., W. C., in course. D. D., W. C., 1877. Trustee W. C., since 1881. Director. Presb. Theol. Sem., N. W., 1870. m. Sarah P. Gulliver, Philadelphia, Oct. 17, 1855; two sons, one living. W. C. Phi Beta Kappa. 76.

1853.

Samuel Davis Barr,   College, Albion, Mich.

Teacher and Lawyer. b. Gouverneur, N. Y., July 7, 1826. f. same place. L. Grad. prize, 1852. Geological o., 1853. Tea. and Law. Gouverneur, N. Y., three yrs.; Watertown, nine yrs.; Albany, four yrs.; Rochester, one yr.; Penn Yan, two yrs.; Cleveland, O., ten yrs.; Prof. Math., Albion, Mich. same time. Surrogate and Sch. Com., Jeff. Co.; M. A.; Dep. N. Y. State Supt. Sch., 1865-9; Pres. N. Y. Tea. Assoc., 1869-70. pub. "Arithmetic," 1870; "Analytic Geometry," (Ms.)

William Cheney,   610 Temple Court, Minneapolis, Minn.

Insurance, Real Estate and Loans. b. Newport, N. H., Oct. 22, 1832. f. Rochester, N. Y. Chi Psi. Pres. T. Salutatory. M. A. Business, Rochester, 1854-61; Minneapolis since 1861. m. Cornelia Walcott, Minneapolis, Mar. 3, 1857; one son.

James Alpheus Clark.

Clergyman and Teacher. b. Washington, Ma., 1828. Delta Upsilon. Pres. L. Phil. o., 1852. Tea. Dudley, 1854-4. Bapt. Minr., Newton, 1857. Pas. Adrian, Mich., 1864-68; Fairfield, 1869-4. Prof. Kalamazoo, 1869-84. d. Iberia, Aug. 17, 1889.

Justus Clement French,   328 Belleville Ave., Newark, N. J.

Clergyman. b. Barre, Vt., May 3, 1827. T. Moonlight. Jun. Ex., 1852. Valedictory. U. T. S., 1854-5. Ord. Cong., Mar. 5, 1857. M. A. Pas. Brooklyn, N. Y., 1857-78; Newark, N. J., since 1878. D. D., Williams, 1874. M. H. S., Long Island. pub. "History Expedition to Restore Flag to Fort Sumter," 1865; "Evidences of Christianity," 1888. m. Mary A. Mather, Williamstown, Dec. 23, 1856; three c., one living.

Charles Franklin Gilson.

Teacher. b. Westminster, Vt., Oct. 1857. Alpha Delta Phi. L. Oration. 1853. Tea., 1854-6. M A. Europe, 1858-9, 1863-6. ref. Modern Lang. and Lit., W. C., 1859-81. d. New York City, June 8, 1882.

Arthur Mitchell, Cor. 5th Ave. and 12th St., New York City.

Clergyman. b. Hudson, N. Y., Aug. 23, 1835. f. Hudson. Sigma Phi. Pres. L. Oration, 1854. U. T. N., 1856-9. Ord., May 9, 1859. Tut. Lafayette, 1858-9. Master's Oration, 1856. Pas. Richmond, Va., 1859-61; Morristown, N. J., 1861-9; Chicago, Ill., 1869-70; Cleveland, O., 1870-1; Secretary Foreign Missions Presb. Ch., since 1884. D. D., Williams, 1873. Trustee W. C., since 1882. m. Harriet E. Post, New York, Oct. 5, 1859; seven c.

Francis Nathan Peloubet, Natick, Mass.

Clergyman and Author. b. New York City, Dec 2, 1831. f. Bloomfield, N. J. L. Missionary o., 1853. Bangor, T. S., 18 7. Pas. Gloucester, Mass., 1857-59; Oakham, 1859-61; Attleboro, 1861-72. Natick, since 1872. D. D., Univ., Tenn., 1884. pub. "Select Notes Inter, S. S. Lessons," 15 vols.; "Question Books," same, 30 vols.; "Quarterlies," 15 vols.; "Select Songs for Sunday Schools." Edition "Smith's Dictionary Bible." m. Mary A. Thaxter, Bangor, Me., Apr. 26, 1859; four c.

Henry Augustus Smith.

Clergyman. b. Palatine, N. Y., May 20, 1830. L. Classical o., 1852. U. T. S., 1852-3. Ord. Presb., Oct., 1854. Pas. Philadelphia, 1854-58. D. D., W. C., 1879. m. Louisa B. Andrews, July 11, 1855. d. Mar. 7, 1883.

1854.

George Lapham Ames.

Physician. b. Barnet, Vt., July 2, 1832. Alpha Delta Phi. Jun. Ex., 1853. L. Geological o., 1854. M. D., Univ., Louisville, 1857. M. A. p. Med., Hector, N. Y., and Manchester, Vt., 1858-60. Pres. Bras. Co. Med. Soc. m. Lizzie Bacon, Aug. 8, 1858, Niles, Mich. d. there, 1860.

James Marshall Anderson, New Vernon, N. J.

Clergyman and Teacher. b. Kilmarnock, Scotland. Sep. 10, 1827. f. Robertstadt, N. Y. Sigma Phi. Pres. L. Jun. Ex., 1853. Historical o., 1854. Europe, 1854-5. Tea., S. C., Ohio and Ala., 1855-61. Law, Cincinnati, 1861-4. P. T. S. 1864-7. Ord., Apr. 1865. Pres. Ohio Fem. Coll., 1864-9. Prof. Math., W. C., 1869-9. Philadelphia, 1869-70; Pas. Belvidere, N. J., 1870-4; Matawan, 1874-82; Around the World, 1882; Brooklyn, N. Y., 1882-4; New Vernon, N. J., since 1884. m. Elizabeth Robbins, Cheshire, Ct., Aug. 15, 1854; four c.

Judson Aspinwall.

Clergyman. b. Owego, N. Y., Feb. 24, 1832. Delta Upsilon. L. Missionary o., 1854. Aub. T. S., 1855-7. Ord. Presb., Dec. 30, 1858. Jordan, N. Y., 1857-8; Keokuk, Ia., 1859-9; Warsaw, Ill., 1859-61; Olathe, Kan., 1861-4. m. Harriet A. McWilliams, Elmira, N. Y., June 29, 1857; five c. d. Oct. 10, 1807.

James Randolph Dewey, 27 So. Ashland Ave., Chicago, Ill.

Teacher and Lawyer. b. Westfield, Mass., Aug. 14, 1830. f. Arad, Westfield, Alpha Delta Phi. Pres. L. Political o., 1854. a. Law, Springfield, 1854-8. Tea. and Law, Chicago, since 1859. M. A. Williams. m. Eliza Jane Kells, Simsbury, Conn., May 10, 1856; five c.

Carlton S. Horton.

Student. b. Palmyra, N. Y., June 12, 1832. T. Classical o., 1854. U. T. S., 1854-7. Invalid, Madeira, Ia., 1859-61. d. Buffalo, N. Y., Dec. 15, 1864.

Edward Payson Hudson.

Manufacturer. b. Vermont Apr. 29, 1832. Alpha Delta Phi. L. Aurora, o., 1854. Publisher, Washington, D. C.; Iron Manf., Port Henry and Troy, N. Y.; U. S. Army; Captain, Chemical Patentee. m. Kate Campbell Rutland, Vt., Jan. 1, 1862. d. City Hospital, Boston, June 16, 1881.

Robert Jackson.

Lawyer. b. Cambridge, N. Y., Nov. 21, 1834. Kappa Alpha. Pres. L. Ed. West. Quar. Val. Adel. Un., 1854. Aesthetical o., 1854. a. Law, Albany; Admitted, Oct., 1856; Law, New York, 1857-77. d. there, July 28, 1877.

William T. R. Marvin, 49 Federal St., Boston, Mass.

Printer and Publisher. b. Boston, Dec. 30, 1832. f. Latin School. Sigma Phi. L. L. S. H. Oration, 1854. res. Boston, 1852-63; Boston Highlands, 1866-73; Brookline, since 1873. School Com. since 1875. M. A., Williams. Charter mem. Phi Beta Kappa. Hon. mem. Am. Num. and Arch. Soc. Corr. mem. Num. and Antiq. Soc., Phila. mem. Num. Soc., Boston. Life mem. Bostonian Soc. pub. "The Arms of the Free Masons," 1880; "The Medals of the Masonic Fraternity," 1880; "The Carrara Medals, with notices of the Duke of Parma," 1880. Ed. "Eliot's Brief Narratives;" "The Grand Masters of Malta;" "American Journal of Numismatics," 10. Annie M. Howe, Boston, Apr. 17, 1861. (d. July 9, 1870.) m. Mary Ritchie, Brookline, Dec. 30, 1874. six c.

Hollis Read Murdock, Stillwater, Minn.

Lawyer. b. Gouverneur, N. Y., Aug. 15, 1832. Alpha Delta Phi. T. Jun. Ex., 1853. Phil. o., 1851. Law, Stillwater, Minn., since 1855. Judge Probate, 1870-8. mem. City Bd. Ed. City Attorney. Mayor, 1865-6. Mass. H. of R., 1872. m. Sarah A. Rice, Wegatchie, N. Y., Nov. 5, 1857. two c.

George Washington Northrup, Morgan Park, Ill.

Teacher and Clergyman. b. Antwerp, N. Y., Oct. 13, 1826. Delta Upsilon. Pres. L. Meta. o., 1854. Roch. T. S., 1857; Prof. Ch. His., same, ten yrs.; Prof. Sys. Theol. and Pres. Baptist T. S., Chicago, twelve yrs. D. D., Univ., Roch., 1864. LL. D., Kalamazoo, 1879. m. and four c.

James Lothrop Rice.

Lawyer. b. Detroit, Mich., Feb. 22, 1832. Chi Psi. L. Salutatory. a. Law, Detroit, 1854-7. M. A. p. Law, Kankuk, Ia., 1857-59. Register of Bankruptcy. Donor Rice prizes, W. C. d. Aug., 1876.

Jarvis Rockwell.

Lawyer. b. Peru, Ms., Mar. 18, 1829. f. Hinsdale. Delta Upsilon. L. Jun. Ex., 1853. Valedictory. a. Law, Pittsfield, 1855-7. M. A. p. Law, Hinsdale and North Adams, 1857-85. Mass. H. of R., 1882. Judge Dist. Court. m. Mary E. Chapin, North Adams, Sep. 15, 1856. two sons. d. May 14, 1885.

Norman Seaver, Park Cong. Ch., St. Paul, Minn.

Clergyman. b. Boston, Apr. 20, 1834. f. Latin School. Sigma Phi. T. Oration, 1854. A. T. S., 1857 etc. Ord. Aug. 20, 1860. Pas. Rutland, Vt., 1860-6; Brooklyn, N. Y., 1866-73; Syracuse, 1873-5; St. Paul, since 1875. D. D., Middlebury, 1883. m. Fanchar R. Daniels, Rutland, Vt.

Charles Augustus Stoddard, 37 Park Row, New York City.

Clergyman and Editor. b. Boston, Mass., May 28, 1833. f. Boston Latin School. Sigma Phi. Logian. Editor Williams Quarterly. President Adelphic Union. Editor Logian Catalogue, 1853. Oration, 1854. Tea P. A. Andover, Mass., 1854. a. Theol. Free Church Seminary, Edinburgh, Scotland, 1855, and U. T. S., 1856-8. M. A. Ord. Presb., Sep. 16, 1858. Pas. Washington Heights, New York City, 1858-65. D. R. Williams, 1851. Assoc. Ed. New York Observer, 1873-85. Editor in Chief and Proprietor, same, since the death of Dr. Prime. mem. Am. Oriental Soc. Director N. Y. Institution for Deaf and Dumb. mem. Evangelical Alliance. Europe, 1855-6, 1872, 1878, 1881-2, 1884, 1887. pub. many articles, sermons, etc. m. Mary Elizabeth, daughter of Rev. Dr. Prime, (W. C., 1829.) New York City, Nov. 16, 1858. six c.

Thomas Macauley Wheeler, 22 Pine St., New York City.

Lawyer. b. New York, July 4, 1831. Chi Psi. Zeta Psi. Jun. Ex., 1853. Math. o., 1854. Law, New York, since 1856. C. S. Army; N. Y. Seventh Regiment; Major 13th N. Y. Cavalry. m. and c. House, Englewood, N. J.

1855.

William Wisner Adams, First Cong. Ch., Fall River, Mass.

Clergyman. b. Palmyrville, O., Aug. 15, 1831. f. Chicago. Mills Theol. Soc. T. Editor Williams Quarterly. Junior Ex., 1854. Adelphic Union Debate, 1855. Metaphysical o., 1855. U. T. S., 1858. Ord Cong. Jan. 24, 1860. Pas. Burlington, Ia., 1860-; Conn., Ill., 1860-69; Briol, Wis., 1864-9; Fall River, Mass., since 1864. D. D., Williams, 1873. Member and Chairman School Board. Trustee, Williams, since 1886. Trustee Public Library. pub. Articles, Reviews, Sermons, etc. m. Mary Augusta Cooper, Wells River, Vt., Oct. 18, 1864.

William Reynolds Dimmock.

Teacher. b. Falmouth, Ma., Feb. 25, 1853. f. Latin School, Boston. Sigma Phi. Jun Ex., 1851. Pres. I. Pres. L N II. Editor *Williams Quarterly*. Pres. Mills T N. Oration, 1855. Hurr. Law Sch., 1854. Master's Oration, 1856. Admitted, 1862. Tea, Latin School, Boston, 1861-4. Prof Gr. Lang and Lit. W. C., 1864-72. Master Adams Acad., Quincy, 1856-8. LL. D., Williams, 1872. Trustee. W. C., 1873. m. Caroline E. Dimmock, Afton, Ill. May 84, 1854, (d. Iowa). d. Mar. 29, 1876

Cyrus Morris Dodd. Williamstown, Mass.

Teacher. b Brooklinhn. N Y., Nov. 19, 1836. f Blooomfield, N J. Delta Upsilon. L. Mathematical o., 1855. Tea. Kalom, N. J., 1857-7. M A. Prof Lat. Lang. and Lit. Jefferson College, 1861-4; Prof Math. and Prof. L.d. Lang and Lit. Univ., Indiana, 1866-70; Prof Math. W. C., since 1864. 1858. m. Mary Collins Latham, Williamtown, Mass., Aug. 17, 1857; three daughters.

Charles Elliott Fitch, Rochester, N. Y.

Editor. b. Syracuse, N. Y., Dec. 8, 1835. Sigma Phi. T. Oration, 1855. s. Law, Albany Law School. p. Law, Syracuse, 1857-61. Clerk Provost Cong't. Southern. N. C. 1864 b. Editor. Standard, Syracuse, N. Y., 1856-74. Democrat and Chronicle, Rochester, since 1874. M. A., Syracuse Univ., 1873. Delegate Repub. Nat. Conv., 1876. Regent Univ. State N. Y., since 1877. Rep. with Comm'n Dept Ment Am. Ilia Soc.; Am. Geog. Soc' pub), "The Press of Onondaga Co.," 1868; "The Risks of Thinking," 1870; "Church and State," 1871; "The Perils of Journalism," 1868; "Migration and Development," 1869; "Moral Limitations," 1882; "Rural and Urban Life," 1864; "The American College," 1861; "Five Lectures on Journalism," Cornell Univ., 1862; "Journalism as a Profession," Rutgers, 1863; "Principles Before Men," 1867; and many others. m. Louise Lawrence Smith, Syracuse, July 21, 1879; three c.

Samuel Baker Forbes. Rockville, Tolland Co., Conn.

Clergyman and Merchant. b. Hopkinton, Ma., Aug. 1, 1830. f. W. H. Easthampton. Delta Upsilon. Jun. Ex., 1851. Adel. U's. Debate, 1853. Pres L. Filikel o., 1855. Theol. Inst., Conn., 1855-7. Ord. Oct. 1857. Merchant, West Winsted. Ct., 1865-81. Pas. Rockville, since 1881. m. Cornelia Beardsley. West Winsted, Oct. 22, 1857; two c.

Ephraim Livingston Lincoln.

Lawyer. b. Plainfield, Mass., Jan. 14, 1830. Delta Upsilon. 1. Jun. Ex., 1854 Salutatory. Law, Pittsfield and Westfield, 1855-8. d. Westfield, Sep. 9, 1858.

Charles Marsh, Pynchon Nat. Bank, Springfield, Mass.

Cashier National Bank b. Hartford, Conn., Apr. 18, 1834. f. Academy, Westfield, and W. N. Easthampton. Greek o. Junior Ex., 1852. Prize Biped. Ex. 1851. Editor *Williams Quarterly*. Pres. Logian. Valedictory. Tea., 1855-6; Insurance, 1856-66; Banking, since 1866. res. Springfield, since 1856. M. A. Williams. m. Helen Pruisman, Oct. 22, 1857; four c.

James Orton.

Teacher and Clergyman b. Seneca Falls, N. Y., Apr. 21, 1830. Delta Upsilon. Junior Ex., 1851. Pres. Technima. Pres. L. N. H. Editor *Williams Quarterly* Phil. o. 1852 Master's o., 1854 A. T. N. 1855-8. Ord. Presb., July 11, 1861. Pas. Greene, N Y., 1861-1; Thomasson, Mo., 1861-3; Brighton, N. Y., 1861-6. Tea. Nat. Sci., Univ., Rochester, 1866-7; Prof. Nat. His., Vassar College, 1866-77. Ph. D., W. C., 1876. pub. "The Andes and the Amazon," 1870; "Underground Treasures," 1872; "The Liberal Education of Women," 1861; "Comparative Zoology," 1876. m. Ellen M Foote, Williamstown. 1859; four c. d. on scientific trip, Lake Titicaca, S. A., Sep. 24, 1877.

William Packer Prentice, 155 Broadway, New York City.

Lawyer. b. Albany, N. Y., Aug. 26, 1834. Chi Psi. T. Oration, 1855. Europe. 1855-9. Albany Law School. U N. Army, 1861-3. Lieut. Col., Rep., 1864. Law, New York, since 1865. Ph. D., Göttingen, 1864. mem. Am. Geog. and Am. Chem. Soc. m. Florence Kelly, New York, Jan. 22, 1865; six c.

Simeon Foster Woodin, Foochow, China.

Missionary. b Hillsdale, N. Y., May 11, 1833. Latin o. Jun Ex., 1854. T. Classical o., 1855 U T. N., 1855-9. Ord. Presb., June 19, 1859. Missionary, since 1860. Trans. in Chinese, "Arithmetic for Beginners;" "Book of Psalms;" "Ruth," etc. m. Sarah L. Ciley, Concord, N. H., Aug. 10, 1859; seven c.

1856.

James Abram Garfield.

President United States. b Orange, O., Nov. 19, 1831. f. Coll. Inst., Hiram. Delta Upsilon. Pres. Logian. Editor Williams Quarterly. Adelphic Union, 1854. Metaphysical o., 1856. Tea., Hiram, O., 1856-9. Master's Oration W. C., 1859. Ohio Senate, 1860, 1861. n Law, Cleveland. U. S. Army, 1861-3. Lieut. Col. Aug. 14, 1861; Maj. Gen. Sep. 20, 1863. M. C., 1863-79. Elected U. S. Senate, Jan., 1880. Elected President United States, 1880. Assassinated as he started for Commencement, July 2, 1881. d. Elberon, N. J., Sep. 19, 1881. Some of the subjects on which he wrote are these: "Free Commerce between the States;" "Public Expenditure and Civil Service;" "Relation of the National Government to Science;" "The Tariff;" "National Aid to Education." Adelphic Union Orator, 1876. Trustee, W. C., 1880. LL. D., Williams, 1872; Univ. Penn., 1881. m. Lucretia Rudolph, Hiram, Ohio, Nov. 11, 1858; seven c., two W. C. men in '85.

Charles Storrs Halsey, Un. Classical Inst., Schenectady, N. Y.

Teacher. b. Cambria, N. Y., son of Rev. Herman Halsey, 1811.1 Dec. 20, 1834. f. Wilson. Jun. Ex., 1855; Pres Logian; Adelphic Un. Debate: Valedictory. Tea., Macedon, N. Y., 1855-6; Newton, N. J. 1856-64; Macedon, 1862-5; Canandaigua, 1865-73; Burlington, Vt., 1873-5; Schenectady, N. Y., since 1875. M. A., Williams. pub. "Genealogical and Chronological Chart of European Rulers," 1871; "Etymology of Latin and Greek," 1882. m. Maria A. Lippincott, Penfield, N. Y., 1869; seven c.

Clement Hugh Hill,   25 Mt. Vernon St., Boston, Mass.

Lawyer. b. London, England. June 7, 1836. f. Oberlin, Ohio. Delta Kappa Epsilon. Adelphic Un. Debate. Logian. Oration, 1856. x and p. Law, Boston, since 1857. Admitted, 1858. Asst Solicitor, Boston, 1866-70. Asst. Att. Gen. U. S., 1866-. mem. Mass. H. of R., 1877, 1878. M. A., Williams. M. H. S. Trustee. Boston Athenaeum.

John Lamberton.

Student. b. Ware, Mass., Feb. 11, 1832. f. W. S., Easthampton. Kappa Alpha. Greek c Jun. Ex., 1855. L. Val. Adelphic Un., 1856. Salutatory. Tea., Philadelphia, 1856-7. d Springfield, Mass., June 28, 1857.

George Benton Newcomb, 17 Lexington Ave., New York City

Clergyman and Teacher. b. Allegheny, Pa., Nov. 21, 1833. Alpha Delta Phi. L. Adelphic Un. Val. Oration, 1856. U. T. S., 1856-60. Ord. Cong. Oct. 15, 1861. Pas. Bloomfield, O., 1861-8; Wakefield(?), 1868-9: New Haven, 1869-79. Prof. Int and Mor Phil College, City of New York, since 1879. Ph. D., Williams, 1881. pub. Reviews, Addresses, etc. m. Eliza W. Harvey; one c.

John Tatlock,   Hoosac Falls, N. Y.

Clergyman. b. Liverpool, Eng., Jan. 20, 1833. f. Hinsdale. Kappa Alpha. Jun. Ex., 1855. T. Editor Williams Quarterly. Mathematical o., 1856. Master's o., 1859. Adl. T. S., 1856 ord., Nov. 29, 1859. Pas. South Adams, Ms., 1856-67; Troy, N. Y., 1867-8; Hoosac Falls, since 1868. M. A. Williams. D. D., Williams, 1880. pub. "Bible in Pictures," 1880. m. Lucy B. Whitman, Williamstown, Dec. 29, 1759; six c., three W. C. sons, '82, '84, '86.

Lavalette Wilson,   Haverstraw, Rockland Co., N. Y.

Teacher and Civil Engineer. b. New York City, June 5, 1835. f. New Haven, Ct. Delta Upsilon. Logian. Astronomical o., 1856. Tea. Clarence, N. Y., 1856-7. Prin. Mountain Institute and Civil Engineer, Haverstraw, since 1858. pub. "The Andre and Arnold Treason." m. Sarah E. DeRonde, Haverstraw, July 26, 1860; one c.

1857.

Rufus Apthorp,   Lyndon, Whitesides Co., Ill.

Clergyman. b. Hinsdale, Ms., Feb. 8, 1830. Delta Upsilon. L. Classical o., 1857. Adl. T. S., 1856-60. Ord. Cong. Oct. 16, 1861. Pas. Cragier, St. Johns, Alpena, Allegan, Mich., 1861-71; DeWitt, Ia., 1871-5; Lamark, Ill., 1876-7; Big Rock, Ia., 1877-80; Rock Falls, Ill., 1880-2; Odell, 1882-3; Lee Center, 1883-5; Lyndon, since 1886. m. Louisa Fay, Rochester, O., May 14, 1861. 5

George Dickinson Goodrich.

Clergyman. b. Ware, Ms., Apr. 89, 1834. Alpha Delta Phi. T. Ethical o., 1857. P. T. S 1861-3; A. T. S., 1863-5. Ord., Sep. 13, 1865. Pas. Denver, Col., 1865-7. d. Hartford, Ct., Ju 23, 1872.

Alexander Hutchins, 796 DeKalb Ave., Brooklyn, N. Y.

Physician. b. New York. Jan. 24, 1835. f. Peekskill, N. Y. Alpha Delta Phi. Prev. Logian. Valedictory. Med. Dept. Harv. Univ., 1856. N. Y. Med. College, 1860. Asst. Surg. U. S. Navy, 1861-5. Brooklyn, since 1862. Visiting Phys. Brooklyn Hospital; Consulting Phys. St. Mary's Hosp., St. John's Hosp., Long Island Coll. Hosp. Prev. Med. Soc., N. Y., 1876; Prev. Med. Soc., Kings Co., 1878-84; pub. Miscellaneous Medical Monographs. m. Mary F. Felton. Poughkeepsie, N. Y., Dec. 15, 1863; seven c.

Edward Swift Isham, 204 Dearborn St., Chicago, Ill.

Lawyer. b. Bennington, Vt., Jan. 15, 1836. f. L. A. Groton, Mass. Chi Psi. T. Editor Williams Quarterly. Moonlight prize, 1856. Oration, 1857. Master's Oration, 1860. a Law, Harvard Law School; p. Law, Chicago. Ill. Legislature, 1864-6. M. A., Williams. 1869. Soc. de Legis. Comparee, Paris. m. Fanzie Burch, Little Falls, N. Y.; four c.

Irving Magee, Rondout, Ulster Co., N. Y.

Clergyman. b. Red Hook, N. Y., July 24, 1831. f. Hartwick Seminary, N. Y. Delta Upsilon. Prev. Logian. Poem, 1857. U. T. N., 1858-60. Ord., Sep. 6, 1858. Pas. Valatie, N. Y., 1860-5; Baltimore, Md., 1865-8; Chambersburgh, Pa., 1868-9; Dayton, O., 1869-70; Albany, N. Y., 1870-82; Rondout, since 1882. D. D., Wittenberg, 1871. Trustee Wittenberg and Hartwick Theol. Sems. M. H. S. Board Examiners. W. C. Prev. Missal Synod, Ohio; Sec. Maryland Synod. pub. "Rise of Evangelical Lutheran Church and History of the Doctrines," 1876; "Liturgy of the Evan. Luth. Ch.," compiled and altered, 1881; "History, Romanist Presbyterian Church," 1865; "History, Class of 1857," 1857. Chaplain Rondout, N. Y.

Francis Le Baron Monroe, 3501 Cottage Grove Ave., Chicago.

Physician, Surgeon, Druggist. b. Medway, Ms., Mar. 20, 1836. f. W. S. Easthampton. Delta Kappa Epsilon. T. Geological o., 1856. M. D., Harvard, 1861. U S Army, 1861-76; Asst. Surg. Boston Light Artillery; Asst. Surg. 1st Mass. Vols.; Surg. 15th Mass. Vols.; Port Phys., Boston; Asst. Surg. Regular Army. Brooklyn, N. Y., 1878-86; Chicago, since 1886. m. Tamson Lavinia Barrows, Medford, N. H., Jan. 1874; two girls.

Andrew Parsons, Knox, Albany Co., N. Y.

Clergyman. b. Sharon Springs, N. Y., Aug. 13, 1830. f. Hemlock. Delta Upsilon. L. Jan. Ex., 1856. Prev. Mills. Historical o., 1857. Aub. T S., 1857-60. Ord. Presb., June, 1860. Pas. Richfield Springs, 1860 6; Ottawa, Kan., 1866-70; Wis., 1870-5; Hunter, N. Y., 1875-86; Sharon Springs, 1886 6; Knox, since 1886. m. Helena White, Auburn, May 24, 1860.

Charles Morgan Pierce, Hardwick, Worcester Co., Mass.

Clergyman. b. Hinsdale, Ms., Oct. 16, 1833. f. Acad., Hinsdale. Delta Upsilon. L. Jun. Ex., 1856. Mathematical o., 1857. A. T. S., 1858-61. Ord., Sep. 9, 1861. Tut. W. C., 1864-5, 1867-8. Pas. W. Boxford, Ms., 1863-7; Middlefield, 1868-81; Salem, 1881-8; Chariton, 1888-5; Hardwick, since 1885. m. Elizabeth M. Peabody, Salem, Aug. 14, 1865; one son.

Samuel Hubbard Scudder, Cambridge, Mass.

Scientist. b. Boston, Mass., Apr. 13, 1837. f. Roxbury Latin School. Prev. and Curator. L. N. H. Prev. Gymnasium. L. Oration, 1857. Lawrence Sci. Sch., Cambridge; B. S., 1858; M. A. Williams. Curator, Museum Soc. Nat. His., Boston, 1864-70. Europe, three years. Asst. Librarian, Harvard, 1870-80. Editor Science, 1883-5. Paleontologist, U. S. Geol. Survey, since 1886. res. Cambridge since 1882. pub. "Catalogue of Orthoptera, described previous to 1867," 1868; "Entomological Notes," 1868; "Entomological Correspondence of T. W. Harris," 1869; "Historical Sketch of the Generic Names Proposed for Butterflies," 1875; "Fossil Butterflies," 1875; "Catalogue of Scientific Serials of all Countries," 1879; "A Century of Orthoptera," 1879; "Paleozoic Cockroaches," 1879; "A Bibliography of Fossil Insects," 1882; "Butterflies: their Structure, Changes and Life Histories," 1881; "Fragments of the Coarser Anatomy of Lepidoptera," 1888; "Nomenclator Zoologicus," 1882 & "Systematische Uebersicht der fossilen Myriopoden Arachnoiden und Insekten," 1885; "Systematic Review of our present Knowledge of Fossil Insects," 1886; "The Winnipeg Country, or Roughing It with an Eclipse Party," 1888. mem. National Acad. Sciences; Am. Acad. Arts and Sci.; Am. Phil. Soc. Hon. mem. Scientific Societies, Boston, New York, Philadelphia, Washington, Chicago, Buffalo, Davenport, Troy and Salem. Also of the Foreign Scientific Societies of Geneva, Vienna, Moscow, London, Belgium and Holland. m. Ethelinda Jane Blatchford, Cambridge, June 65, 1867; one son.

Homer Bemis Stevens,   Westfield, Mass.

Lawyer, b. Norwich, Ma., Sep. 9, 1835. f. W. N. Easthampton, Ms. Alpha Delta Phi. Editor *Williams Quarterly*. L. Jun. Ex., 1854. Salutatory. Prin. H. S., Westfield, 1857-8. Law, Boston, 1859. Law, Westfield, since 1859. Judge Dist. Court, West. Hampden, since 1860. n., Mariette Hamnto. Huntington, Mass., Apr. 10, 1861; one daughter.

William Tatlock,   Stamford, Conn.

Clergyman. b. Liverpool, Eng., May 65, 1833. f. under Cowperware and Howson. ord at Wm. Kappa Alpha. Jun. Ex., 1856. T. Editor *Williams Quarterly*. Philosophical o., 1857. Gen. Theol. Sem. Epis. Ch., New York, 1857-60. M. A. Ord., Nov. 11, 1860. Rector, North Adams, Ms., 1860-6. Albany, N. Y., 1863-6; Stamford, Ct., since 1866. Archdeacon of Fairfield since 1877. D. D. Union, 1878. Rev. House of Bishops, P. E. Ch. Trustee, Trinity College and Gen. Theol. Sem. m. Florence Perry, Albany, N. Y., Sep. 10, 1860; five c.

Horace Herman Wells,

Lawyer, b. Northville, N. Y., Apr. 62, 1833. Delta Upsilon. L. Metaphysical o., 1857. Law, New Haven, Ct., and Huntington, N. Y. m. Frances E. Wells, Dec. 61, 1852; one son. d. Aug. 62, 1862.

Samuel Wood,   Westport, Fairfield Co., Conn.

Lawyer, b. Albany, N. Y., Nov. 90, 1803. f. P. A, Andover. Chi Psi. T. Jun. Ex., 1864. Aesthetical o., 1857. LL. H. Univ., Albany, 1859. Law, New York City. res New York, 1862-6. Personal, N. Y., 1868-77; Westport, Ct., since 1877 M. A., Williams. m. Anna D. Babcock, Stonington, Ct., Apr. 25, 1861; two c., one living.

1858.

James McKinney Alexander, Haiku, Maui, Hawaiian Islands.

Missionary Planter. b. Waihuka, H. I., Jan. 29, 1835. Alpha Delta Phi. Pres. Mills, L. Adel. Un. Debate. Mathematical o., 1856. U. T. S., 1859-61. Ord., June 11, 1863. Pas. San Leandro, Cal., 1863-70; Centreville, 1870-2. For. Missionary and Sugar Planter, Sandwich Islands, since 1872. m. and four c.

John Griffith Ames,   Interior Dept., Washington, D. C.

Clergyman and Librarian. b. East Dorset, Vt., Dec. 11, 1834. f. Burr N. Manchester. Alpha Delta Phi. T. Salutatory. Theol. Sem., P. E. Ch., Gambier, O. Morristown, N. J., 1864-5; Springfield, O., 1866-9; New York City, 1869-3; Washington, D. C., since 1874. Prof. and Hosd. House of Evangelists, New York. Librarian and Supt. Documents, Dept. of the Interior, Washington. pub. Official Reports on Public Documents. Official Register U. S., 1873, '77, '79, '81, '83, '85. m. Elizabeth Delano, Mt. Vernon, O., Oct. 4, 1861; five c.

Samuel McCoskry Cleveland, 252 S. 21st St., Philadelphia, Pa.

Teacher and Physician. b. Philadelphia, Dec. 7, 1837. f. P. A. Andover. Kappa Alpha. Moonlight, 1856. Jun. Ex., 1857. Metaphysical o., 1858. Prof. Rhet., Univ., Pa. M. D., Hahn Med. Coll., Phila., 1878. Physician, Phila., since 1872. m. Julia H. Conover, Philadelphia, Aug. 14, 1870; one c.

Justin Dewey,   Judge Sup. Court, Springfield, Mass.

Lawyer, b. Alford, Ms., June 12, 1836. f. Gt. Barrington. Alpha Delta Phi. L. Adel. Un. Debate, 1857. Philosophical o., 1858. Law, Gt. Barrington, 1858-9; Springfield, since 1887. Judge Superior Court, Mass., since 1886. m. Jane Stanley, Gt. Barrington, Feb. 8, 1866; three daughters.

Henry Hopkins,   916 Holmes St., Kansas City, Mo.

Clergyman. b. Williamstown, Mass., Nov. 80, 1837. T. Moonlight, 1856. Adel Un Deb., 1857. Vice Adel. Un., 1858. Pres. Gymnasium, 1858. Master's Oration, 1861. U. T. S., 1862-61. Ord., Sep. 22, 1861. Chaplain U. S. A., 1861-3. Pas. Westfield, Mass., 1866-90; Kansas City, Mo., since 1890. Companion, "The Loyal Legion, U. S." D. D., Williams, 1887. Trustee Williams since 1887. m. Alice Knight, Easthampton, Mass., Sep. 20, 1866. m. Jeanette M. Southworth, Cohoes, N. Y., Oct. 10, 1879; four c.

Henry Munson Lyman, 583 W. Adams St., Chicago, Ill.

Physician. b. Hilo, H. I., Nov. 26, 1855. Alpha Delta Phi. L. Pres. L. N. H. Editor Williams Quarterly. Valedictory. M. D. Coll. Phys and Surg., New York, 1861. Act. Asst. Surg. U. S. A., 1862-5. Chicago, since 1866. Prof. Chem. Rush Med. Coll., 1871-6; Prof. Physiol. and Nerv. Dis., same, since 1876. Prof. Theory and Prac. Med., Woman's Med. Coll. Chicago, since 1877. Phys. Cook Co. Hosp. and Presb. Hosp. M. H. S., Ill. pub. "Anaesthesia and Anaesthetics," 1881; "Insomnia and the Disorders of Sleep," 1885. Ed. Chicago Medical Journal. mem. Am. Acad. Med. and Assoc. Am. Phys. m. Sarah K. Clark, Roxbury, Mass., May 27, 1866; four daughters.

Curtis Jerre Lyons, Honolulu, Hawaiian Islands.

Assistant Gov. Survey. b. Waimea, H. I., June 16, 1833. Alpha Delta Phi. Pres. Mills. Pres. L. Historical o., 1856. U. T. S., 1858-60. Business, Honolulu, since 1874. m. and two c.

Horace Elisha Scudder, Cambridge, Mass.

Author. b. Boston, Mass., Oct. 16, 1838. f. Latin School, Roxbury and Boston. Greek o. Jun. Ex., 1857. L. N. A. Editor Williams Quarterly. L. Oration, 1858. res New York, 1858-63; Boston, 1863-73; Cambridge, since 1873. M. A. Europe, 1865. Ed. Riverside Magazine, 1867-71. Firm of Hurd & Houghton, 1874-5. Literary work since 1875. pub. "Seven Little People and their Friends," 1862; "Dream Children," 1863; "Life and Letters of David Coit Scudder," 1864; "Stories from my Attic," 1869; "Doings of the Bodley Family in Town and Country," 1875; "Men and Manners in America One Hundred Years Ago," (Ed.) 1876; "The Dwellers in Five Sisters Court," 1876; "Recollections of Samuel Breck," (Ed.) 1877; "The Bodleys Telling Stories," 1877; "The Bodleys on Wheels," 1878; "American Poems," (Ed.) 1879; "The Bodleys Afoot," 1879; "American Prose," (Ed.) 1880; "The Bodleys Abroad," 1880; "Stories and Romances," 1880; "Boston Town," 1881; "The Children's Book," (Ed.) 1881; "Noah Webster," 1882; "The Book of Fables," 1882; "The Bodley Grandchildren and their Journey in Holland," 1882; "The English Bodley Family," 1883; "A History of the United States of America," 1884; "Life and Letters of Bayard Taylor," (with Mrs. Taylor.) 1884; "The Viking Bodleys," 1884; "The Book of Folk Stories," 1887; "Men and Letters: Essays in Criticism and Characterization," 1887. Many Articles in Magazines. mem. Mass. Board Education, M. H. S. Trustee Williams since 1884. m. Grace Owen, Cambridge, Mass., Oct. 30, 1873; two c.

William Phillips Strickland, Northampton, Mass.

Lawyer. b. Marshfield, Mo., Jan. 24, 1835. f. Acad., Gt. Barrington and W. R. Easthampton. Delta Kappa Epsilon. Pres. L. Classical o., 1858. Law, Ware, Mass., 1861-5; Northampton, since 1865. Judge Dist. Court, Hampshire Co. Trustee Clarke Inst., Public Library, etc. Deacon First Cong. Church. m. Mary A. Dutton, Lee, 1861; five c.

Stephen Higginson Tyng, 44 E. 43rd St., New York City.

Clergyman. b. New York City, June 30, 1839. Chi Psi. T. Oration, 1859. mem. Epis. Ch., Alexandria, Va., 1859-61. M. A. Chaplain U. S. A. Rector, New York, 1864-80. Europe, 1866-7. Trustee, Williams, 1873-84. D. D., Williams, 1878. pub. "Peoples Pulpit;" "Square of Life;" "He Will Come;" "Life Insurance does Insure." m. Fanny Rollins Tappan, New York, Dec. 16, 1865; two sons. W. C., M. '85.

Richard Halsted Ward, 53 Fourth St., Troy, N. Y.

Physician. b. Bloomfield, N. J., June 17, 1837. L. N. H. Florida Expedition, 1857. Pres. T. Editor Williams Quarterly. Oration, 1858. M. D. Coll. Phys. and Surg., New York, 1863. M. A., in course. Asst. Surg. U. S. Hosp., Nashville, Tenn., 1862. Physician, Troy, N. Y., since 1863. Inst. Botany, Rens. Pol. Inst., 1867-9; Prof. Botany, same, since 1869. Ed. American Naturalist, 1876-80; "Microscope," (App. Cyc.); "Microscope in Botany," 1865; "Microscopical Slide Catalogue," 1884. mem. Rens. Co. Med. Soc., Pres. same, 1876-8; Am. Soc., Mic., Pres. same, 1879-80; Mic. Soc., London, Belgium, etc. m. Charlotte A. Baldwin, Bloomfield, N. J., 1866; four c.

1859.

Humphrey Stevenson Anderson.

Lawyer. b. Glover, Vt., Oct. 23, 1833. f. Swan's Sch., Wa. Delta Kappa Epsilon. Greek o. Jun. Ex., 1858. Pres. Lorian. Captain Base Ball Nine. Valedictory. Tea., Poughkeepsie, N. Y., and Tuskegee, Ala., 1859-61. s. Law, New York; Admitted, 1861. p. Law, New York, 1862-80. m. Katharine Anna Demuler, Lyons, N. Y., Oct. 24, 1869. d. Brooklyn, May 14, 1884.

Timothy Manning Brown, Springfield, Mass.

Lawyer. b. Williamstown, Ms., May 8, 1868. f. Swan's Sch., Wn. Delta Kappa Epsilon. Orator, Adel. Un., 1858. Jun. Ex., 1858. l. Marshal, 1858. Honorary o., 1858. s. Law, Harvard. M. A. p. Law, Springfield. U. S. Attorney; City School Board; Director Bank, etc. m. Elizabeth Chapman, Springfield, Apr. 16, 1868; two sons.

Hiram Burr Crandall, 93 Pemberton Square, Boston, Mass.

Lawyer. b. Adams, Mass., Oct. 27, 1854. f. Fort Edward, N. Y. Delta Kappa Epsilon. Librarian Technician. Oration, 1858. s. Law, Boston; Admitted Apr. 8, 1861. U. S. Army; Adj. 1st Mass., 1861-5. M. A., Williams. p. Law, Boston, since 1864. Trustee State Hospital, Public Adm. Suffolk Co. Pres. Boston W. C. Alumni. mem. Hist. Genral. Soc. mem. Webster Soc., Boston.

Edwin Harris Darling, 23 Court St., Boston, Mass.

Lawyer. b. Calais, Me., Jan. 24, 1858. Kappa Alpha. Jun. Ex., 1858. L. Adel. Un. Ex., 1858. Honorary o., 1858. s. Law, Portland, Me., and New York City; Admitted, 1881. p. Law, New York and Boston. Ed. Chronicle, Charlestown, Mass. Bail Com., Suffolk Co. Sec. and Pres. W. C. Alumni, Boston. Master in Chancery since 1863. m. Julia F. Kinney, Cincinnati, O., Nov. 24, 1868. m. George A. Smith, New Market, N. H., Feb. 1, 1868; three c.

Hiram Madison Dickinson.

Lawyer. b. Wilmington, Vt., July 21, 1858. Delta Upsilon. T. Jun. Ex., 1858. Editor Williams Quarterly. Honorary o., 1858. LL. B., Univ., Mich., 1862. p. Law and Probate Judge, Omaha, Neb., 1863-5. d. there, July 20, 1865.

Charles Hall Everest, 1020 Broad St., Newark, N. J.

Clergyman. b. New Lebanon, N. Y., Feb. 14, 1857. f. Sem., Auburn, N. Y. L. Moonlight, 1857. Adel Un Part, 1858. Jun. Ex., 1858. Honorary poem, 1859. U. T S. 1859-61. Ord., Dec. 30, 1861. Pas. Oswego, N. Y., 1861-5; Puritan Ch., Brooklyn, 1865-75; Plymouth Ch., Chicago, 1867-82; Norwalk, Ct., 1884-6; Meriden, 1885; Newark since 1886. Europe, 1884-5. Farm of 1,000 acres in Dakota. pub. poems, music, newspaper articles, etc. D. D., Maryville, 1882. m. Maria L. Wadhams, Hartford, Ct., Feb. 11, 1862; two c.

Washington Gladden, Columbus, Ohio.

Clergyman. Journalist and Author. b. Pottsgrove, Pa., Feb. 11, 1836. f. Acad., Owego, N. Y. Adel. Un., Orator, 1857. l. Jun. Ex., 1858. Editor Williams Quarterly. Conductor Metalogian Soc. Honorary, poem, 1859. Ord., Nov. 15, 1860. Pas Cong., Brooklyn, N. Y., 1860-1; Morrisania, 1861-6; North Adams, Mass., 1866-71; North Ch. Springfield, 1875-82; First Ch., Columbus, O., since 1882. Ed. N. Y. Independent, 1871-4; Ed. Sunday Afternoon and Good Company, 1878-81. pub. "Songs of Williams," 1859; "Plain Thoughts on the Art of Living," 1868; "From the Hub to the Hudson," 1869; "Working People and their Employers," 1876; "Being a Christian," 1876; "The Christian Way," 1877; "The Lord's Prayer," 1880; "The Christian League of Connecticut," 1883; "Things New and Old," 1884; "Applied Christianity," 1886; "Parish Problems," 1887; and many magazine articles. LL. D., Univ., Wis., 1891. D. D., Roanoke, 1882. Trustee Marietta. Trustee, Williams, since 1886. Lectureship, Yale Univ., 1887. m. Jennie O. Cohoon, Brooklyn, Dec. 5, 1860; four c.

Henry Charles Haskell, Bulgaria, Turkey.

Missionary. b. Anson, Me., Dec. 29, 1835. f. Hinsdale, Ms. Delta Upsilon. Jun. Ex., 1858. Pres. L. Pres Mills. Philosophical o., 1858. A. T. S., 1858-61. Ord., Aug. 18, 1861. F. M., Turkey, 1862-72, and since 1887. Pas. Huntington, O., 1873-5; Columbus, 1875-7; N. Amherst, 1877-81; Hanmar, 1881-7. m. Margaret H. Bell, S. Deerfield, Ms., Aug. 13, 1861; three c.

Jacob F. Miller, 120 Broadway, New York City.

Lawyer. b. Claverack, N. Y., Nov. 65, 1837. f. H. R. Inst., Claverack. Delta Upsilon. Jun. Ex., 1858. Sec. and Disputant Adel. Un., 1858. Adel Un. Ex., 1859. L. Honorary o., 1859. s. Law, New York; Admitted. May, 1861. p. Law, New York, since 1861. Pres. N. Y. Medico-Legal Soc.; Y. M. C. A.; mem. Free Trade Club, New York; State Bar Association, etc. Assembly, N. Y., 1878. m. Laura Augusta Chace, Claverack, N. Y., Oct. 61, 1861; three c.

Horace Hills Morgan,   P. O. Box 397, St. Louis, Mo.

Teacher and Author. b. Auburn, N. Y., Jan. 24, 1920, f. Geneva. Alpha Delta Phi. T. Classical o., 1920. Tea High School, St. Louis, Mo., 1850-80; Prin. same, 1880-86; pub. "Representative Names in English Literature;" "Literary Studies in Great British Authors;" "Topical Shakespeariana;" "Bascom's Philosophy of Rhetoric;" "Premium Essays;" "Keys to Standard Elementary" and "Standard Practical Arithmetics." Many Educational Reports, Addresses, Articles, etc. M. A., Williams, 1882. LL. D. Univ. Wis., 1881 M. H. S. Va. Ed. The Western, 1873 sl. mem. Acad. Sci.; Acad. Art.; Am. Assoc. Sci.; Civil Service Ref. Assoc.; University Club, etc. m. Mary Ellen Smith, St. Louis, Mo., June 24, 1880; d. Jan. 26, 1893; one son.

Henry F. C. Nichols,   New Lisbon, Wis.

Lumber Manufacturer and Dealer. b. Kingston, N. H., Feb. 9, 1832. f. Acad., Pembroke. Jun Ex., 1856. Pres. I., Pres. Mills Honorary o., 1856. Tea. Canton, N. Y., 1870-61; U. T. K., 1861-6. Christian Com., U. S., 1861-5; Norfolk, N. Y., 1865-7; New Lisbon, Wis. since 1867. M. A., Williams Wis. Assembly, 1872, 1873, 1876. Trustee. Clerk and H. H. Supt. Cong. Ch. m. Nettie Williams, Concord, N. H., May 14, 1866; five c.

Eben Burt Parsons,   Baldwinsville, Onondaga Co., N. Y.

Clergyman. b. Pittsfield, Me., Mar. 3, 1833. f. H. S., Pittsfield Delta Kappa Epsilon. Jun. Ex., 1858. f. Pres. I. N. H. Editor Williams Quarterly. Mathematical o., 1860. Prin. H. K., Greenfield, Ms., 1860-61; Harvard and Amherst, 1861-2. Master's o., 1864. M. A., U. T. K., 1861-4; Ans. T. K., 1864-5. Ord. Preab., New York City, Apr. 11, 1865; Chaplain U. S. A. H. M., 1865-8. Pas. Baldwinsville, N. Y. since 1869 D. D., Maryville, 1881. pub. "Memorials," "Class Reports," "Alumni Lists." Phi Beta Kappa Catalogue, 1887. Necrologist W. C. Alumni, since 1881. m. Clara Bigelow, June 18, 1867; four c.

Henry Albert Schauffler,   1532 Broadway, Cleveland, O.

Missionary b. Constantinople, Sep. 4, 1837. Social Fraternity. Latin o., Jun. Ex., 1858. I. Pres. Mills Salutatory. A. T. K., 1862. M. A., W. C., 1862. LL. B., Harv., 1858. Prof. Robert College. Ord. June 8, 1865. F. M. Turkey, 1865-70; Austria, 1870-73. A. H. M., Supt. Slavonic work, Cleveland, O., since 1883. M. Clara E. Gray. Springfield, Ms., Nov. 15, 1865; d. Aug. 8, 1881; eight c.

William White Williams,   New York City.

Clergyman. b. Tuscaloosa, Ala. Jan. 8, 1834. Delta Upsilon. Jun. Ex., 1858. Pres. I. Honorary o., 1859. U. T. K., 1861. Europe U. S. San. Com. Ord., May 14, 1865. Indian for many years. m. Charlotte L. Ford, Morristown, N. J., June 21, 1863; one daughter.

1860.

James Madison Barker,   Judge Sup. Court, Pittsfield, Mass.

Lawyer b. Pittsfield, Oct. 29, 1839. f. H. S., Pittsfield; Acad., Hinsdale; W. S. Easthampton. Delta Kappa Epsilon. Latin o. Jun. Ex., 1859. T. Class Marshal. pub. Classical o., 1860. s. Law, Ham. N. Y., 1861-2; Harvard Law Sch., 1862-3; Admitted, 1863. p. Law, Pittsfield, since 1863. Town Clerk, Pittsfield, 1864-73; Justice Peace, 1865-84; Notary Public. 1864-85. mem. Mass. H. of R., 1874, 1875. Commissioner to Revise Tax Laws, 1873-5 Commissioner to Consolidate Public Statutes, Mass., 1879-81. Judge Superior Court, Mass., since 1882. pub. "Report of Com. to Revise Tax Laws," 1875; "Public Statutes of Mass.," 1881, ment Clerk. Co. Ha. Soc. Trustee, Williams, since 1881. m. Helena Whiting, Bath, N. Y., Sep. 21, 1864; seven c., five living.

William Wilberforce Chapin.

Missionary. b. Somers, Ct., Dec. 2, 1835 f. Acad., Monson, Ms. Delta Upsilon, L. Nat. His. o., 1860. A. T. K., 1860-1. Ord., Sep 30, 1862 F. M., W. India, 1863-5. m. Katharine J. Hayes, Derry, N. H., Sep. 26, 1862. d. Ahmednuggur, Mar. 22, 1865.

Edward Trumbull Hooker.

Clergyman. b. Bennington, Vt., Oct. 31, 1837. f. P. A. Andover. Alpha Delta Phi. L' Salutatory. Theol. Inst., Ct., 1860-1. Banf., Vt., 1861-3 8th Vt. Vols., 1863-5. Chl. T. K., 1865-7. Pas. Broad Brook, Ct., 1868-9; Windfield, 1869-72; New Orleans, La., 1874-; Castleton, Vt., 1876-81; Charleston, S. C., 1882-3; Los Angeles, Cal., 1883-6. m. Susan C. Atwater, Brooklyn, N. Y., Dec. 31, 1868; four c. d. West Salem, Wis., (with Clark, W. C., '43.) Oct. 2, 1886.

Joseph William Hyde, Waterville, Oneida Co., N. Y.

Clergyman. b. New York, Dec. 4, 1838. Kappa Alpha. Jun. Ex., 1858. Prov. I. Editor *Williams Quarterly*. Aesthetical o., 1860. Tea. New Brighton, Pa., 1860-2; Brooklyn, N. Y., 1862-3. Ord., 1865. Rector, North and New Castle, N. Y., 1865-7; Stamford, Ct., 1867-71; Sharon, 1871-3; Stamford, 1873-82; W. Hartford, 1882-7; Waterville, N. Y., since 1887. m. Mary Porter, July 31, 1865. Id. 1874; three c.

George Russell Leavitt, 413 North Perry St., Cleveland, O.

Clergyman. b. Lowell, Mass., June 7, 1839. Delta Upsilon. Moonlight, 1859. Prov. T. Philosophical o., 1864. A. T. S., 1864-1. Tea. W. C. 1862-4. N. A. A. T. S., 1864-5. Ord., Mar. 22, 1865. Pas., Lancaster, Ma., 1865-70; Cambridgeport, 1870-80; Cleveland, O., since 1880. pub. Sunday Club Sermons. D. D., Williams, 1885. m. Henrietta Swan Kendrick, Lancaster, Ma., Oct. 2, 1865; seven c.

Edward Williams Morley, Adelbert College, Cleveland, Ohio.

Teacher. b. Newark, N. J., Jan. 29, 1838. Jun. Ex., 1859. T. Valedictory. A. T. S., 1861-1. U. S. San. Com., 1864-5. Tea. New Marlboro, Ma., 1865-8. Prof. Nat. His. and Chem. West. Res. (now Adelbert) Coll., since 1868. Prof. Chem. and Tox. Cleveland Med. Coll., since 1873. M. D., same. m. Isabella K. Birdsall, Hillsdale, N. Y., Dec. 24, 1868.

John Crosby Olmsted, 1130 South Main St., Los Angeles, Cal.

Bookseller and Stationer. b. New York, Mar. 10, 1838. f. Hinsdale, Mass. Delta Kappa Epsilon. Moonlight, 1859. L. Jun. Ex., 1858. Prest. Adelphia Union. Ethical o., 1861. Business, San Francisco, Cal., fifteen years; Southern Cal., twelve years. Elder Presb. Ch. m. Millicent Hickcox, San Francisco, June 17, 1865.

Charles Eleazer Wright.

Lawyer. b. Rodman, N. Y., Sep. 30, 1838. Jun. Ex., 1858. Prest. T. Mathematical o., 1860. s. and p. Law, Chicago, 1860-4. d. 1864.

1861.

William Penn Alcott, Boxford, Essex Co., Mass.

Clergyman. b. Dorchester, Ma., July 11, 1838. f. F. A., Andover. Delta Upsilon. L. Curator I. N. H., Jun. Ex., 1860. Nat. History o., 1861. A. T. S., 1861-3. Tea. Chem and Mineral, W. C., 1862. Ord., Feb. 10, 1864. Pas., W. Greenwich, Ct., 1864-7; Barton Landing, Vt., 1867; North Chelmsford, Ma., 1870-80; Boxford, since 1880. Supt. of Schools. Vice-Pres. Am. Veget. Soc.; mem. Keg. Veget. Soc. pub. "Natural History" of Schaff's Bible Dict., 1880; "The Book of Esther," (new trans. and com.), 1885. m. Sarah J. Merrill, Peacham, Vt., Aug. 30, 1864. m. Lucy R. Davis, Boston, Ma., Sep. 18, 1878; five c., two living.

Zenas Rogers Farrington, 33 Smith St., Portland, Me.

Merchant. b. Holden, Me., Mar. 31, 1833. Jun. Ex., 1860. L. Prea. Mills. Philosophical o., 1861. Impaired Eyesight. Farming, Holden, Me., 1861-76. Merchant, Port'd wl, since 1876. Supt. of Schools. Patriarch, Sons of Temperance. First Selectman. Deacon Cong. Ch. m. Ella F. Rowe, Eddington, Me., Aug., 1865; seven c., six living.

Chauncey Goodrich, Tungcho, China.

Missionary. b. Hinsdale, Ma., June 4, 1836. Delta Upsilon. T. Missionary o., 1861. A. T. S., 1861-4. Ord., Sep. 21, 1865. F. M., Pekin and Tungcho, China, since 1865. three m.; one c.

Warren Luke Hayden, 122 Washington St., Johnstown, Pa.

Clergyman. b. Deerfield, O., May 30, 1835. f. Hiram, th. Prest. L. Ethical o., 1861. Ord. (Disciples.) Sep. 1, 1861. Pas. W. Rupert, Vt., 1861-7; Danbury, Ct., 1867-70; Philadelphia, 1870-3; Canton, O., 1873-7; Washington, Pa., 1877-83; Johnstown, since 1883. M. A. In course Pres. Dist. Co-operation. m. Anna F. Sherman, Salem, N. Y., Oct. 28, 1862; five c., two living.

Charles Lewis Hutchins, Medford, Middlesex Co., Mass.

Clergyman. b. Concord, N. H., Aug. 5, 1838. Delta Kappa Epsilon. Jun. Ex., 1860. T. Editor *Williams Quarterly*. Graduate, 1861. Gen. Epis. Theol. Sem., New York, 1864-5. Rector, Lowell, Ma., 1865-8; Buffalo, N. Y., 1868-72; Medford, since 1872. M. A., Williams. also Trinity, 1868. Sec. House of Dep. Gen. Conv. Epis. Ch. pub. "The Church Hymnal" (67th thousand); "S. S. Hymnal," 10th thousand). Ed. and pub. "The Parish Choir." Much Ch. and Festival Music. m. Mary Groom, Oct. 4, 1865; two c.

Gavin Langmuir.

Clergyman. b. Kilmarnock, Scotland, Nov. 1, 1840. [Geneseo, N. Y. Kappa Alpha. Moonlight, 1858. Jun Ex., 1860. Class day Pres., 1861. Valedictory. P. T. R., 1858-6; Ord., May 22, 1870; Pas. Morristown, N. J ; Deac.; Europe, 1880-81; Pas. Aux. Ch., Rome, Italy, 1873-4; Florence, 1879-81. D. D., Williams, 1881. m. Laura J. Baker, Paris, France, Sep. 3, 1867, (d. Feb. 22, 1871) d. Florence, Oct. 16, 1881.

Charles Stewart Maurice,   Athens, Bradford Co., Pa.

Civil Engineer and Manufacturer. b. Perth Amboy, N. J., June 23, 1840. [King Ring, N. Y. Kigran Phi Greek a. Jun. Ex., 1861 T. Salgiatory. Rens. Polyt. Inst., Troy, N. Y., 1861-2. U. S. Navy, 1862-6; Asst. Engineer, Mobile and Fort Fisher. Athens, Pa., 1867-70; King Ring, N. Y., 1871-3; Union Bridge Co., Athens, Pa., since 1871. mem. Am. Soc. Civil Eng. m. Charlotte M. Holbrooke, New York, Apr. 25, 1866; also c., eight living.

James Farrar Stone,   1906 Green St., Philadelphia, Pa.

Physician. b. Nashua, India, Nov. 8, 1838. [P. A., Andover. Alpha Delta Phi. Jun Ex., 1860. L. Chemical a., 1861. a. Med. Univ. Pa., and Bellevue Hosp. Med. College. M. D., Bellevue Med. Coll. 1864. M. A., in course. p. Med., Manchester, Vt., 1867; Philadelphia, since 1871. Lecturer, Med. Chir. Coll., Phila. m. Isabel McIlvaine, Philadelphia, Sep. 6, 1866; one c.

1862.

Henry Anstice,   132 South Fitzhugh St., Rochester, N. Y.

Clergyman. b. New York City, Oct 7, 1841. Delta Kappa Epsilon. Jun. Ex., 1861. L. Adel. Un. Debate. Astronomical a., 1862 A T. K. one year; Phila. Divinity Sch., two years. Ord., July 2, 1865; Ht. Barnabas' Ch., Irvington, N. Y., 1865-8; St. Luke's Ch., Rochester, since 1868. M. A., Williams. D. D., Rochester Univ., 1873. mem. Gen. Conv. Epis. Ch. and Asst. Sec., since 1877.

Samuel Chapman Armstrong,   Hampton, Va.

Teacher. b. Honolulu, Mar. 30, 1840. Adel. Un Debate. Pres. T. Elklical o., 1862. Army U. S., 1862-6; Capt. 125th N. Y. Vols., 1862; Brig. Gen. U. S. C. L., 1865. Freedmen's Bureau, Fortress Monroe, 1866. Tra. and Pres. Hampton Institute, since 1868. M A., in course. LL. D., Williams, 1887.

William Parmenter Bennett.   Crete, Saline Co., Neb.

Clergyman. b. Groton, Ma., Nov. 6, 1838. [Groton and P. A., Exeter. Jun. Ex., 1861. T. Honorary o., 1862. Tra. South Abington, Ma., 1862-3; Lexington, 1863-4; Millbury, 1864-5; Bradford, Ia., 1865-70. Ord. Cong., Dec. 8, 1870. Pas. Mason city, Ia., 1870-3; A. T. K., 1873-5; Lyndonville, Vt., 1875-80; Ames, Ia., 1880-1; Crete, Neb., since 1881. pub. sermons and trans paper articles. m. Hattie Irene Blodgett, Randolph, Vt., Aug. 4, 1864; seven c., six living.

Edward Stanley Brewster.

Student. b. Pittsfield, Mass., Dec. 12, 1841. [H. S., Pittsfield. Jun. Ex., 1861. Pres. L. N. H. I., Mathematical o., 1862 U. S. Army, 1862-5; Quartermaster, Baltimore, Md. d. Pittsfield, June 20, 1865.

Franklin Carter,   Williamstown, Mass.

President Williams College. b. Waterbury, Ct., Sep 30, 1837. [P. A., Andover. Editor Williams Quarterly T. Pres. Art Association. Pres. Class Day. Aesthetical o., 1862. Europe, 1863. Prof. Latin and French lang., W. C., 1865-8; Mass. Prof. Latin Lang. and Lit., W. C., 1868-72; Europe, 1872-3; Prof. German Lang., Yale, 1873-81. President Williams College, since 1881. Prof. Theology, W. C. since 1882. M. A., Williams, also Jefferson, 1862, and Yale, 1872. Ph. D., Williams, 1872; LL. D., Union, 1881. Trustee Williams, since 1881. Trustee Andover Theol. Sem., since 1881. pub. Translations, Reviews, Addresses, Reports, etc. m. Sarah L. Kingsbury, Waterbury, Ct. Feb. 24, 1862; four c.

John Henry Denison,   Williamstown, Mass.

Clergyman. b. Boston, Mar 8, 1841. [P. A., Amherst. Alpha Delta Phi Adel. Un. Ora tor. Editor Williams Quarterly. T. Class Day Orator. Poet. Honorary o., 1862. A T. K., 1864-6; Hampton, Va., 1866-7; South Williamstown, Ma., 1868-71; Ord., Jan. 30, 1870; Pas. New Britain, Ct., 1871-8; Hampton, Va., 1879-81. Europe, 1881-2. Prof. Theology and College Pastor, W. C., since 1884. D. D., Williams, 1884. m. Caroline H opkins, Apr. 16, 1867; one son, W. C., '86.

John Abbott French.   Flushing, Queens Co., N. Y.

Clergyman. b. Boscawen, N. Y., Mar 59, 1843. f. Nashaa. Kappa Alpha. T. Jun. Ex.,
1861 Prof. Class Day. Historical o., 1862. U. T. S., 1862-4; Ord., Apr., 1865; Pas. Morristown,
N. J., 1865-77; Chicago, Ill., 1877-80; Flushing. N. Y., since 1881. M. A., in course. m. Emily
W. Leavitt, 1870.

John Howard Goodhue.

Student. b. Boston, Ma., Feb. 21, 1843. Delta Upsilon. L. Philosophical o., 1862. Work
for Freedmen, 1863-4. d. Aug 29, 1864.

Edward Herrick Griffin,   Williamstown, Mass.

Teacher and Clergyman. b. Williamstown, Nov. 18, 1843. f. by his father, Prof. N. H. Griffin, D. D., Class of 31. Kappa Alpha. Jun. Ex., 1861. Pres. L. Metaphysical o., 1861 P. T.
S., 1863-4; Tutor W. C., 1864-5; P. T. S., 1865-6; D. T. S., 1866-7; Ord., Feb. 6, 1868; Pas. First
Cong. Ch., Burlington, Vt., 1868-72 Mass. Prof. Latin Lang and Lit., W. C., 1872-81; Morris
Prof. Rhet., W. C., 1881-4; Prof. Philosophy, W. C., since 1886. M. A., in course. D. D. Amherst, 1886. Europe, 1878 m. Rebekah, daughter of Rev. Dr. Wheeler, Burlington, Vt., May
23, 1872; two sons.

Everett Edward Lewis,   Haddam, Middlesex Co., Conn.

Clergyman. b. Bristol, Ct., June 4, 1837. f. E. Windsor Hill. Delta Upsilon. Jun. Ex.,
1861. T. Adel. Un. Debate. Natural History o., 1862. A T. S., 1864-7; Bethel, Vt., 1868-71;
Ord., Jan. 17, 1872; Pas. Haddam, Ct., since 1872 M. A., in course. pub. "History of Haddam Cong. Church," 1879. m. Ellen A. Hurd, Bristol, Ct., June 21, 1870; one daughter.

George Franklin Mills,   South Williamstown, Mass.

Teacher. b. South Wn., Aug. 25, 1840. f. at home and W. H. Easthampton. Alpha Delta
Phi, Moonlight, 1861. Lat. o Jun. Ex., 1861. Pres. T. Rehistory. Tro. and Principal Grey-
lock Institute, S. Williamstown, since 1865. M. A., in course. Europe, 1871-2. Treasurer Phi
Beta Kappa, since 1884. m. Jennie L. Hubbell, Fort Edward, N. Y., Apr. 16, 1868; one son.

Francis Huntington Snow,   State University, Lawrence, Kan.

Teacher. b. Fitchburg, Ma., June 29, 1840. f. H. S., Fitchburg. Delta Upsilon. Greek o.
Jun. Ex., 1861. Pres. L. Adel. Un. Debate. Pres. L. N. H. Valedictory. A. T. S., 1863-6.
Prof. Math. and Nat. Science and Prof. Nat. History, Univ., Kansas, since 1866. M. A., in
course. Ph. D., Williams, 1881. Pres. Kan. Acad. Sci. Fellow Am. Assoc. Sci. Kansas Legislature in 1883 built a $10,000 Nat. His. building and called it "Snow Hall." pub. Historical
and Scientific Papers. m. Jennie A. Aiken, Andover, Ma., July 2, 1868; five c.

James Field Spalding,   13 Follen St., Cambridge, Mass.

Clergyman. b. Enfield, Ct., Dec. 5, 1839. f. W. H., Easthampton. Kappa Alpha. Moon-
light, 1861 L. Editor Williams Quarterly. Classical o., 1862. Tra. Cookill, S. Y., 1862-4;
Tutor W. C., 1865-6; Assoc Prin. Round Hill Sch., Northampton, Ma., 1866-70, Rector, Ithaca,
N. Y., 1870-6; Portland, Ct., 1876-9; Cambridge, Ma., since 1879 M. A., in course; D. D., Wil-
liams, 1887. pub. "The Ordinance of Confirmation," 1880; "The Teaching and Influence of
St. Augustine," 1886. m. Mary A. Harper, Enfield, Ct., Apr. 28, 1864; three sons.

Albert True.

Clergyman. b. Owego, N. Y., Oct. 20, 1839. Jun. Ex., 1861. L. Logical o., 1862. Aub. T.
S., 1864-5. Ord., 1866. Pas. Cedar Falls, Ia., 1865-8; Ethridge, N. Y., 1868-71. m. Maria Pitcher,
Warren, Pa., May 16, 1865. d. Saratoga, N. Y., Oct. 18, 1871.

1863.

George Center Brown,   19 West Sixth St., Cincinnati, Ohio.

Lawyer and Journalist. b. Pittsfield, Mass., Feb 15, 1840 Delta Kappa Epsilon. Pres. L.
Ed. Univ. Quarterly. Law, St. Louis, Mo. Journalism, Cincinnati, Ohio.

John Gaylord Davenport, Waterbury, New Haven Co., Conn.

Clergyman. b. Wilton, Ct., Nov. 24, 1840 f. Acad. Wilton. Pres. Logian. Rehistory.
Prin. Jewett Acad., 1863-5. U. T. S., 1865-8. Tut. W. C. and a Theol. under Dr. Hopkins,
1865-7. Ord., July 7, 1868. Pas. Bridgeport, Ct., 1868-81; Waterbury, since 1881. M. A., Williams. pub. "After Twenty Years," 1883, and Poems, Articles, etc. Europe, 1882. m. Alice
Westcott, Wilton, Ct., Nov. 29, 1866; three c.

Samuel Warren Dike,   Auburndale, Middlesex Co., Mass.

Clergyman and Author. b. Thompson, Ct., Feb. 18, 1839. f. Dudley, Mr. Anti-Secret Society. Logian Metaphysical o., 1863. H. T. H., 1863-5; A. T. N., pub.8; ord... Feb 8, 1866. Pas. West Randolph, Vt., pan-70; Royalton, 1870-82. Secretary Divorce Reform League since 1881. res. Royalton, 1882-; Auburndale, since 1875. pub. "Facts as to Divorce in New England," 1881; "The Effect of lax Divorce Legislation upon Am. Publ. Institutions," 1881; "Some Aspect of the Divorce Question," 1881; "The Religious Problem of the Country Town," 1884, 1885; "The Family in the History of Christianity," 1885; "The Home Department of the Sunday School," 1888. m. Augusta M. Smith, Montpelier, Vt., Oct. 20, 1870; four c.

Myron Samuel Dudley,   N. Wilbraham, Hampden Co., Mass.

Clergyman. b. Peru, Vt., Feb. 20, 1837. f. B. and B. Sem., Manchester, Vt. Logian. Ortbodox, 1863. Private, Lieut. and Capt., U. S. Army, 1863-5. A. T. N., 1868-9. Tea. B. and B. Sem., Manchester, 1869-?. U. T. N., 1865-9. Ord., Sep. 28, 1871. Pas. Peacham, Vt., 1870-?; Cromwell, Ct., 1874-9; Pittsfield, Mass., 1869-?; North Wilbraham, since 1884. pub. History of Cromwell, Ct., 1880. Justice of Peace in Vt. m. Martha M. Hair, Peacham, Vt., Aug. 31, 1872. (d. July 31, 1878.) m. Sarah D. Field, Pittsfield, Mass., Apr. 28, 1882. (d. Oct. 85, 1884.)

William Arnett Dunning,   Lawrenceville, Ulster Co., N. Y.

Clergyman. b. Middletown, N. Y., Mar. 24, 1840. f. Franklin. Pres. I.. Oration, 1882. U. T. N., 1862-5. Ord. Presb., Sep. 13, 1865. Pas. Conklin, N. Y., 1865-9; Williamsport, Pa., 1869-81; Ellenville, Ill., 1881-5. res. Lawrenceville, N. Y. m. Maria Hunt, Gilbertsville, N. Y., Jan. 16, 1873; one c.

Addison Pinneo Foster,   Immanuel Cong. Ch., Boston, Mass.

Clergyman. b. Hanover, N. H.. Sep. 25, 1841. f. H. R., Lowell and P. A., Andover, Mass. Logian. Aesthetical o., 1862. P. T. N., 1863-5; A. T. H., 1865-6; Ord., Oct. 8, 1866. Pas. Lowell, Ma., 1865-8; Malden, 1871-2; Chelsea, 1872-?; Jersey City, N. J., 1877-80; Roxbury, since 1880. M. A. and D. D., (1884.) Williams. pub. "Four Pastorates of E. B. Foster," 1881; (Contributions to Sunday Club Sermons, 1878-87; "A Bird's Eye View of the Truths of Christianity," 1887. m. Harriet Day, Springfield, Ma., Aug. 8, 1866; four c.

Daniel Merriman,   Central Church, Worcester, Mass.

Clergyman. b. Manchester, Vt., Dec., 1838. f. Manchester, Vt., and Chicago, Ill. Logian. Ethical o., 1862. First Lieut. 168nd Ill. Vols. C. T. N., 1865-6; A. T. S., 1865-8; Ord., Rep. 26, 1868. Pas. Norwich, Ct., 1868-70; Worcester, Ma., since 1870. Europe, 1871, 1874. M. A.. Williams; D. D., Williams, 1884, also Ripon, 1881. mem. Am. Antiq. Soc., Trustee And Sec Free Inst. Indus. Sci., Worcester. pub. Sermons and Essays. m. Helen Bigelow, New, England, Sep. 1, 1864; one c.

John Henry Morley,   Supt. A, H. M S., Minneapolis, Minn.

Clergyman. b. Hartford, Conn., Jan. 8, 1840. Pres. Technian. Historical o., 1862. A. T. N., 1862-5. Ord. Cong. Jan. 2, 1867. Pas. Magnolia, Ia., 1868-9; Sioux City, 1869-78; Winona, Minn., 1878-83; St. Paul, 1883-5. Supt. A. H. M. S., Minneapolis, since 1885. M. A., Williams. Trustee Carlton College. pub. History of the Winona Church, Addresses, etc. m. Edith T. Johnson, Magnolia, Ill., Oct. 16, 1871; three c.

William Bement Putney,   115 Broadway, New York City.

Lawyer. b. Ashfield, Mass., June 2, 1857. f. Shelburne Falls. Pres. Technian. Honorary o., 1881. Tea. Hoosicktown, N. Y., 1883-4. Supt. Schools, Gallipolis, O., 1884-6. Admitted, Dec., 1887. Law, New York City, since 1888. m. Emma L. Edmunds, New York, Nov., 1880. (d Mar. 16, 1887.) m. Rebecca E. Fuller, Aug. 23, 1887; three c.

Leverett Wilson Spring,   Williamstown, Mass.

Tea her and Clergyman. b. Grafton, Vt. Jan. 5, 1840. f. B. and B. Sem., Manchester. Delta Upsilon. Logian. Philosophical o., 1863. U. T. N., 1863; A. T. N., 1867. Ord., Apr. 30, 1868. Pas. Fitchburg, Ma., 1868-75; Plymouth Ch., Lawrence, Kan., 1876-80. Prof. Eng. Lit Univ., Kan., 1881-6; Morris Prof. Rhet., W. C., since 1886. D. D., Univ., Kansas, 1888. pub. "History of Kansas," 1885 and other Historical papers. m. Sarah Elizabeth Thompson, East Windsor Hill, Ct., Sep. 25, 1867; two c.

Charles Warren Stone,   Warren, Warren Co., Pa.

Lawyer. b. Groton, Ma., June 29, 1843. f. L. A., Groton. Delta Upsilon. Logian. Honorary o., 1863. Tea. Warren, Pa., 1863-5. Supt. Schools, Warren Co., 1865. s. Law, Warren; Admitted, Aug., 1865. p. Law, Warren. since 1865. Pa. H. of R., 1870, 1871. Pa. Senate, 1877, 1878. Lieut. Governor, Pa., 1879-83. Secretary of State, Pa., since 1891. m. Lizzie Morehead, Bordville, Pa., Jan. 30, 1868; six c.

William Swan,   Lambertville, Hunterdon Co., N. J.

Clergyman. b. Fair Haven, Ct., Nov. 4, 1841. f. Bridgeport, Ct., and Bennington, Vt. Delta Psi. Technian. Prize Rhet. Ex. Jun Ex., 1863. Honorary o., 1863. Tea. Lawrenceville, N. J., 1863-5. P. T. S., 1865-8. Ord. Presb., June 2, 1868. Pas. Stockton, N. J., 1868-70. Batavia, N. Y., 1870-87; Lambertville, N. J., since 1887. M. A., Williams. m. Emma C. Nassau, Lawrenceville, N. J., Dec. 62, 1868.

William Henry Swift,   Portland Block, Chicago, Ill.

Lawyer. b. Nantucket, Ma., Mar. 27, 1841. f. H. S., Nantucket. Alpha Delta Phi. Technian. Valedictory. S. Law, Harvard; Admitted, 1866. Pittsfield, Mass., 1866-70; Chicago, since 1870. Trustee, Kane College. Director, Theol. Sem. N. W. m. m. Presb. Bd. Aid for Colleges. m. Grace Campbell, Pittsfield, Ma., May 1, 1867.

Charles Russell Treat,   St. Thomas Ch., New York City.

Clergyman. b. Newark, N. J., Oct. 6, 1843. f. Lat. Sch. Boston. Alpha Delta Phi. Technian. A. T. S., 1864-7. Prof. Physiol and Var. and Phys. Coll., W. C., 1868-9. Ord., Mar. 31, 1870. Pas. Martha's, Ma., 1870-3; Greenwich, Ct., 1874-80. Chap. Res. F. R., Antwerp, 1881-3. Asst. Rector, Stamford, Ct., 1883-5. Rec., Brooklyn, N. Y., 1885-7. Assoc. Rector, St. Thomas Ch., New York, since 1887. m. Julia J. Hubbell. Newark, N. J., Apr. 17, 1883; one c.

1864.

Edwin Smith Adams.

Journalist. b. Mill River, Ma., Nov. 23, 1841. Logian. Salutatory. Teacher and Journalist. New York Times. New York Dispatch. Prin. H. S., New Marlboro. d. Ashley Falls, Aug. 20, 1872.

Charles Ezra Ames.

Manufacturer. b. Niles, Mich., Jan. 62, 1841. f. Harvdfull, Ma. Pres Logian. Phil. o., 1864. Tea. Math., U. S. Naval Acad., Annapolis, Md., 1864-7. Merchant, Jackson, Mich., 1867-70. Stove Works, Detroit, 1870-80. m. Ada O. Chapman. Jackson, Mich., July 18, 1867; two c. Trustee and S. S. Supt., Unit. Ch. d. Dec. 17, 1880.

Stuart Manwaring Buck,   Hampton, Kanawha Co., W. Va.

Mining Engineer. b. Boston, Ma., Oct. 24, 1841. f. Lat. Sch. Boston. Pres L. N. H. Nat History o., 1864. s. Mass. Inst., Technology; Royal Mining Acad., Saxony, M. A., in course. Mich. Copper Mines, 1864-5; Freiburg, Saxony, 1865-8; Van Buren Furnace, Va., 1869-71; Coalburgh, W. Va., since 1871. mem. Am. Inst. Mining Eng. m. Grace Ross, Bangor, Me., Oct. 30, 1871; three c.

Timothy Grenville Darling,   Auburn, N. Y.

Clergyman. b. Nassau, N. P., Bahama Islands, Oct. 3, 1842. f. W. H., Easthampton, Ma. Kappa Alpha. Moonlight, 1864. Editor Williams Quarterly. Class Orator. Pres L. N. H. Ethical o., 1861. P. T. S., 1864-8. U. T. S., 1868-9. Ord. Presb., June 18, 1870. Asst. Pas. Baltimore, Md., 1870-3. Pas. Schenectady, N. Y., 1873-87. D. D., Williams, 1879. Act. Prof. Phil. Union. Prof. Rhet. and Pas. Theol. Aub. T. S., since 1887.

Charles Stoddard Durfee, East Bloomfield, Ontario Co., N. Y.

Clergyman. b. Norwood, Ma., July 22, 1841. f. Williamstown. Logian. Honorary o., 1864. Teacher, 1864-7. H. T. S., 1867-9. Ord. Presb., Sep. 8, 1869. Pas. Newburyport, Ma., 1869-70; Troy, N. Y., 1870-1; Glenwood, 1871-81; Liverpool, 1881-1; East Bloomfield, since 1884. M. A., in course. pub. Sermons and Class Reports. m. Ellen R. Greeley. Schaghticoke, N. Y., June 13, 1871.

William LaRoy Haven,   Morristown, Morris Co., N. J.

Teacher. b. Athol, Ma., May 21, 1833. f. Athol. Logian. Honorary o., 1884. Tea. Brick.
Wis., 1864-5; Noughton, 1865-6; Plattsburg, N. Y., 1868-9; Morristown. S. J., since 1869. Supt.
Public Schools. M. A., in course. m. Florence A Watson, Dec. 24, 1887, (d. 1878) m. Lizzie
N. Turvel, Dec. 22, 1878; two c.

Francis Theodore Ingalls,   Emporia, Lyons Co., Kan.

Clergyman. b. Haverhill, Ma., Jan. 6, 1844. f. Haverhill. Kappa Alpha. Pres. T. Ivy
Orator Valedictory. P. T. N., 1861-3. Teacher. 1863-7. Europe, 1867-8. A. T N., 1869-70.
Ord., Dec. 25, 1870. Pas. Olathe, Kan., 1870-2; Atchison, 1872-84; Emporia, since 1884. Ku-
ropa, 1880-1. Regent Univ., Kan. pub. Sermons, etc.

Joel Drury Miller,   Leominster, Worcester Co., Mass.

Teacher and Clergyman. b. Athol, Ma., Oct. 10, 1837. f. Athol and Bernardston. Pres. L.
Honorary o., 1884   Tea A thol, 1865-7.   M. A., in course.   Tea. Leominster, since 1887.   Ord.
Cong., 1888.   m. Maria L. Sanderson, Athol, July 18, 1888; two daughters.

John Marshall Paul.

Physician. b. Philadelphia, Dec 1, 1842. f P. A. Andover. Oration. 1864. U. R. Ras. Com.
1861-2. a. Med. Univ., Penn., 1865-8. p. Med., Belvidere, N. J., 1868-87. m. Miss Nishwitz,
Brooklyn, N. Y., Nov. 1878; two c. d. Mar. 17, 1887.

Franklin Almond Rising,   Winona, Minn.

Treasurer Savings Bank. b. New Marlboro. Ma., Feb 19, 1842. f. W. R., Easthampton.
Delta Kappa Epsilon. Pres Technian. Metaphysical o., 1864. Prof. Inst. It and D., New
York, 1864-8. Pria Inst. Improved Instruction D and D, New York, 1868-73. Treas. Sav.
Bank, Winona, since 1871. M. A., in course. m. Augusta B. Camp, Winsted, Ct., Oct. 17, 1871;
three c.

Charles Lyman Shaw,   Astoria, Queens Co., N. Y.

Teacher. b. Plainfield. Ma., Feb. 7, 1842. L. L. H. Curator Botany. Astronomical o., 1864.
Tea. Norwalk, Ct., 1864-7. Plainfield, Ma., 1867-8. Harv. Sci. Sch., 1872. Astoria, N. Y., 1864-78,
and since 1873. M. A., in course.

DeWitt Hurd Thomas.

Student. b. Metuchen, N. J., Oct. 20, 1841. Logian. Honorary o., 1864. d. U. T. S. New
York, Dec. ?, 1864.

Charles Chapin Tracy,   Marsovan, Turkey.

Missionary. b. East Smithfield, Pa., Oct. 81, 1838. Logian. Aesthetical Poem, 1864. U. T.
S., 1864-7. Ord. Presb., July 5, 1867. Missionary A. B. C. F. M., since 1867. m. Myra A. Park,
Athens, Pa., Aug. 14, 1867; two boys.

John L. R. Trask,   9 Jackson Terrace, Lawrence, Mass.

Clergyman. b. Hampden, Me., Dec. 19, 1842. f. Dummer Acad. Byfield. Ma. and Athla-
ons, N. H. Logian. Honorary o., 1864. P. T. S., 1864-5. A. T. S., 1865-7. Ord. Cong., Dec. 4,
1867. Pas. Holyoke, Ma., 1867-83; Lawrence, since 1884. Europe, 1873. M. A., in course.
Trustee Mt. Holyoke Fem. Sem., since 1878. m. Jane Parker, Dunbarton, N. H., Aug. 1, 1871;
three c.

Edward Phineas Wells,   710 Lawrence St., Denver, Col.

Clergyman. b. Salisbury, Ct., Mar. 4, 1844. f. Knox College. Logian. Honorary o., 1864.
U. T. S., 1864-5. Ord. Presb., Apr. 18, 1868. Pas. E. Berlhan, Mr., 1868-7; Williamstown, Ma.,
1867-8; Denver, Col., 1868-73; Chicago, Ill., 1873-8; Mechanicsville, Ia., 1878-88; Denver, Col.,
since 1888. Trustee Colorado College, Longmont College. Vice-Pres. Cos College. m. Ade-
laide V. Badger, Williamstown, Ma., May 19, 1868; four c.

1865.

John Strawn Bayne,   Portland, Middlesex Co., Conn.

Clergyman. b. Lacon, Ill., Jan. 29, 1842. f. H. S., Lacon. Prea. Logian. Prea. Mills. Ed. College Quarterly. Historical o., 1865. U. T. s., 1868-9. Ord. Cong., May 16, 1869. Pas Stanwich, Ct., 1867-71; Greenwich, 1873-5; Portland, since 1875. Europe, 1879. M. A., in course. Visitor School Board. pub. "History First Cong. Ch. of Portland," 1876; "History of the L. B. R.," 1883. m. Julia C. Taft, Sag Harbor, N. Y., May 24, 1869; five c.

Samuel Seward Benedict,   Benedict, Wilson Co., Kan.

Ranchman and Civil Engineer. b. Manchester, Vt., Nov. 9, 1843. f. B. and R. Seminary. Alpha Delta Phi. T. Honorary o., 1865. Nebraska 1865-6; Wy. Ter., 1866-7; Kansas, since 1867. U. S. Indian Inspector, four yrs. Regent Univ., Kan. Kan. Senate, eight yrs. m. Dora Farwell, Guilford, Kan., Mar. 12, 1874; three c.

John Edwin Bradley,   Supt. Schools, Minneapolis, Minn.

Teacher and Supt. Schools. b. Lee, Ms., Aug. 8, 1839. f. Lee. Ms., and Claremock, N. Y. L. Honorary o., 1865. Prin. H. S., Pittsfield, Ms., 1865-8. Prin. H. S., Albany, N. Y., 1868-88 Supt. Schools, Minneapolis, Minn., since 1888. M. A., Williams. Ph. D., Univ. State N. Y. 1879. Ed. Mass Teacher. Commissioner Paris Exposition, 1878. Chairman Ex. Com. Univ. Conv. State N. Y., 1884-6. Trustee and Deacon Cong. Ch., Albany. Deacon Plymouth Ch., Minneapolis. Moderator N. Y. Cong. Assoc., 1895. Alumni Visitor W. C. pub. "The Healthfulness of Intellectual Pursuits;" "Educational Methods;" "Classical Studies;" "The Teacher's Preparation;" "Report on the Educational Exhibits at Paris, 1878;" "The Personal Element in Education;" "Manual Training," and other educational papers. m. Martha Jeanette Gould, Albany. July 7, 1870.

William Danforth Bradley.

Lawyer. b. Lanesboro, Ms., June 20, 1843. Oration, 1865. s. Law. Albany. p. Law. New York. d. Aug. 8, 1870.

Frederick Perry Brown.

Lawyer. b. Whitingham, Vt., Mar. 31, 1840. f. Bernardston, Ms. Prea. L. Class Poet. Oration, 1865. Law. North Adams, 1867-87. Mass. H. of M., 1871, 1872. Mass. Senate, 1878. Invex. Sch. Committee. Baptist Church. m. Ella Annette Preston, North Adams, May 1, 1868; four c., W. C., son '90.

Abner Wheeler Buttrick.

Physician. b. Lowell, Ms., Aug. 29, 1841. f. P. A., Andover. Oration, 1865. s. Med., Harvard, 1868-9. Europe, 1869-71. M. A., in course. p. Med., Lowell, 1871-82. d. there, Mar. 27, 1882.

Orestes Gardner Eldridge.

Teacher. b. Hancock, Ms., Apr. 22, 1842. f. P. A., Andover. L. Honorary o., 1865. Teawulawau, N. J., 1867-9; Worcester, Ms., 1869-9. res. Hancock, 1869-75. d. there, Mar. 30, 1875.

Justin Edwards Emerson,   128 Henry St., Detroit, Mich.

Physician. b. Hawaiian Islands, Aug. 31, 1841. f. Oahu College. Logian. Honorary o., 1865. M. A., Williams. M. D., Harvard, 1868. W. Warren, Ms., 1869. Asst. Phys. Mich. Asylum, Kalamazoo, 1870-6. Europe, 1870-9. Detroit, Mich., since 1888. Mich. State Med. Soc.; Am. Acad. Med.; Am. Med. Assoc. m. Williemena H. Elliott. M. A. (Vassar.) M. D. (Woman's Med. Coll., N. Y.) Kalamazoo, Dec. 68, 1877; three boys.

Nathaniel Bright Emerson,   Honolulu, Hawaiian Islands.

Physician. b. Hawaiian Islands, July 1, 1839. f. Oahu College. Delta Kappa Epsilon. Logian. U. S. Army, 1861-4. Honorary o., 1865. s. Med. Coll. Phys. and Surg. New York and Harv. Med. School. p. Med., New York, 1869-78. Honolulu, since 1878. M. A., Williams; M. D., Columbia, 1869. m. Sarah E. Pierce, M. D., Honolulu, Jan. 31, 1885; one boy.

Thomas Lafon Gulick,   Paia, Maui, Hawaiian Islands.

Clergyman. b. Kauai, H. I., Apr. 10, 1839. Prea. Logian. Honorary o., 1865. U. T. S. 1865-8. A. T. S., 1867-8. Ord. Cong., May 13, 1870. Missionary, Spain, 1872-81; Cuba, 1883-1; Las Vegas, N. M., 1885-7. H. Islands, since 1887.

Thomas Hooker,   75 East Fayette St., Syracuse, N. Y.

Manufacturer. b. Hottville, N. Y., Sep. 1, 1840. Pres. Legion. Honorary n., 1885. Resident, Syracuse, N. Y., since 1862. Elder Presb. Church. in. Sept. 30, 1872. Cleveland, O.; wife died, June, 1878.

Albert Brown Lyons,   428 Second St., Detroit, Mich.

Pharmacist and Chemist. b. Waitown. Haw. Is., Apr. 1, 1841. f. Honolulu. Valedictory, Tea. N. J., 1885-4. Univ. Mich., Ann Arbor, 1875-8. Detroit, since 1884. Prof. Chem. Med. Coll., 1888-91. M. A., Williams. M. D., Univ. Mich. and Detroit Med. College, F. C. S. Editor Pharmaceutical Era. mem. A. P. A.; Mich. St. P. A.; Detroit Acad. Med., etc. pub. "Manual of Pharmaceutical Assaying," 1886. m. Edith M. Eddy, Detroit. Apr. 15, 1878; two c.

Charles T. F. Spoor,   95 Tweddle Building, Albany, N. Y.

Lawyer. b. Cooxackie, N. Y. Jan. 1, 1842. f. Lansingburgh. Alpha Delta Phi. Pres. T. Rshistoriy. Tea. Lake Forest, Ill., 1865-6. s. Law. Catskill, N. Y., 1866-7; Albany, 1868 to Law. Catskill, 1868-70; Albany, since 1871. Lect. Alb. Law Sch.; Practice, since 1871; Practice, Real Estate and Wills, since 1874. R. A., Williams.

Emory Washburn West.

Architect. b. New York City, Feb. 11, 1844. Kappa Alpha. T. Pres. L. N. H. Honorary n., 1883. s. Law, Columbia, 1865-6. d. Jan. 22, 1868.

Fernando Cortez Willett.

Student. b. Bakersfield, Vt., Dec. 7, 1842. U. S. Army, 1864-5. Legion. Honorary n., 1886. Prin. Schools, Evansville, Ind., 1865-6. Lect T. N., 1870 i. Sec. Legation, Cordova, Mexico. d. there, June 14, 1873.

1866.

John Milton Bigelow,   Albany, N. Y.

Physician and Surgeon. b. Albany. N. Y., Aug. 22, 1847. f. Academy, Albany. Alpha Delta Phi. Pres. T. Metaphysical n., 1869. s. Med. Coll. Phys. and Surg. New York, and Med. Coll., Albany. p. Med., Albany, since 1869. Prof. Mat. Med. and Ther.; Prof. Diseases Throat and Nose, Albany Med. College. M. A., W. C., 1869; M. D., Columbia, 1869; Alb. Med. Coll., 1870. m. Sarah Amelia Crook, Albany, Feb. 14, 1874. (d.)

George Hamlin Bradford,   Sheffield, Mass.

Business. b. Sheffield, Ms., son of Judge Bradford. Legion. Honorary n., 1872. M A., in course. Business in Chicago.

Ethan Curtis,   350 Mulberry St., Syracuse, N. Y.

Clergyman. b. East Palmyra, N. Y., Feb. 15, 1841. Legion. L. N. H. Mills. Jun. Ex., 1863. Honorary n., 1884. H. T. S., 1865-7; A. T. S., 1867-8. Ord., Oct. 14, 1868. Pas. Cong., Camden, N. Y., 1868-82. Danforth Cong. Ch., Syracuse, since 1882. m. Maria Howard, Hartford, Ct., June 9, 1869, (d. Feb. 26, 1890.) m. Jessie D. Kingsley, Hamilton. N. Y., Aug. 19, 1893; five c.

Virgil Polk Kline,   219 Superior St., Cleveland, Ohio.

Lawyer. Entered College from Ottawa, O. Techalas. Oration, 1888. Law, Cleveland.

Dexter Asa Knowlton,   Freeport, Stephenson Co., Ill.

Banker. b. Freeport, Ill., Aug. 24, 1845. f. P. A., Andover and privately. Pres. T. Honorary n., 1888. res. Freeport, 1863-85; Winnfield, N. Y., 1885-89; Saratoga Springs, 1891-4; Brooklyn, 1894-9; Freeport, Ill., since 1899. Trustee, Beloit. mem. "Board Aid for Colleges." Elder Presb. Ch. m. Mary L. Myers, Brooklyn, N. Y., June 7, 1871; five daughters.

Oscar Frederick Lund.

Physician. b. Boston, Ms., Nov. 30, 1844. f. L. A. Groton. Legion. Honorary n., 1888. M. D., Harvard, 1869. p. Med., Jersey City, N. J., 1869-75. Europe, 1874. LL t. m. Sarah W. Palmer, Canterbury, Ct., June, 1880; two c. d. June 29, 1878.

Alfred Edwards Myers, 617 Chestnut St., Syracuse, N. Y.

Clergyman. b. New York City, Dec. 29, 1844. f. Coll. and Polyt. Inst., Brooklyn. Delta Psi. Prize Techolan. Salutatory. X. B. T. S., 1869-7; P. T. K., 1869-9; U. T. K., 1869-70, Ord., May, 1870. Brooklyn, N. Y., 1870-1. Europe 1871-2. Pas. Brownville, N. Y., 1872-4; Owasco, 1874-5; Syracuse, since 1865. Pastor Westminster Presb. Ch. M. A. Williams, pub. "The Noviciate, the Entertainment and the Bazaar," 1868. m. Mary Moffat, Brooklyn, June 3, 1873; four c.

William C. P. Rhoades, 400 Putnam St., Brooklyn, N. Y.

Clergyman. b. Elbridge, N. Y., Apr. 6, 1843. f. M. C. I. Elbridge Delta Kappa Epsilon. Logian. Valedictory. Rochester Theol. Sem. Tutor W. C., 1867-8. Mission Work. 1868-9. Pas. Bapt. Granville, O., 1871-6; Brooklyn, N. Y., since 1876. D. D., Bapt. Theol. Sem., Chicago, 1884. Trustee, Denison.

Benjamin Day Skinner.

Broker's Clerk. b. Cincinnati, O., July, 1845. Pres. Logian. Business, New York. d. from overdose of morphine, Sep. 21, 1866. wife and one c.

Rufus Scofield Underwood, Northampton, Mass.

Clergyman and Evangelist. b. Newark, N. J., Nov. 24, 1846. Pres. Logian. Pres. Millennary o., 1868. H. T. S., 1866-7. Ord., Nov. 1867. Evangelist, Wilbraham, Ms. 1867-8; Lawrence, 1868-9; Somers and East Hartford, Ct., 1869-70; Springfield, Mo. 1870-3; New York City, 1873-4; Brooklyn, 1874-6; Irvington, N. J., 1875-85; Northampton, Ms., since 1885. pub. Volume of Sermons, 1870. m. Almira J. Kent, Wilbraham, May 19, 1868; five daughters.

1867.

Charles Augustus Davenport, Herald Bldg., Boston, Mass.

Manufacturer. Entered College from West Killingly, Ct. Logian. Honorary o., 1867. Cotton Mauf., Lewiston, Me.; Manchester, N. H.; Waterville, Me.; Piedmont, S. C.

Frederick William Gunster, Scranton, Pa.

Lawyer. b. Lackwanna, Prussia, Sept. 15, 1845. f. Scranton. 1st Lat. Prize, 1865. Pres. Logian. Philosophical o., 1867. Law. Admitted Nov. 1869. Scranton, Pa. Europe, 1872. Law H. of R., Pa., 1873, 1874. Out Att. Lack. Co., Pa., 1876, 1879. Pres. Lack. Hospital. M. A., Williams. m. Maggie Rechl, Wilkesbarre, Pa., Oct. 10, 1875; six c., four living.

Granville Stanley Hall, J. H. University, Baltimore, Md.

Teacher. b. Ashfield, Ms., Feb. 1, 1845. f. W. R. Easthampton. Alpha Delta Phi. Class Poet. Pres Technolan. U. T. S., 1867-8; Bonn, Ger., 1868-70; U. T. S., 1870-1. Prof. Ant. Coll. Yellow Springs, O., 1872-6. Tea. Harvard, 1876-8. Europe, 1878-80. Lecturer, Harvard and Johns Hopkins Univs., 1881-4. Lect. W. C. 1881-4. Prof. J. H. Univ. since 1884. M. A., Williams. Ph. D., Harvard, 1878. LL. D., Wesleyan Univ., 1887. pub. "Rosenkranz's Hegel and Nationalphilosoph," (tr.) 1872; "Aspects of German Culture," 1881; "How to Teach History," 1883; "Philosophy of Education," 1885; "American Journal of Psychology," (Ed.) m. Cornelia M. Fisher, (Cincinnati.) Berlin, Ger., Sept., 1879; two c.

Rollin Eugene Harmon, Lynn, Essex Co., Mass.

Lawyer. b. Lawrence, Ms. f. H. S., Lawrence. Valedictory. Tut. Wis. Univ., 1867-8. s. Law, Lawrence; Admitted, 1870. p. Law, Lynn, since 1870. m. Maria O. Batchelder, Lynn, Feb. 17, 1870

Hamilton Wright Mabie, 30 Lafayette Place, New York City.

Lawyer and Editor. b. Cold Springs, N. Y., Dec. 13, 1846. f. privately. Brooklyn. Alpha Delta Phi. Technolan. Editor Williams Quarterly. Literary Oration. Pres. Adelphic Union. Oration, 1867. Columbia Law School, 1867-9; Admitted, May, 1869. p. Law, Tarrytown, N. Y., 1869-78. Journalism and Literary Work, since 1878. Editor Christian Union, New York, res. University Pl. O., since 1879. pub. "Norse Stories," 1882; "Michaud's History of the Crusades," (Ed.) m. Jeannette Trivett, New York City, Oct. 11, 1876; two c.

Henry Clay Miller,   1479-1485 Broadway, New York City.

Teacher. b. Philadelphia, Pa., May 19, 1844. Kappa Alpha. Techniau. Val. Adelphic Union. Aesthetical o., 1865. Prin. Hasbrouck Inst., Jersey City, N. J., 1872-80. Prin. School of Languages, New York, since 1880, mem. Consol Stock and Petroleum Exch. Am. Numis. and Arch. Soc.

Obed Hatch Sanderson,   18 Wall St., New York City.

Lawyer. b. Littleton, Mass., May 16, 1845. f. I. A., Groton, Mass. Logian. Honorary o., 1867. n. Law, New York; Admitted to N. Y. Bar, Nov., 1868. p Law, New York, since 1868.

Albert Cole Sewall.   Schenectady, N. Y.

Clergyman. b. Blackbill, Me., Mar. 25, 1845. f. North Granville, N. Y., Middlebury, Vt., and Wn. Logian. Mills. Honorary o., 1867. Auburn T S., 1867-70. Ord. Presb., Oct. 15, 1871. Pas. Newark, N. Y., 1872. Williamstown, Mass., 1874-80. Schenectady, N. Y., since 1880. pub. "Life of Prof. Albert Hopkins," 1879. m. Helen S. Ives, South Easton, N. Y., Jan. 12, 1871; one son.

John Ford Smith,   18 North Fourth St., St. Louis, Mo.

Lawyer. b. Granville, Ma., Mar 6, 1847. f. Knox Coll., Galesburg, Ill. Techniau. Honorary o., 1867. n. Law, Harvard. p. Law. St. Louis. U S. Army, 1861-5. M. A., Williams. m. Carrie D. Lathrop, St. Louis, Mo., June 11, 1874; two c.

Francis Lynde Stetson,   45 William St., New York City.

Lawyer. b. Keeseville, N. Y., Apr. 23, 1846. f. Acad., Plattsburgh. Alpha Delta Phi. Techniau. Honorary o., 1867. n. Law, Columbia; LL. B., 1869. p. Law, New York City. Assistant Counsel to the Corporation, N. Y. City. Commissioner to Revise City Ordinances. M A., Williams. President W. C. Alumni. m. Elizabeth Wright Ruff, Rahway, N. J., June 26, 1873.

Gilbert Milligan Tucker, 138 Washington Ave., Albany, N. Y.

Editor. b. Albany, N. Y., Aug 28, 1847. f. Acad., Albany. Logian. L. S. H. Art Association. Metaphysical o., 1867. M A., in course. Editor and one of the Publishers, Country Gentleman. m. Sarah Edwards Miller, Albany, June 7, 1877; two c.

Jonathan Wadhams,   Ashfield, Franklin Co., Mass.

Clergyman. b. Clarkson, N. Y., Dec. 4, 1846. f. Brockport. Pres Techniau. Salutatory. A. T. S., 1867-71. Ord. Dec. 20, 1871. Pas Oswego, Ill., 1871-3. Belle Plain, Ia., 1873-4. Charles City, 1874-8. Ashfield, Mass., since 1878. m. Lucy M. Kneeley, Albany, Aug 7, 1871; two c.

1868.

Charles Henry Burr,   121 West 34th St., New York City.

Clergyman. b. Astoria, N. Y., Dec. 19, 1847. f. St. P. Acad., Sing Sing. Delta Psi. Techniau. P. T. S., 1868-70. Edinburgh, 1870-1; (German), 1871-3. Ord., Mar. 5, 1871. Pas Sing Sing, N. Y., 1872-4. Riverdale, 1874-8. Bethany Cong. Ch., New York, since 1880. m. Laura C. Hoyle, Champlain, N. Y., Aug. 19, 1874; two c.

James Hulme Canfield,   State University, Lawrence, Kan.

Lawyer and Teacher. b. Delaware, O., Mar. 18, 1847. f. Coll and Polyt. Inst., Brooklyn, N Y. L. N. d. Rhet. Prize, 1868 Philosophical o., 1868. R R. Construction, Ia. and Minn., 1868-71. Law, Jackson, Mich., 1871-2; St Joseph, 1872-7. Prof. His. and Eng. Lang. and Lit., Univ. Kan., 1877-8. Prof. His. and Polit. Sci., same, since 1881. M. A., Williams. Circ. Court Com. Dist , Mich., 1875-7. Supt. Schools, 1875-7. mem. Am His. Assoc.: Am. Economic Assoc. Pres. Kan. Teachers Assoc., 1885. Sec. National Ed. Assoc., 1881-7. 1887-8. pub. "School History of Kansas," 1884; "Local Government in Kansas," 1885. m. Flavia A. Camp. Clear Lake, Ia., June 21, 1873; two c.

Charles Worth Folger.

Clerk. b. Geneva, N. Y., Oct. 8, 1846. f. Peekskill. Sigma Phi. Oration, 1868. Farmer, Minn. and Clerk, Washington, D. C. m. Susie Depew, Baltimore, Md., Nov. 14, 1875; six c. d. Geneva, N. Y., Jan 11, 1885.

William Ball Gilbert, Portland, Oregon.

Lawyer. b. Fairfax Co., Va., July 4, 1847. f. Zanesville, O. Logian. Oration, 1868. a. Law, Univ., Mich. Ohio Geological Survey, 1870-3. p. Law. since 1873. res. Zanesville, O., 1868-78; Portland, Ore. since 1878. m. Julia W. Lindsley, Portland. Sep. 6, 1878; four c.

George Field Lawton, Lowell, Mass.

Lawyer and Supt. Public Schools. b. Lowell, Oct. 17, 1846. Pres. Logian. L. N. H. Honorary o., 1868. Law. Lowell. City Solicitor, '81, '82, '85, '86. Supt. Public Schools, '88, '89. M. A., Williams. m. Ida A. Hill, Lowell, 1867; two c.

George Perkins Lawton, Saratoga Springs, N. Y.

Lawyer. b. Albany, N. Y., Aug. 19, 1847. f. Vt. Epis. Inst. Burlington. Chi Psi. Prize Rhet., 1868. Technian. Oration, 1868. Law, Troy, Albany and Saratoga. Lieut. Col 3rd Div N. G. S. N. Y. m. Jeannie M. W. Lathrop, Albany, N. Y., Nov. 5, 1873; one son.

Burke Fay Leavitt, 409 Orchard St., Chicago, Ill.

Clergyman. b. Lowell, Ms. Sep. 21, 1841. Pres Logian. L. N. H. Honorary o., 1868. A. T. K., 1867-71. Ord. May 8, 1871. Pas. Portland, Me., 1871-3. Lincoln Park Ch. Chicago, since 1873. m. Lucine M. Day, Lancaster, Ms., Jan. 3, 1878; six c.

Edward Walter Rice, Mt. Vernon, Westchester Co., N. Y.

Teacher. b. Wayland, Mass., Sep. 3, 1846. f. Lee. Alpha Delta Phi. Technian. Valedictory. Tet. Lev. Ms., 1868-70. Cambridge, 1870-3. Mt. Vernon, N. Y., since 1873. M. A. Williams. m. Mary M. Levy, Mt. Vernon, Dec. 28, 1873. (d.); one c.

Charles T. R. Smith, Lansingburgh, N. Y.

Teacher. b. Pittsford, Vt., Dec. 3, 1846. f. Acad. Plattsburgh, N. Y. Technian. L. N. H. Honorary o., 1868. Prin Leavenworth Inst., Wolcott, N. Y., 1869-70. Acad., Fort Byron, 1870-1. Acad., Fayetteville, 1871-3. Acad., Lansingburg, since 1873. M. A., Williams. m. Cornelia A. Hibbard, South Butler, N. Y., Nov. 88, 1876; two c.

Henry Schmaltz Van Ingen, 53 Dearborn St., Chicago, Ill.

Civil Engineer. b. Schenectady, N. Y., Mar. 28, 1847. f. Coll. and Polyt. Inst., Brooklyn. Delta Psi. Pres Technian. Honorary o., 1868. Sch. Mines, Columbia, 1868-70. Asst. Eng. U. R. A., Newport, R. I., 1870-6. Supt. Penn. Coal Co., Chicago, since 1876. Pres. Anthracite Coal Assoc. res. Kenosha, Wis., since 1884. Vestryman Epis. Ch. m. Emma C. Lawton, Newport, R. I., May 24, 1877; four c.

John Seymour Walton, Chicago, Ill.

Banker. Entered College from New Orleans, La. Sigma Phi. Technian. Classical o., 1868.

George Franklin Woodward, Lowell, Mass.

Lawyer. Entered College from Lowell. Pres. Logian. Mathematical o., 1868. Law. Boston. Infirm for some years.

1869.

Avery Leeds Billings, Minneapolis, Minn.

Merchant. Entered College from Rutland, Vt. Logian. Oration, 1869. Tau. Excelsior, Minn. Merchant, Minneapolis.

Alfred Clark Chapin, Mayor's Office, Brooklyn, N. Y.

Lawyer. b. South Hadley, Mass., Mar. 8, 1848. f. 41. L., South Williamstown. Alpha Delta Phi. Logian. Rhet. Prize, 1868. a. Law, Harvard: LL. B. 1871. p Law. New York City, since 1871. res. Brooklyn, since 1873. N. Y. Assembly, 1882, 1883; Speaker, same, 1883. Comptroller, State N. Y., 1883-7, (16,000 majority.) Elected Mayor of Brooklyn, Nov., 1887. Adelphic Union Orator, 1884. N. Y. Office, 115 Broadway. m. Grace Stebbins, New York, Feb. 29, 1881; one c.

Edward Herman Cole,   Nyack, Rockland Co., N. Y.

Lawyer. b. Pratsburgh, N. Y., Oct 13, 1847. f. Pobyt. Inst., Brooklyn. Alpha Delta Phi. Oration, 1869. Law, (Gov); Sec. Furnace Co., 1870-10; Law, since 1880. m. Caroline P. Chamberlin, Nyack, Nov. 5, 1879; one c.

James Seth Cooley,   Glen Cove, Long Island, N. Y.

Physician. b. South Hartford, N. Y., June 29, 1845. f. Coll. Inst., Fort Edward. Logian. L. N. H. Moonlight. Salutatory. Tea. Fort Edward, 1869-75; Glens Falls, 1875-8. n. Med., Univ., Vt., 1878; Univ., City N. Y., 1877. p. Med., Sandy Hill, 1877-80; Luzerne, 1880-8. (the Cove, since 1888. M. A., Williams. M. D., Univ. City N. Y., 1877. Coroner, 1884-6 Health Officer, 1884-6, mem. Washington Co. Med. Soc. Queens Co. Med. Soc. Trustee and Elder Presb. Ch. m. M. Reba Clark, Wilsboro Point, N. Y., June 30, 1878; two c.

Charles Dewey Howk.

Lawyer. b. Charlestown, Ind., Dec. 4, 1849. Logian. Oration, 1869. Law, New Albany. Ind. and Louisville, Ky. d. Feb. 5, 1873.

Henry Ketcham,   Menomonie, Dunn Co., Wis.

Clergyman. b. Indianapolis, Ind., May 5, 1846. Prm. Trcholan. Oration, 1869 Law T. S., 1869-70; A. T. S., 1870-3; Ord. Cong. Oct. 30, 1873. Pas. Wolfsborough. N. H., 1875-9; Menomonie, Wis., since 1879. m. Sarah Dickson Hendricks, Oct. 8, 1879; three c.

Charles Wolcott Loomis,   Binghamton, N. Y.

Lawyer. b. Binghamton. Sigma Phi. Logian. Philosophical o., 1869.

Elisha Barclay Powell,   Oswego, N. Y.

Lawyer. b. Milton, N. Y., Sep. 1, 1848. L. H. R., Oswego Sigma Phi. Valedictory. Lumber Trade, Oswego, 1869-78. Law, Oswego, since 1879. City Att., Oswego. M. A., Williams. m. Addie Hoy Wright, Oswego, Oct. d. 1875; three boys.

William Ward Wight,   159 Insurance Bldg., Milwaukee, Wis.

Lawyer. b. Troy, N. Y., Jan. 11, 1849. f Troy, Bennington and Homer. Delta Kappa Epsilon. Prm. Trchaisu. Philosophical o., 1869. Tea. D. L. I., Franklin, N. Y., 1869-71, a Law. Union Univ., Albany, 1871-3; Admitted, 1873. New York City, 1873-4. Milwaukee, since 1874. Europe, 1880. Special Ex. Civil Service Com. mem. N. E. His. General Soc.; Wis. His. Soc. M. A., Williams, 1882. pub "Table of Wisconsin Law Cases," 1878. m. Sarah E. West, June 30, 1878. (d. Feb. 1, 1877.) m Mary O. Brockway, June 16, 1881, (d. July 24, 1883;) one son.

William Page Winslow.

Editor. b. Pittsford, Vt., Feb. 17, 1847. Logian. Philosophical o., 1869. Clerk, Rutland Bank, 1869-73. Europe, 1873. Ed. Herald, Rutland, 1873. d. May 4, 1875.

1870.

William Keith Brooks,   J. H. Univ., Baltimore, Md.

Teacher. Entered College from Cleveland, O. Prm. Logian. Oration, 1870. Assoc. Biol. J. H. Univ. Ph. D., Harvard, 1875.

Francis Henry Davenport,   5 Park Square, Boston, Mass.

Physician. b. Roxbury, Ms., Mar. 17, 1851. f Lat. Sch., Roxbury. Kappa Alpha. Moonlight, 1869. Prm. Logian. Philosophical o., 1870. s. Med., Harvard; M. D., 1874. p. Med., Boston, since 1877. Europe, 1874-5. Asst. Prof. Gynecology. Harv. Med. Sch., since 1881. M. M. S. m. Elizabeth A. Brewster, Roxbury, June 4, 1879; two c.

Melville Egleston,   18 Cortlandt St., New York City.

Lawyer. b. Ellington, Ct., July 27, 1845. f Stockbridge, Ms. Delta Psi. Benedict Prize Rhet., 1870. Historical o., 1870. s Law, Columbia. n. Univ., Berlin; Univ., Gottingen. Law, New York, 1870-6 and since 1879. Act. Prof. W. C., 1876-9. Special Lecturer, Law Sch., Univ., City N. Y., since 1886. U. S. Army; 2nd Lieut., 10th Mass.; 1st Lieut and Adj., same, 1863-5. M. A., Yale, 1886. pub "Land System of N. E. Colonies," 1880, reprinted in 4th Series, J. H. Univ.: "Studies in Historical and Political Science," 1886. m. Jane Shelton Dunbar, Hartford, Ct., May 4, 1882; three c.

Robert Gershom Fitch, City Hall, Boston, Mass.

Journalist. b. Sheffield, Ma., May 18, 1848. f. New Marlboro. Logian. Oration. 1870. Journalist, 1870-80. Chairman Bd. Fire Commissioners, since 1880. m. Emma H. Emmons, Detroit, Mich., Sep. 18, 1876; three c.

John Charles Haines, Seattle, Wash. Ter.

Lawyer. b. Hainesville, Ill., Feb. 14, 1849. f. Lake Forest. Kappa Alpha. Moonlight. 1871. Class Poet. Logian. Philosophical o., 1870. z. Law, Chicago Univ. p. Law, Chicago, 1870-80. Seattle, since 1880. Justice Peace, 1871-2. Colonel 1st Reg., Nat. Guard. 1887. m. Belle Barton, Waukegan, Ill., Jan. 16, 1879; one and.

Robert Beales Hall.

Clergyman. b. Ashfield, Ma., Dec. 20, 1848. Pres. Logian. Salutatory. U. T. S., 1871-3; Ord. Cong., Nov. 18, 1873. Pas. Wolfboro, N. H., 1873-5; Cambridgeport, Ma., 1875-6. m. Sarah D. Lord, Rockland, 1871; one c. d. Nov. 3, 1876.

William Henry Hollister, Jr., 17 First St., Troy, N. Y.

Lawyer. b. Cornwallis, N. Y. f. P. A., Andover, and H. R. L., Claverack, N. Y. Delta Kappa Epsilon. Moonlight, 1869. Editor Williams Quarterly. Pres. Logian. Oration, 1870. Law, Troy, N. Y., since 1871. Elder and Trustee Presb. Ch. m. Julia Frances Hillman, Troy, Oct. 16, 1876; one c.

Harry Pratt Judson, State Univ., Minneapolis, Minn.

Teacher. b. Jamestown, N. Y., Dec. 20, 1849. f. Geneva and Lansingburg. Delta Kappa Epsilon. Logian. Prizes, Greek and German. Philosophical o., 1870. Tea. Troy, N. Y., 1870-85. Prof. History Univ. Minn., since 1885. M. A. Williams. pub. "History of Cæsar's Corps. Troy, N. Y." 1884; "Cæsar's Gallic War" (Ed.) 1886; "Cæsar's Army." 1888. m. Rebecca A. Gilbert, Troy, Jan. 15, 1879; two c.

Arthur Robinson, North Adams, Mass,

Journalist. Entered College from North Adams. Logian. Hist. Prize, 1869. Oration, 1870. Transcript, North Adams.

1871.

James Robert Dunbar, Westfield, Mass.

Lawyer. b. Pittsfield, Mass., Dec. 22, 1847. f. H. S. Pittsfield. L. N. H. Pres. Technian. Honorary o., 1871. z. Law, Harvard; Admitted Apr. 1874. p. Law, Westfield, since 1874. Mass. Senate, 1880, 1881. Dist. Attorney. m. Harriet P. Walton, Westfield, May 15, 1873; three c.

Frank Foxcroft, Journal Office, Boston, Mass.

Journalist. b. Boston, Jan. 21, 1850. f. H. S. Pittsfield. Technian. Class Poet. Oration, 1871. res. Cambridge, Ma., since 1871. Asst. Editor Boston Journal, pub. "Transcript Pieces," etc., 1886; "Resurgit, Hymns and Songs of the Resurrection," 1879. mem. Cambridge School Board, 1878-9. Deacon, Cong. Ch. since 1878. m. Elizabeth True Howard, Cambridge, Sep. 11, 1878; als c., three living.

Herbert Russell Gibbs, Riverside Press, Cambridge, Mass.

Clerk. b. Pittsfield, Mass., Dec. 20, 1850. f. H. S. Lee. Alpha Delta Phi. Technian. Philosophical o., 1871. Post-graduate Course, Yale. M. A. Yale, 1884. Cambridge, since 1878. Aud. and Assessor, Pilgrim Cong. Ch., Cambridgeport. m. Sarah M. Calvd, Cambridge, Jan 1, 1875; three c.

William Hale Herrick, State College, Centre Co., Pa.

Teacher. b. Essex, Vt., Oct. 18, 1849. f. K. U. A. Meriden, S. H. Logian. Hist. Prize, 1870. Philosophical o., 1871. Sheffield Sci. Sch., Yale, 1874. M. A. Williams. Prof. Chem. Iowa Coll., 1874-5. Prof. Chem. Penn. State Coll. since 1885. mem. Iowa Acad. Sci. pub. Classen's "Quantitative Analysis by Electrolysis," (trans.) 1886. m. Jennie A. Tuttle, New Haven, Ct., June 30, 1876.

George Edwin MacLean,   State Univ., Minneapolis Minn.

Clergyman and Teacher. Entered College from Gt. Barrington, Ms. Delta Kappa Epsilon. Pres. Logian Rhet. Prize. Philosophical o., 1871. Y. T. S. 1874-4. Ord. Rep. 1875, 1874 Pas New Orleans, N. Y., 1874-7; Troy, 1877-81. Europe, 1881-3. Prof. Eng. Lang. and Lit. Univ., Minn., since 1884. M. A., William. Ph. D., Leipzig. 1883. m. Clara N. Taylor, Gt. Barrington, Ms. May 30, 1874.

Wilhelmus Mynderse,   54 Wall St., New York City.

Lawyer. b. Seneca Falls, N. Y., Nov. 25, 1849. f. Mt. P. Mil. Acad., Sing Sing, N. Y. Sigma Phi. Math. Prize. 1869; German, 1870. Salutatory. Civil Eng., 1871-3. a. Law. Columbia, 1874; LL. B., 1875. p. Law, New York City since 1875. res Brooklyn since 1883. M. A. William. m. Mary E Swan, Geneva, N. Y., Mar. 10, 1883; d Apr 8, 1885); one daughter.

Robert Wilson Patterson,   Tribune Office, Chicago, Ill.

Editor. b. Chicago, Ill., Nov. 30, 1850. f. Lake Forest. Sigma Phi. Pres Technian. Philosophical o., 1871. Editor Interior, 1871-3; Tribune, since 1873, now Managing Editor. m. Elinor Medill, Chicago, Jan. 17, 1878; two c.

Claude Lasell Smith.

Lawyer. b Rhinebeck, N. Y., Feb. 8, 1851. f. Rugby Acad., Phila. Technian. Philosophical o., 1871 Law, Philadelphia till 1879, San Francisco, Cal., 1879-83. d. there Oct. 2, 1883.

John Lawson Stoddard, 230 Westchester Park, Boston, Mass.

Teacher and Lecturer. b. Brooklyn, Ms., Apr. 24, 1850. Delta Phi. First Language Prizes; Rhet Prize 1869. Valedictory. Y. T. S., 1872-4. Tea. Boston Lat Sch., 1874-7. Europe, 1877. Tea Boston, 1878-81, Lecturer, Europe each Summer. pub. "Red Letter Days Abroad," 1884. m. Mary H. Brown. Bangor, Me., Dec. 14, 1877; one son.

Henry Tallock,   98 Locust Hill Ave., Yonkers, N. Y.

Teacher. b. Dublin, Ireland, May 27, 1849. f. with Prof. Griffin, Williamstown. Disgus tot Adel. Union. Pres. Logian. Pres. II. S. Gleston, Ms., 1871-3. Prin. and Proprietor, Park Inst., Rye. N. Y., 1872-4. Gen Epis Thrid. Sem., 1844-5. Teacher and Student, New York since 1883. M. A. William. Vestryman Epis. Ch.. Rye m Margaret Tallock. Stamford, Ct., Aug. 15, 1874; five c., three living.

1872.

Francis Collins Eaton,   591 North High St., Columbus, Ohio.

Manufacturer. b. Montkville, N. Y., June 28, 1851. f. Brooklyn. Sigma Phi Moonlight; 1870. Library Oration. Pres. Logian. Oration, 1872. Merchant, Indianapolis, Ind., 1872-82. Manf., Columbus, O., since 1882. Deacon First Cong. Ch. Trus. Univ. Club. m. Alice Wright, Indianapolis. June 11, 1872; two daughters.

Frederick William Fiske,   514 Ashland Ave., St. Paul, Minn.

Teacher. b. Southbridge, Ms., Sep. 12, 1848. Six Prizes and Prize for Prizes. Pres. Technian. Valedictory. Teacher G L., Ms. Williamstown, 1872-83; Southbridge, 1884-5; 1886-6; St. Paul, Minn., 1886 L and since 1887. M. A. William. m. Belle T. Hartwell, Southbridge, Ms., Dec. 25, 1874; two c.

Charles Cuthbert Hall,   126 Henry St., Brooklyn, N. Y.

Clergyman. b. New York City, Sep. 3, 1851. f. Newburgh, N. Y. Delta Psi. Rosorary a., 1872. U. T. S., 1872-3; Presb. College, London, and Free Ch. College, Edinburgh, 1873-4; Ord., Dec. 4, 1873. Pas. Newburgh, N. Y., 1873-7; First Presb. Ch., Brooklyn, since 1877. pub. "Evangelical Hymnal," compiled 1880; Occasional Sermons, etc. Trustee W. C., since 1884. Trustee Presb. Ed. Ch. Erection. Director U. T. S. m. Jennie Harwart Boyd, Newburgh, N. Y., Aug. 8, 1877; one c.

Frederic Beach Jennings,   2 Nassau St., New York City.

Lawyer. b. Bennington Centre, Vt, Aug. 4, 1853. Delta Kappa Epsilon. Oration, 1872. a. Law, Harvard, and Univ., City N. Y. Opening Address and First Prize Law School. LL. B., Harvard, 1874; LL. B. Univ. City N. Y., 1875. p. Law, New York City, res. 87 East 55th street, since 1879. M. A., William. Vice-Pres. and Director B. and B. R. R. Co. Vice-Pres. and Director Manhattan Watch Co., etc. m. Laura Hall Park, Bennington, Vt., July 31, 1880; two c.

George William Morey.

Student. b. Williamstown, Ma., Jan. 17, 1852. f. G. I., Bo. Wa. Technian. Oration, 1872
Europe, 1873-4. d. Na. Wa. Sep. 1, 1872.

George Dole Rumsey, 10 Pacific Ave., Chicago, Ill.

Merchant. b. Chicago, May 20, 1849. Kappa Alpha. Technian. Moonlight, 1871. Oration,
1871. Commission Merchant. m. Alice C. Garfield, Chicago, June 18, 1878; one daughter.

John Langdon Tupper, 136 West 29th St., New York City.

Lawyer and Teacher. Entered College from North Granville, N. Y. Delta Kappa Epsilon.
Logian. Salutatory. Law and Teaching, New York.

William H. K. Tuttle, 53 Devonshire St., Boston, Mass.

Lawyer. b Littleton, Ma., Aug. Aug 17, 1845. f. with Prof. Griffin, Wa. Alpha Delta Phi
Math. Prize, 1869; Rhet. Prize, 1870. Class Day Oration. Philosophical o., 1872. a. Law, Harvard; LL. B. 1877. p. Law, Boston. res Arlington, Mass.; 1874-7; Boston, 1877-9; Arlington
since 1869; M. A., Williams.

Luther Dana Woodbridge, Williamstown, Mass.

Teacher and Physician. b. Perth Amboy. N. J., Dec. 27, 1850. f. Elizabeth, N. J. Logian
President Class Day. Philosophical o., 1872. Tutor Robert Coll. 1873-3. Instructor Phys
Coll. W. C., 1873-4. M D., Columbia, 1877. Europe, 1879-80. New York City, 1881 I. Prof.
Anat and Phys , W. C., since 1881. M. A., Williams. pub "Syllabus of a Course of Lectures
on Anatomy and Physiology." Vice-Pres. Phi Beta Kappa, since 1885. m. Abbie M. Mather,
Williamstown, July 20, 1879; three c.

1873.

Edward Asahel Birge, State Univ., Madison, Wis.

Teacher. b. Troy, N. Y . Sep. 7, 1851. f. H. S., Troy. Prize, German, 1872. Pres. Logian.
Salutatory. Mason Comp Zool., Harvard, 1873-5. Inst. Nat His., Wis Univ., 1875-9, Phys
Institute, Leipzig, 1880-1. Prof. Zoology, Wis Univ., since 1879. M. A., Williams 1876; Ph
D., Harvard, 1878. Sec. Wis. Acad. Sci. Arts and Let., 1881-7. pub. "Revision of Cladocera
Zoology," 1878, and other Scientific papers. m. Anna W. Grant, Troy, N. Y., July 15, 1880;
two c.

Robert Meech Chamberlain, 56 Moffat Block, Detroit, Mich.

Lawyer. b. LeRoy, N. Y., Mar. 16, 1852. f. LeRoy. Alpha Delta Phi. Logian. Prize,
Greek, Latin and German. Undergraduate Address Inaug. Pres. Chautauqua. Philosophical
o., 1872 Law, Admitted, Nov., 1875. Williamsport, Pa., 1876-6; Chicago, 1876; Ridgway, Pa.,
1876-7; Detroit, Mich., since 1877. Vestryman Epis. Ch. m. Florence A. Lee, Detroit, June 7,
1881; two c.

Charles May, 32 Nassau St., New York City.

Lawyer. b. Lev. Mass., Dec. 11, 1851. f. H. S., Lev. Alpha Delta Phi. Prize, Rhet and
French. Philosophical o., 1872. Tea. G. I., So. Williamstown, 1873-5. LL. B. Columbia, 1874.
New York City, since 1874.

Franklin Marcellus Olds, 721 Broad St., Newark, N. J.

Lawyer. b Port Byron, N. Y., Aug. 30, 1851. f. H. S., Auburn, N. Y. Prize, Latin, Greek,
and Math. Pres. Technian Valedictory res. Newark, since 1878. M A Williams. LL. B.,
Columbia, 1877. mem. His. Soc., N. J. m. Carrie A. Walker, Newark, Dec. 25, 1878.

John Myers Olin, Madison, Wis.

Lawyer and Teacher. b. Belleville, O., July 30, 1851. f. Oberlin Pres. Logian Moonlight,
1872. Prize, His and Pol. Econ., 1871. Philosophical o., 1872. Mansfield, O., 1873-4. Bastion
sch. Oratory, 1874-6. Prof. Oratory and Rhet Univ., Wis. M. A., Williams, 1877. LL. B.
Univ., Wis., 1878. Supt S. S Cong. Church. Prohibition Candidate for Congress, 1884, for
Governor, 1886. Prof of Law, Univ., Wis. m. Helen M. Remington, Baraboo, Wis., June 14,
1881.

William Francis Place,   College, Milton, Wis.

Teacher and Clergyman. b. Alfred, N. Y., May 6, 1848. f. Alfred Univ. Technian. Editor Vidette. Milk. 1. N. H. Oration. 1878 Tut. Latin, Alfred Univ., 1876-7. M. A. Williams B. D., Alfred Univ., 1877. Prin. Acad. Walworth, Wis., 1877-9. Prof. Lat. Phys. Sci. and Chem., Milton College, since 1879. Cor. Sec. S. D. B. Gen. Conference, 1884. m. Alice A. Dunham, Shiloh, N. J., Aug. 28, 1877; five c.

Truman Wilcox Saunders.

Lawyer and Teacher. b. Berlin, N. Y., Jan. 22, 1847. Technian. Oration, 1873. Prof. Greek and Ger., Milton Coll., 1873-8. Law, Admitted 1879. Milwaukee, Wis., 1879-82. m. Lucy C. Titsworth, Plainfield, N. J., July 6, 1878; one c. d. Feb. 19, 1884.

Henry Truax Scholl,   Springfield, Otsego Co., N. Y.

Clergyman. b. Rhinebeck, N. Y., May 31, 1851. f. Hartwick Seminary, N. Y. Prize, Latin, Greek, Math., His. and Nat His. Moonlight. R. B. Nine, Rowenor, College Regatta, 1872. College Choir. Philosophical o., 1878. U. T. S., 1874-7. Ord. Feb. 19, 1878. Pas. Chautauquay, N. Y., 1877-9; Milford, 1879-81; Lawrenceville, Pa., 1881-5; Springfield, N. Y., since 1885. m. Lillian F. McKee, West Milton, N. Y., Dec. 25, 1878; five c.

Peter Miles Snyder,   Middletown, Conn.

Clergyman. b. Watertown, N. Y., Nov. 28, 1853. f. H. B. Watertown. Technian. Prizes, Rhet., Math., German and His. Philosophical o., 1873. Edinburgh, 1873-6; U. T. S., 1876-8. Ord. Presb. May 11, 1880. Pas. Carthage, N. Y., 1879-83; South Cong. Ch., Middletown, Ct., since 1883. m. Grace E. Bliss, New Haven, Ct., Sep. 30, 1880; two c.

Morton Smith Wardner,   Chicago, Ill.

Clergyman. Physician. Pharmacist. b. Shanghai, China, Jan. 14, 1850. f. Alfred Univ., N. Y. I. N. H. Moonlight. Oration. 1873. s. Theol. and Assi. Lat., Alfred Univ., 1873-6. Europe, 1876-7. Pas. Little Genesee, N. Y., 1878-9. Villa Ridge, Ill., 1881-2. s. Med. Rush. Med. Coll., Chicago, 1884-4. Phys. and Surg., 1884-5. Pharmacist since 1885. A. M. Williams. B. D., Alfred Univ. Med. S. D. D. Wred. Assoc., 1884-5. pub. "Communion," 1881, m. Sarah L. Summerbell, Berlin, N. Y., July 16, 1878; four c.

1874.

John Benjamin Adams,   19 Bryant Ave., Chicago, Ill.

Merchant. b. Chicago, May 4, 1852. f. H S., Chicago. Technian. Oration, 1874. Journalist and Grain Merchant. m. Olive E. White, Chicago, Sep. 30, 1883; one daughter.

Lilian Herbert Andrews,   132 Nassau St., New York City.

Teacher. Lawyer. Author. b. Saratoga, N. Y., Feb. 23, 1853. Technian. Eight First Prizes and Prize for Prizes. Valedictory. Private Tutor, 1874-6. Europe, 1876-8. Prof. Latin, W. U., 1878. Law, New York, since 1879. M. A., Williams. pub "Only a Farmer's Daughter," a Novel, 1882.

Harlan Hoge Ballard,   50 South St., Pittsfield, Mass.

Teacher and Editor. b. Athens, O., May 26, 1853. f. Williamstown and Detroit. Logician. 1st Greek and 1st Latin. Olivet, Mich. 1st Junior Moonlight. Williams. Philosophical o., 1874. Prin. Acad., Lenox, Mass., 1874-85. res. Pittsfield. since 1885. Founder and President Agassiz Association. pub. "Words and How to Put Them Together," 1879; "Harpers' First and Second Readers;" "American Plant Book," 1879; "1,000 Blunders in English," 1884; "Hand Book of the Agassiz Association," 1884. Editor of "The Swiss Cross." M. A., Williams. Secretary Phi Beta Kappa Society.

David Campbell,   107 Dearborn St., Chicago, Ill.

Lawyer. b. Pittsfield, Mass., July 31, 1854. Alpha Delta Phi. Salutatory. Chicago, since 1874.

Rudolph C. F. Dunhaupt,   4022 Peck St., St. Louis, Mo.

Teacher. b. Germany, Nov. 25, 1849. f. H. S., St. Louis. Technian. Prize in History. Philosophical o., 1874. Teacher in St. Louis, since 1874. M. A., Williams. Deacon and S. S. Supd. Park Cong. Ch. m. Nellie Schwer, St. Louis, Mo., Dec. 26, 1877; three c.

Walter Doumaux Edmonds, Temple Court, New York City,

Lawyer. b Utica, N. Y., Jan. 29, 1851. f. Free Acad., Utica. Sigma Phi. Legian. Class Day Orator. Prizes, Math. and History. Philosophical o., 1874. s. Law, Columbia; LL. B., 1876. p. Law, New York City, since 1876. M. A., Williams. Civil Service Examiner, State N. Y.

Charles Sumner Holt, 97 Clark St., Chicago, Ill.

Lawyer. b Chicago, Oct. 21, 1854. f. Acad., Lake Forest. Kappa Alpha. Prizes, Rhet., German and Nat. His. Adel Un. Ex., 1874. Editor Vidette. Oration, 1874. Traveling, 1874-5. s. Law, Harvard, 1877-8; Admitted, Oct., 1878. p. Law, Chicago, since 1878. Elder Presb. Ch., Lake Forest.

Charles Henry Watson.

Lawyer. b. Brooklyn, N. Y., Aug. 19, 1851. f. O. L., Bo. Williamstown. Prizes, Greek, Ger., Latin, His. and Rhet. Philosophical o., 1874. Law, Maysville, Cal. d. there, Dec. 11, 1880.

Julius Edward Werner, Haddonfield, N. J.

Clergyman. b. Prussia, Europe, July 17, 1848. French Prize. Philosophical o., 1874. Anb. T. S., 1874-7; Ord., 1877. Pas. Oaks Corners, N. Y., 1877-81; Haddonfield, N. J., since 1881. m. Mary Robinson, Canandaigua, N. Y., Oct. 4, 1880; two c.

1875.

Charles Bulkley Bullard, Parsippany, N. J.

Clergyman. b. Lee, Mass., Oct. 13, 1853. f. H. S., Lee. Chi Psi. Technian. His Prizes and Prize for Prizes. Valedictory. Teacher, So. Wm., 1873-4; Parkersburgh, Pa., 1876-7; Poughkeepsie, N. Y., 1878-9. U. T. S., 1878-80. Ord Presb., Jan. 17, 1882. Pas. Parsippany, N. J., since 1882. m. Minnie W. Atkins, Poughkeepsie, N. Y., Dec. 28, 1882; two c.

Henry Selden Hitchcock.

Teacher. Entered College from Lincoln, Neb. Philosophical o., 1875. Teacher, Philadelphia. d. Chicago, Sept., 1887.

Jeremiah Fuller Locke, Fall River, Mass.

Business. b. Williamstown, Ma., Dec. 10, 1849. f. O. L., So. Wm. Technian. Prizes, Greek. German and Nat. His. Nahatory. M. A., Williams. Business at Fall River. m. and two c.

Adair Pleasants, Buford Block, Rock Island, Ill.

Lawyer. b. Rock Island, Apr. 8, 1854. f. H. S., Rock Island. Kappa Alpha. Legian. Prizes German and Rhet. Ivy Orator, 1875. Philosophical o., 1875. Lawyer, Rock Island, Ill. Admitted, July, 1876.

Willard Scott, 805 South 27th St., Omaha, Neb.

Clergyman. b. Amsterdam, N. Y., June 23, 1850. f. Acad., Amsterdam, and private Tutor. Prizes, History. Polit. Econ. and Nal. His. Moonlight, 1874. Pres. Logian. Philosophical o., 1874. U. T. S., 1875-8; Ord. Presb., Oct. 24, 1879. Pas. Bethany Cong., New York, 1878-9; West Farms, Presb., New York, 1879-85; St. Mary's Ave. Cong., Omaha, Neb., since 1885. Mod. Gen. Assoc., Neb., 1886-8; Pres. Neb. H. M. Soc., since 1886. Director Neb. B. S. Assembly Assoc., since 1884; Chairman Neb. Ed. Com., since 1887; Trustee Doane College, since 1887. m. Mary Bell Stewart, Amsterdam, N. Y., Oct. 4, 1878.

Joseph Tomlinson, Roadstown, Cumberland Co., N. J.

Physician. b. Roadstown, N. J., Aug. 15, 1854. f. Shiloh. Technian. Philosophical o., 1875. M. D., Columbia, 1878. Plainfield, 1880-1; New York City, 1881-7; Roadstown, N. J., since 1887. m. Caroline M. Lawrence, Troy, N. Y., June 19, 1881; two c.

1876.

George Frederic Chipperfield, Battle Creek, Mich.

Clergyman. b. Wrexford, Eng., Dec. 12, 1854. f. privately. Technian. Prizes, French, His. and Ex. Speaking. Library Orator, 1876. Philosophical o., 1876. C. T. S., 1881. Clifton, Ill., three years; Sterling, three years. Pas. Presb. Battle Creek, Mich., since 1884. m. Minnie E. Smith, Paterson, N. J., May 2, 1878. m. Marie J. Delaiour, Chicago, Oct. 11, 1881; two c.

Emanuel Cohen, Minneapolis, Minn.

Lawyer. b. Carbondale, Pa., May 11, 1858. Leg, Prize, Rhet. and Ex. Speaking. Salutatory. Law, Philadelphia, 1878-80; Scranton, 1881-2; Philadelphia, 1882-6; Minneapolis, since 1886. m. Nora Morris, Philadelphia, Dec. 15, 1880.

Francis Henshaw Dewey, Jr., 405 Main St., Worcester, Mass.

Lawyer. b. Worcester, Mass., (son of Judge Dewey. Class '50) Mar. 20, 1856. f. M. Mark's School, Southboro, Mass. Kappa Alpha. Moonlight, 1873. Philosophical o., 1878. LL. B., Harvard Law School, 1878. M A., Williams Law, Worcester, Mass. Chairman Parish Com mittee. m. Lizzie D. Bliss, Worcester, Mass., Dec. 15, 1878; two c.

Edgar Rollin Downs, South Weymouth, Norfolk Co., Mass.

Teacher. b. Lowell, Mass., July 26, 1855. f. H. S., Fitchburg. Technolan. L N. H. Prize, Greek and Math. Philosophical o., 1878. Prin. Acad., Deerfield, Ma., 1876-7; Prin. H. S., Cheshire, 1877-8; Bingham, 1879-80; South Weymouth, since 1880. Prin. South High School. M. A., Williams. m. Isabella Parker Howland, Boston, Mass., Oct. 8, 1881.

James Francis Eaton, College, Ripon, Wis.

Clergyman and Teacher. b. Hamden, N. Y., Oct. 16, 1850. f. D. L. L, Franklin. Technolan. L. N. H. Prize, Math. and Nat. His. Philosophical o., 1878. Y. T. S., 1878-9; Oberlin T. S., 1879-9. Ord. Cong., 1879. Tut. Oberlin, 1878-9. Pas. Madrid and Lisbon, N. Y., 1879-80; Bridge port, Vt., 1881-4; Linden, Mich., 1884-4. Prin. Prep Dept. and Prof. Ancient Lang., Ripon College, since 1884. m. Agora Kent, Brooklyn, N. Y., Oct. 16, 1879; three c.

Charles White Huntington, 85 George St., Providence, R. I.

Clergyman. b. Stockbridge, Mass., May 22, 1854. f. W. S., Easthampton. Kappa Alpha. Prize, French, Math., History and Nat. His. Pres. Logian. Editor Athenaeum. Valedictory. Harvard Law Sch., 1877. A. T. S., 1878-81. Ord. Cong., Sep. 6, 1881. Pas. Ellsworth, Me., 1881-4; Central Cong. Ch., Providence, R. L, since 1884. m. Della Frances Bliss, Boston, Nov. 16, 1881.

William Alexander Platt, Mail and Express, New York City.

Journalist and Teacher. b. Zanesville, O., Jan. 23, 1855. f. Math, N. Y., and Trenton, N. J. Delta Psi. 1st Prize, German. Moonlight. Philosophical o., 1878. Tea. Newkirby, Pa., 1877-80; Tidioute, 1880-1; Babylon, N. Y., 1881-2. Ed. Staff Mail and Express, since 1882. mem. Presb. Church. M. A., Williams. m. Julia Hankinson, Hoboken, Dec. 24, 1879; two sons

Clarence Burgess Roote, Greenwich, Fairfield Co., Conn.

Teacher and Lawyer. b. Francestown, N. H., Oct 5, 1858. f. Acad., Francestown. Chi Psi. Logian. 8½ Prizes and Prize for Prizes. Class Day Oration. Philosophical o., 1878. Assoc. Prin. L. G. Sch., Ft. Edward, N. Y., 1877-9; Prin. H. S., Barre, Mass., 1879-80; Assoc. Prin. Acad., Greenwich, Ct., 1880-4. a Law, Barre, and Boston Univ. Law School, 1884-1. p. Law, Barre and Warr, 1884-5. Assoc. Prin. Acad., Greenwich, since 1885. M. A., Williams. m. Idella M. Bothwell, Barre, Mass., Oct. 3, 1882.

1877.

William Williston Carter, Stockbridge, Mass.

Teacher. b. Stockbridge, Sep 18, 1854. f. H. S., Stockbridge. Logian. First Eng. Ora tion, 1877. White Plains, N. Y., 1878-81; Lawrenceville, N. J., 1881-2; Rye, N. Y., 1883. Eu rope, 1884-5. m. Nellie Russell Curtis, Lenox, Mass., Oct. 1, 1885; one c.

Gaylord Parsons Clark, 126 South Salina St., Syracuse, N. Y.

Physician. b. Syracuse, N. Y., Nov. 12, 1856. f. Syracuse Classical School. Kappa Alpha. Logian. 1st Prize German. Philosophical o., 1877. a Med. Syracuse Univ., 1877-80. M. D. and Diploma Prize, Syr. Univ., 1880. p. Med. Syracuse, since 1880. Inst Anat., Med. College, Syr. Univ., 1880-1. Prof. Anatomy, same, since 1881. U. S. Pension Ex. Surgeon. M. A., Wil liams. Elder 1st Presb. Ch., Syracuse. m. Jennie H. Baydam, Baldwinsville, N. Y., June 16, 1881.

Herbert Wendell Gleason, Minneapolis, Minn.

Clergyman and Law Stenographer. b. Malden, Mass., June 5, 1855. f. H. S., Malden. Prize, German and Nat His. Pres. Logian. Oration, 1877. U. T. S., 1877-80; A. T. S., 1879-81. Ord. Cong., 1882. Pas. Pillsbury Rapids, Minn., 1882-5; Como Ave. Cong. Ch., Minneapolis, since 1885. m. Lulie Wadsworth Rounds, Malden, Mass., Oct. 16, 1882.

Rufus Henry Halsey,   **Oshkosh, Winnebago Co., Wis.**

Teacher. b. Washingtonville, N. Y., Mar. 9, 1856. f. Adelphai Acad., Brooklyn. Cl'd Pol. Technian. Philosophical o., 1877. Tea. Newtonville, N. Y., 1877-8; Brooklyn, 1878-81; O a-kosh, Wis., since 1881. s. Long Island College Hospital, Brooklyn. m. Emma Lavinia Cole, Claverack, N. Y., Jan. 16, 1881; four c.

Emerson Wadsworth Judd,   **Bradstreet's Journal, Boston.**

Journalist. b. Westhampton, Mass., Sep. 29, 1856. f. W. R., Easthampton. Technian. Seven Prizes and Prize for Prizes. Valedictory. Republican, Springfield, Ms., 1877-80; Globe, Boston, 1881; Globe Democrat, St. Louis, Mo., 1881-4; N. E. Correspondent Bradstreet's Journal, Boston, since 1884. Secretary Free Trade League, Mo., 1883-4. pub. "Economic Fact Book," (con..) 1886. Deacon Catholic Apostolic Church. m. Mary E. Wheeler, Williamstown, Aug. 28, 1879; two c.

Rollo Ogden,   **Ramapo, Rockland Co., N. Y.**

Clergyman and Journalist. b. Sand Lake, N. Y., Jan 19, 1856. f. High School. Technian. Prizes Latin, French and Essays. Philosophical o., 1877. A. T. S., 1877 9; U. T. S., 1879-80. Ord. May 11, 1881. Pas. Cleveland, O., 1881-1, 1883-5; P. M. in City of Mexico, 1881-3. Literary work in New York City since 1886. m. Susan M. Mitchell, Cleveland, O., Nov. 30, 1881; two c., one living.

Stephen Stedman,   **Herald Office, Syracuse, N. Y.**

Journalist. b. Pomfret, Vt., Apr. 17, 1856. f. Newark, N. J., and privately. Technian. Prizes Greek Latin, Math. and Nat. His. Philosophical o., 1877. Mercury, Newport, R. I., 1877-8; Herald, Syracuse, N. Y., since 1881. m. Frances L. Johnson, Fredonia, S. Y., May 2, 1880.

Albert Harris Tolman,   **College, Ripon, Wis.**

Teacher. b. Lanesboro, Mass., June 17, 1856. f. H. S., Pittsfield. Seven Prizes. Pres. Logian. Salutatory. Tea. Hampton, Va., 1877-8; Troy, N. Y., 1878-9; Prin H. S. Chicopee Falls, Mass., 1879-82. Student J. H. Univ., Baltimore, Md., 1882-4; Fellow, same, 1884. Prof. Rhet. and Eng. Lit., Ripon College, since 1884.

1878.

Arthur Graves Canfield,   **State Univ., Lawrence, Kan.**

Teacher. b. Sunderland, Vt., Mar. 27, 1859. f. B. and B S., Manchester. Logian. First Prize Jun. Rhet. Oration. 1878. s. Berlin, Goltingen and Paris, 1879-82. Inst. Mod. Lang., Univ., Kan., 1883-7; Prof. French, same, since 1887. M. A. Williams.

Walter Geer, Terra Cotta Co., 38 Park Row, New York City.

Lawyer. b. Williamstown, Mass., Aug. 19, 1857. f. G. I. So. Wn. Delta Psi. Logian. 1st Prize French. Philosophical o., 1878 s. Boston Univ. Oratory, 1878. Nat. Univ. Law Sch., Washington; LL. M., 1881. Asst. Manager Wood M. and R Co., Chicago, 1882-6. Pres. N. Y. Arch. Terra Cotta Co., since 1886. M. A. Williams. m. Mary Potter, N. Y. City, Sep. 25, 1884; one daughter.

Charles Gross,   **(Europe,) 28 Fourth St., Troy, N. Y.**

Author. b. Troy, N Y., Feb. 10, 1857. f. H. S. Troy. Eight Prizes and Prize for Prizes. Pres. Logian. Valedictory. Tea Troy, N. Y., 1878-9. s. Leipsic, Berlin, Goltingen and Paris, 1879-83. London, since 1884. M. A. and Ph. D., Goltingen, 1883. pub. "Gilda Mercatoria," 1883; "The Affiliation of Mediæval Boroughs," 1885; "The Exchequer of the Jews of England in the Middle Ages," 1887; "The Gild Merchant," 1887.

Rufus Buel McClenon,   **Beloit, Wis.**

Teacher. b. Franklin, N. Y., Nov. 18, 1852. f. Walton. Five Technian. Honorary o., 1878. Tea Mil. Acad., North Granville, N. Y., 1878-81; Lake Geneva, Wis., Sem., 1881-3; Prin H. S. Oconto, Wis., 1884-7; Inst. Nat. Sci. and English, College Acad., Beloit, Wis., since 1887. M. A. Williams. m. Adeline White, Walton, N. Y., July 27, 1881; two c.

Carlton Putnam Mills,   **Newton Highlands, Mass.**

Clergyman. b. South Williamstown, Mass., Apr. 29, 1857. f. G. I. So. Wn. Alpha Delta Phi. Technian. Bonn schol. 1878. Oras. Prize intercoll., 1878. Class Day Orator, 1878. Oration. 1878. Epis. Theol. Sch., Cambridge, three years. So. Wn, 1879-81; Waltham, 1883-6; Newton Highlands since 1886. m. Helen LeRoy Briggs, East Douglas, Mass., Sep. 30, 1885; one c.

Howe Paige,   **12 Third St., Minneapolis, Minn.**

Lawyer. b. St. Louis, Mo., Sep. M. 1857. (son of Rev. Trustees. f. Jacksonville, Ill. Pres. Technics. Graves Prize. Philosophical o., 1878. s. Law, St. Louis Law School. p Law. Minneapolis, since 1880.

Charles Malcolm Platt,   **Asheville, Buncombe Co., N. C.**

Lawyer. b. Sweden. N. Y., Feb. 21, 1853. f. Acad., Dryden. Technics. Pres. Adel. Union. Moonlight. 1877. Library Orator. 1878. Philosophical o., 1878. Law, Syracuse, N. Y., 1878-82. Stock Raising, Asheville, N. C., since 1888.

Waldo Selden Pratt,   **82 Niles St., Hartford, Conn.**

Teacher. b. Philadelphia, Pa., Nov. 30, 1857. (son of Rev. Dr. Pratt, '34.) f. R. R., North Adams, and P. A., Andover, Mass. Chl Phl. Greek Prize, 1878. Gen. Prize, Moonlight, 1877. Graves Essay and Prize for Delivery, 1878. Philosophical o., 1878. s. J. H. Univ., Baltimore, 1878-80; Fellow of the same. N. Y. City Metro. Mus. of Art, 1880-2. Assoc. Prof. Music and Hymnology, R. T. S., since 1882. M. A., Williams. pub. "Essays on Egyptian Columnar Architecture," 1883; "St. Nicholas Songs," (Ed.) 1895; "Songs of Worship for the Sunday School," (Ed.) 1887. m. Mary E. Seayly. New York City, July 5, 1887.

William Edgar Roe,   **King's Ferry, Cayuga Co., N. Y.**

Clergyman. b. Cornwell. N. Y., Nov. 8, 1857. f. Newburgh Chl Phl. Eight Prizes and Prize for Prizes. Pres. Logian. Salutatory. U. T. S., 1882-5. Ord. Presb., Feb. 10, 1887. Brooklyn, N. Y., 1878-83; Pottstown, Pa., 1883-5; New York City, 1884-5; Jacksonville, Fla., 1886-7; King's Ferry. since 1887.

Halsey Bidwell Stevenson,   **Geneva, N. Y.**

Clergyman. b. Montezuma, N. Y., Feb. 9, 1854. f. H. S., Auburn. Chl Phl. Prizes, Math., Rhet. and Essay. Pres. Class Day. Philosophical o., 1878. Aub T. S., 1878-9; U. T. S., 1879-80; Aub. T. S., 1880-1. Ord. Presb., Nov. 7, 1881. Fas. Pottstown, Pa., 1881-7; Geneva, N. Y., since 1887. m. Nellie M. Roe, Cornwall-on-Hudson, N. Y., Oct. 6, 1881; two c.

1879.

George Asa Bruce,   **South Shaftsbury, Bennington Co., Vt.**

Merchant. b. Danby, Vt., June 17, 1857. f. B. and B., Manchester. Logian. Oration, 1879. res Williamsford, 1879-80; Sioux City, Ia., 1880-3; Waterbury, Ct., 1883-7; So Shaftsbury, Vt., since 1887. m. Ro. Shaftsbury. May 24, 1880.

Charles Albert Fiske,   **High School, St. Paul, Minn.**

Teacher. Entered College from Southbridge, Mass. Prizes, German, Greek and Latin. Philosophical o., 1879. Teacher, St. Paul, Minn.

Herbert Hervey Fletcher,   **Associated Press, Boston, Mass.**

Journalist. b. Granby, Mass., Aug. 10, 1855. Technics. Seven Prizes and Prize for Prizes. Philosophical o., 1879. Springfield, Mass., 1879-83; Boston, since 1884. m. Alice N. Kellogg. Granby, Mass., Dec. 25, 1881; one c.

Horace Greenwood Hill,   **3416 Baring St., Philadelphia, Pa.**

Physician. h Philadelphia, Nov. 6, 1858. f. Acad., W Phila. Chl Phl. Logian. Prizes, German and History Valedictory. s. Med. Jefferson Med. College, Phila., 1879-83. M. D., same, 1883. Resident Phys. Presb. Hospital, 1883-4. Phys. Phila. Home for Incurables. Med. Director, Fidelity Mut. Life Assoc M A., Williams. m. M. Louise Bennett, Philadelphia, Apr. 30, 1885; one c.

Robert Ellis Jones,   **St. Luke's Rectory, Kalamazoo, Mich.**

Clergyman. b. Liverpool, Eng., Mar. 14, 1856. f. Alexandria, Va. Chl Phl Prizes, Essays and Delivery. Pres. Logian. Oration, 1879. Asst. Topographer U. S. Geological Survey. s. Theol. three years. Epis. Church. Rector St. Luke's P. E. Ch., Kalamazoo, Mich.

Charles Albert Perkins,   **Bryn Mawr, Montgomery Co., Pa.**

Teacher. b Ware, Mass., Oct. 31, 1858. f. H. S., Ware. Technics. Prizes, French and History. Oration, 1879. Prof. Math. Lawrence Univ., Appleton, Wis., 1880-1. s J. H. Univ., Baltimore, Md., 1881-3; Fellow, same, 1883, 1885; Ph D, same, 1884-7; Asst. Physics, same, 1884-7. Associate Prof. Physics, Bryn Mawr College, since 1887 m Angie V. Warren, Danielsonville, Ct., Sep. 19, 1885; one c.

Henry Poor Perkins, Tientsin, North China.

Missionary, A. B. C. F. M. b. Ware, Mass., Dec. 24, 1856. f. H. R. Ware. Techmian. Four Prizes, Naturatory. H. T. S., 1879-81; U. T. S. and Med. Dept. Univ. N. Y. City, 1881-3. China since 1883. m. L. Estella Abere, M. D., Tientain, Oct. 29, 1883.

Milton Goslee Pond.

Clergyman. b. Jewett, N. Y., Nov. 18, 1855. f. L. A. Grates. Prize Logian. Philosophical o., 1879. Tra. Cheshire, 1879-80. a. Dudley Obs., Albany, 1880-1. U. T. S., 1881-4. Ord. Cong. Oct. 8, 1884. Pastor Royalston, Mass., 1884-5. m. Mary M. Jewett, Pepperell, Mass., Sep 4 1884; one daughter. d. Sep. 16, 1885.

1880.

John Grey Campbell, Wellington, Sumner Co., Kan.

Journalist. b. Mendon, Ill., Apr 7, 1860. f. H. S. Cleveland O. Chi Psi. Graves Prize, 1880. Prize Logian. Oration, 1880. Litchfield, Ill., 1881-3. Editor and Publisher Monitor, Wellington, Kas., since 1885.

Frederick Hale Cooke, 1301 Conn. Ave., Washington, D. C.

Lawyer. b. Winnunchet, R. I., Mar. 17, 1858. f. R. S. Horton, Mass. Six Prizes and Prize for Prize. Prize Logian. Valedictory. a. J. H. Univ., Baltimore, Md., 1881. Tra. Saratoga, Yonkers and Cornwall-on-Hudson, N. Y., 1881-2. Law, Brooklyn, 1886-7; Admitted 1884. Editor "Abbott's Cases Criticised." 1887. Washington, D. C., since 1887.

Edward Danforth Hale, N. E. Conserv Music, Boston, Mass.

Teacher. b. Aquebogue, L. I., N. Y., Feb 1, 1858. f. Acad. Southold. Prizes. French, Greek, Latin, and Nat. His. Logian. Salutatory. Prof. Harmony and Comp. N. E. Conserv. Music. Boston. M. A. Williams.

Lowell Mason Hallock.

Student. b. Hartford, L. I., N. Y., Nov. 8, 1858. Logian. Philosophical o., 1880. A. T. S., 1880. d. Ada, Kan., Feb 14, 1881.

Frank Gaylord Hubbard, Oswego, N. Y.

Student and Business. b. Oswego, N. Y., Jan. 24, 1859. f. Eng. and Clas. School, Oswego. Chi Psi Prizes. Math., Rhet., His. and German. Logian. Philosophical o., 1880. Business Oswego, 1880 f. J. H. Univ., Baltimore, Md., 1884-7; Ph. D., same, 1887.

Hermann Lewis Matz, 98 Park Row, New York City.

Business. b. Chicago, Ill., Feb. 2, 1859. f. H. S. Chicago. Alpha Delta Phi Techsian. Prize, French. Tra. two years; Business, Hoosick Falls, N. Y., five years. N. Y. Arch Terra Cotta Co., New York, since 1885. m. Elizabeth Dunsbury, Oct. 12, 1887.

Willis Waldo Mead, Marash, Turkey.

Missionary, A. B. C. F. M. b. Fayetteville, N. Y., Mar. 9, 1854. Techsian. Oration, 1880. U. T. S., 1881-4; Ord. Cong., 1884. Pas. Clarion and Sibley, Ia., 1884.

Alfred Tyler Perry, Ware, Hampshire Co., Mass.

Clergyman. b. Geneseo, Ill., Aug. 19, 1858. f. North Adams. Techsian. Prizes, Math., Rhet. and German. Philosophical o., 1880. H. T. S., 1883. Ord. Cong., Dec. 29, 1883. Asst. Pas. Memorial Ch., Springfield, Mass., 1883. Pas. East Church, Ware, since 1885. m. Anna Morris, Hartford, Ct., Apr. 19, 1887.

Raymond Hoyt Stearns, Charlton, Saratoga Co., N. Y.

Clergyman. b. Albany, N. Y., Nov. 6, 1859. f. H. S., Albany. Delta Kappa Epsilon. Prizes. History, German and Essays. Philosophical o., 1880. U. T. S., 1880-3. Ord. Presb., Sept. 23, 1884. Pas. Charlton, N. Y., since 1884. m. Emma A. Frensham, Albany, June 22, 1885

1881.

Austin Bradley Bassett, **Williamstown, Mass.**

Clergyman. b. Allegan, Mich., Jan. 23, 1858. f. H. R., Albany, N. Y., Alpha Beta Phi. 1st Prize Nat. Hist.; Graves' Essay Prize. Pres. Logian. Philosophical o., 1881. Tea. Saratoga, 1881-3; Prof. Math. and Physics. Agr. Coll., Amherst, Mass., 1883-4. H. T. N., 1884-6; Chicago T. S., 1886-7. Ord., Sep. 11, 1887. Europe, 1887. Pas. Cong. Ch., Williamstown, since 1887.

Elliot White Bumstead, **12 Berkeley St., Cambridge, Mass.**

Clergyman. b. New York City, Nov. 28, 1861. Sigma Phi. Prize, Latin, History and German. Salutatory. Gen. Theol. Sem. Epis. Ch., New York, 1883-6. Trenton, N. J., 1885-6; Cambridge, since 1887. M. A., Williams.

Willard Starr Cutting, **Deerfield, Franklin Co., Mass.**

Teacher. b. West Brattleboro, Vt., Oct. 14, 1858. f. Acad., West Brattleboro. Logian. Prize, German and Rhet. Philosophical o., 1881. Prin. Acad., Deerfield, Mass., 1881-6. x. Univ., Leipsig, Germany, since 1886.

Charles Mason Demond, **52 William St., New York City.**

Lawyer. b. Boston, Mass., Jan. 23, 1860. f. Roxbury Latin School. Alpha Delta Phi. Several Prizes and Prize for Prize. Pres. Logian. Valedictory. Tea. W. H., Easthampton, Ms., 1881-4. x. Law, Columbia. 1883-5; LL. B., 1885. p. Law, New York City.

Frederic Jennings Parsons, **Berlin, Germany.**

Teacher. b. Sicomedia, Turkey, Dec. 3, 1860. f. H. S., Newton, Mass. Kappa Alpha. Logian. Fire Prizes. Philosophical o., 1881. x. Astro., W. C., 1881-2; Instructor French and Math., W. C., 1882-1; Ph. D., Williams, 1884. Europe, 1884-6. Prof. Physics, N. W. Univ., Evanston, Ill., 1886-7. x. Electricity. "Imperial Polytechnikum." three miles from Berlin.

Bliss Perry, **(Europe,) Williamstown, Mass.**

Teacher. (son of Prof. Perry, W. C., 1852.) Entered College from Williamstown. Prizes, Essays, Delivery and Ex-Speaking. Pres. Logian. Oration, 1881. Instructor Oratory, W. C., 1881-4. Europe, 1886-7. Prof. Oratory, W. C., since 1887.

Frank Pierce, **152 Main St., Salt Lake City, Utah.**

Lawyer. b. Londonderry, Vt., Apr. 3, 1857. f. B. and B Sem., Manchester. Logian. Philosophical o., 1881. Manchester, Vt., 1881-2; Salt Lake City, since 1882. U. S. Commissioner for Utah. mem. 1st Presb. Church.

Walter Clark Roe, **The Hill School, Pottstown, Pa.**

Teacher. b. Cornwall-on-Hudson, N. Y., May, 18, 1860. f. Coll. Inst., Newburgh. Chi Psi. Techninan. Prizes, Greek and German. Class President. Philosophical o., 1881. Tea. Brooklyn. N. Y., 1881-4; Pottstown, Pa., since 1884. m. Mary Wickham Roe, Brooklyn, N. Y., Oct. 22, 1887.

Cleon Josiah Sawyer, **Signal Office, Washington, D. C.**

Lawyer, Librarian, Bibliographer. b. Salem, N. H., May 28, 1858. f. Acad., Derby, N. H., and H. S., Lawrence, Mass. Logian. Philosophical o., 1881. Librarian, 1881-3. Bibliographer, since 1884. LL. M., Columbian Univ., Law School, 1885. m. Jennie M. Roberts, Pownal, Vt., Apr. 18, 1881; three c.

Edward Carroll Wiley, **North Granville, N. Y.**

Teacher and Theol. Student. b. Dorset, Vt., June 11, 1859. f. N. Granville. Logian. 1st Prize French, Philosophical o., 1881. Tea. North Granville, N. Y., 1881-3; Argyle, 1883-4. res. N. Granville, since 1884. U. T. S., 1886-7; Aab. T. S., 1887.

1882.

Frank Alexander Erwin, **38 West 59th St., New York City.**

Teacher. b. West Point, N. Y., Jan. 9, 1859. f. S. P. S., Newburgh. Chi Psi. Techninan. 1st Prize German. Philosophical o., 1882. Head Master, Mil. Acad., Peekskill, N. Y., 1882-5. Tea. Eng. Lit. and Classics, Coll. Inst., New York, since 1885. A. M., Williams. m. Nellie R. Briggs, Peekskill, N. Y., June 24, 1886; one son.

Thomas Sarsfield Fagan, 17 First St., Troy, N. Y.

Lawyer and Teacher. b. Troy, N. Y., Jan. 18, 1862. f. H. R., Troy. Reeve Prizes and Prize for Prizes. Pres. Logian. Salutatory. Tre. H. R., Troy, 1882-6. Law. Troy, since 1886.

Franklin Fuller Gunn, - (Europe,) Andover, Mass.

Clergyman. b. Greenwich, N. Y., Aug. 19, 1858. f. I. C. Sch., Fort Edward. Delta Kappa Epsilon. Technian. Six Prizes. Valedictory. Tea. Peekskill, N. Y., 1882-3. A. T. S., 1883-6. Winkley Fellowship, A. T. S., 1886-8.

Edwards Platt Ingersoll, 41 Malden Lane, New York City.

Librarian. Entered College from Cleveland, O. Philosophical o., 1882. Literary Work, New York City.

Francis Lockwood Kendall, Leipsic, Germany.

Teacher. b. Lenox, Mass., Mar. 27, 1860. f. Germany and Armel., Lake Forest, Ill. Zeta Psi. Prizes, Greek, Latin and French. Technian. Philosophical o., 1882. Prof. German and French, Iowa Coll., Crete, Neb., 1882-7. Europe, 1884-5, 1887-9. Asst. Prof. Modern Languages, W. C., after 1888.

Rudolph Matz, 431 Oak St., Chicago, Ill.

Lawyer and Teacher. b. Chicago, Dec. 11, 1860. Alpha Delta Phi. Technian. Prizes, Math. and Essay. Oration, 1882. Tea. Chicago, 1882-4; Law, 1884-6. LL. B. Union College of Law, Chicago, 1886.

Nathaniel Fisher Wilcox, Northboro, Mass.

Teacher. b. East Bridgewater, Ma., Dec. 8, 1857. f. H. S., Westboro. Logian. Greek and German Prizes. Philosophical o., 1882. Bennington, Vt., 1882-5; Hopkinton, Mass., 1885-6; Hadley, 1886-7; Northboro, since 1887. m. Effie I. Coates, North Adams, Aug. 5, 1886.

1883.

Frederick Geller, 20 Nassau St., New York City.

Lawyer. b. Albany, N. Y., June 4, 1861. f. H. S., Albany. Zeta Psi. Logian. Eight Prizes and Prize for Prizes. Valedictory. a. Law, Columbia Coll. Law Sch.; LL. B., 1885; First Prize in Municipal Law, p. Law, New York, since 1885. res. Brooklyn.

Frederick Morris Herrick, Robert College, Constantinople.

Librarian. b. Constantinople, Dec. 17, 1862. f. H. t., Newton, Mass. Logian. Three Prizes. Philosophical o., 1883. Helper, Robert College.

Samuel Van Vranken Holmes, Richfield Springs, N. Y.

Clergyman. b. Brooklyn, N. Y., Mar. 25, 1862. f. Boy's Acad., Albany. Alpha Delta Phi. Logian. Prizes, Essay and Ex-Speaking. Class Orator, 1883. Oration, 1883. P. T. S. and Berlin Univ., Richfield Springs, N. Y., since 1887. m. Helen Stanton, Bridgeport Ct., June 11, 1887.

Henry Lefavour, Williamstown, Mass.

Teacher. b. Salem, Mass., Sep. 1, 1862. f. H. S., Salem. Five Prizes. Pres. Logian. Pres. First Class, 1883. Salutatory. Tea. W. H., Easthampton, Ms., 1883-4. Instructor, French and Math., W. C., since 1884. Ph. D., Williams, 1886.

Francis Vergnies Pike, 76 State St., Newburyport, Mass.

Lawyer. b. Newburyport, Feb. 10, 1863. Moonlight, 1882. Pres. Logian. Oration, 1883. a. Law, Boston Univ. Tre. Cleveland, O., 1883-5; Newburyport, Ms., 1885-6. p. Law, Newburyport, since 1886.

Davie Butler Pratt, Andover, Mass.

Theol. Student. b. Dudley, Ma., Sep. 26, 1861. f. N. Acad., Dudley. Cobden Club Medal. Pres. Logian. Philosophical o., 1883. Harvard Observatory, 1883-4. A. T. S., 1884-7. Andover Fellowship.

Fred Martin Rice,   Hampstead, Rockingham Co., N. H.

Teacher. b. Natick, Mass., July 4, 1851. f. H. S., Newton. Logian. Philosophical o., 1878. Tra. Greenwich, Ct., 1880-4; Cranbury. N. J., 1883-4; Master H. S., Hampstead, N. H., since 1885 M. A., Williams, 1879.

Lewis Goold Rogers,   Arcade, Wyoming Co., N. Y.

Clergyman. b. Albion, N. Y., Mar. 11, 1861. f. H. S., Albion. Technian. Oration, 1882. P. T. R., 1884-7.

Fred DeLysle Smith,   18 Cortlandt St., New York City.

Lawyer. b. North Hebron N. Y., Oct. 4, 1858. f. Troy Conf. Acad., Poultney, Vt. Zeta Psi. Logian. Moonlight, 1883. Library Orator, 1883. Philosophical o., 1883. Rec. Gen. Hare, 1883-5. Columbian Law School, Washington, D. C.; LL. B. and LL. M., 1885. p. law. New York, since 1886. m. Florence Hamilton, Brooklyn, Apr. 27, 1887.

Herbert Shapleigh Underwood,   Advertiser Office, Boston.

Journalist. b. Fort Edward, N. Y., June 8, 1861. f. Acad., Glens Falls. Technian. Vice Prim. Class Historian. First Eng. Oration, 1883. Democrat. Amsterdam. N. Y., 1883-5; Republican, Springfield, Mass., 1885-8; Advertiser, Boston, since 1888 mem. Grillron Club of Washington. D. C'. Correspondents.

1884.
Percy Favor Bicknell,   Gottingen, Prussia.

Teacher. Entered College from Rowe, Mass. Logian. Five Prizes and Prize for Prizes. Valedictory. Tea. W. H., Easthampton, 1884-5; lost, W. C., 1885-7. Europe, since 1887

Walter Parke Bradley,   Williamstown, Mass.

Teacher. b. Lee, Mass., July 7, 1862. f. H. S. Lee. Zeta Psi. Technian. Outdoor Club Social. Philosophical o., 1884 s Chemistry, Gottingen, 1884-6. Asst. Chem., W. C., since 1886.

Calvin Montague Clark,   West Salem. Wis.

Theol Student. b Hartford, Wis., Jan. 30, 1861. f. Beloit. Delta Upsilon. Logian. Philosophical o., 1884. Tra. Saratoga, N. Y., 1884-5. A. T. S., 1885 K

William James Foster,   Pottstown, Montgomery Co., Pa.

Teacher. b. Argyle. N. Y., Sep. 17, 1860 f. I. O. R., Fort Edward. Technian. Three Prizes Philosophical o., 1884, rec. Grad., W. C., 1884-5. Tea. Manchester, Vt., 1885 & Pottstown, Pa., since 1886.

Nathan Gest.

Student. b Rock Island, Ill., June 30, 1863 f. P. A. Andover. Delta Kappa Epsilon German Prize. Killed in coasting, Jan. 16, 1884.

Charles Edward Greenman,   107 First St., Troy, N. Y.

Lawyer. b. Berlin, N. Y., July 81, 1861. f. H R., Troy. Delta Kappa Epsilon Logian. Moonlight, 1883. Oration, 1884 s. Law. Troy; Admitted, 1886

Walter Foxcroft Hawkins,   Pittsfield, Mass.

Lawyer. b. Pittsfield, July 18, 1859 Chi Psi. Moonlight, 1883. Prize Essay. Ivy Orator, 1884 Philosophical o., 1884. LL. B., Columbia Law Sch. 1886 p. law, Pittsfield.

Thomas Samuel Holmes, Jr., 115 Broadway, New York City.

Lawyer. b. Newark, N. J., Jan. 17, 1861. f. Jersey City, Technian. French Prize. First English o., 1884. LL. B., Columbia Law Sch., 1886. M. A., Williams. res. the Fifth St., Jersey City, N. J.

Arthur Waring Underwood,   Eagle River, Lincoln Co., Wis.

Lumber Manufacturer. b. Fort Edward, N. Y., June 6, 1862, f. Acad., Glens Falls. Technian. ola Prize. Salutatory. Tea Poltersmerville. Ia., 1843. Manf. Lumber, Appleton. Wis., 1885-7; Eagle River. since 1887.

William Hill Williams, Lake Forest, Ill.

Teacher. b. North Argyle, N. Y., Nov 4, 1861. f. 1. G. S., Fort Edward. Techaian. Tre.
Port Byron, Ill., 1884-7; Lake Forest, since 1887.

1885.

Herbert Dexter Bailey, 6 Keenan Building, Troy, N. Y.

Lawyer. b. Chester, Vt., Oct. 8, 1863. f. Saxton's River, Vt. Logian. Four Prizes. Philosophical o., 1885. Law, Troy, N. Y.; Admitted, Sep. 16, 1887. President Troy Law Assoc-
new. 1st Supt. Ch., Troy. m. Grace Galusha, Albany, Oct. 8, 1887; one boy.

Robert Anderson Clark, Harrisburg, Pa.

Teacher and Clerk. b. Williamstown, Mass., Oct. 15, 1863. f. Geo. Kem., Wn. Techaian.
Oration, 1885. Washington, D. C., 1886-7; Erie, Pa.; Omaha, Neb.; Harrisburg, Pa.

Charles Carroll Cobb, 348 LaSalle Ave., Chicago, Ill.

Teacher. b. Abington, Mass., Nov 26, 1863. f. Quincy. Four Prizes. Valedictory. Tea.
Chicago.

David Soudder Herrick, Pasumalai, South India.

Teacher. b. India, Mar. 20, 1862. f. U. S., Newton, Ms. Logian. Two Prizes. Oration,
1885. Tea. India.

John Campbell Martin, 679 Madison Ave., New York City

Lawyer. b. New York City, Sep. 2, 1864. f. U. S., So, Wn. Techaian. Oration, 1885 Law,
Columbia, New York.

Stephen B. L. Penrose, Theol. Sem., Princeton, N. J.

Teacher and Theol. Student. b. Germantown, Pa., Dec. 20, 1864. f. Germantown. Delta
Kappa Epsilon. Logian. Six Prizes and Prize for Prizes. Philosophical o., 1885. Tea. Potts-
town, Pa., 1885-6; 2nd Greek and Elocution, W. C., 1886-7. P. T. S., 1887. Hon. Mem. Whig
Soc., Princeton College. Sec. and Treas. W. C. Alumni, Philadelphia.

Alfred Ernest Street, Theol. Sem., Auburn, N. Y.

Theol. Student. b. Salem, O., Nov. 11, 1860. f. Ripon, Wis. Techaian. French Prize.
Philosophical o., 1885 Aub. T. S., 1885-8.

Henry Baldwin Ward, High School, Troy, N. Y.

Teacher. b. Troy, N. Y., Mar. 4, 1865. f. H. S., Troy. Techaian. L. N. H. Six Prizes and
Prize for Prize. Salutatory. Tea and Prin. H. S., Troy.

Levi Francis Warner, South Glastonbury, Conn.

Med Student. b. So. Glastonbury, Nov. 11, 1864. f. Acad., Glastonbury. German Prize;
Gibson Scholarship, 1884. Philosophical o., 1885. Coll. Phys. and Surg., New York City.

Henry Harding Wentworth, 162 Washington St., Chicago, Ill.

Teacher and Lawyer. b. Nashville, Tenn., Aug. 13, 1859. f. P. Exeter Acad. Zeta Psi.
Techaian. Hive Prize, 1884. Gulden Club Medal, 1884. Oration, 1885. Tea. and Supt. Sch.,
Bristol, Ct., 1885-7. Law, Chicago, since 1887.

1886.

George Weston Anderson, Nashua, N. H.

Teacher. b. Acworth, N. H., Sep. 1, 1861. f. Cushing Acad., Ashburnham, Ms. Logian.
Four Prizes. Gulden Club Medal Philosophical o., 1886. Tea. Springfield, Vt., 1886-7; Prin.
Mt. Pleasant School, Nashua, N. H., since 1887.

Edward Luther Dixon,   53 Prospect Ave., Milwaukee, Wis.

Law Student. b. Madison, Wis. Apr. 29, 1865. f Milwaukee. Chi Psi. Seven Prizes and Prize for Prizes. Valedictory. Law, Columbus Law School.

George Henry Flint,   Lincoln, Middlesex Co., Mass.

Teacher. h. Livonia, Me., Jan. 23, 1845. f P. A., Andover, Delta Upsilon. Techoian. Latin and Greek Prizes. Oration, 1845. Tea Peekskill, N. Y., 1845-7; Monson, Mass., since 1845.

John Luther Kilbon, Jr.,   Theol. Sem., Hartford, Conn.

Theol. Student. h. Springfield, Mass. June 29, 1862. f. H. S., Law. Logian. Six Prizes. Philosophical o. 1882. If T. S., since 1882

Walter Decker Mapes,   Williamstown, Mass.

Teacher. h. Matamoras, Pa., Sep. 23, 1863. f. Port Jervis, N. Y., and Cleveland, O. Phi Delta Theta. Logian. Four Prizes. Philosophical o., 1882. Inst. Math. Kenyon Mil. Acad., Gambier, O., 1886-7. Inst. Math. and Elocution, W. C., since 1887

Paul Carlton Ransom,   1298 Main St., Buffalo, N. Y.

Law Student. b. Earlville, N. Y., Mar. 1, 1862. f. Buffalo. Kappa Alpha. Greek Prize. Philosophical o., 1882. Law, Harvard Law School.

Arthur Vincent Taylor,   69 Sherman Ave., Newark, N. J.

Teacher. h. Newark, N. J., July 22, 1863. f. H. S., Newark. Delta Upsilon. Four Prizes. Thomann Scholarship. Salutatory. Tea. U. I. Inst. Wm., 1882-7; Classical Institute, Paterson, N. J., since 1887.

Sanborn Gove Tenney,   Williamstown, Ms., or New York.

Teacher. b. Cambridge, Ms., Feb. 24, 1864. f. Glen Penn, Wis., and H. S., Newton, Ms. Delta Kappa Epsilon. Techoian. L. N. H. Five Prizes. Gibson Scholarship. Ivy Orator. Oration, 1882. Tea. Lenox and New York City.

John Jenks Thomas,   Columbus, Ohio.

Med. Student. h. Columbus, O., Sep. 6, 1861. f privately. Logian. Oration, 1882. Harvard Med. School, Boston, since 1882.

Harry Vreeland Youngman, 135 Lancaster St., Albany, N. Y.

Merchant. h. Albany, N. Y., June 30, 1863. f Acad., Albany. Chi Psi. Prize. Math. and Graves. Philosophical o., 1882. Leonard and Youngman, Coal Merchants, Albany, N. Y.

1887.

Robert Grant Aitken,   Oakland, Cal.

Teacher. h. Jackson, Cal., Dec. 31, 1864. f. H. S., Oakland. Prizes. German and Nat. His. Pres. Technian. Pres. Y. M. C. A. Philosophical o., 1887. Inst. German and Mech. Drawing, Oakland, Cal.

Frank Coe Barnes,   514 Fulton St., Troy, N. Y.

Teacher. b. Troy, N. Y., Nov. 24, 1864. f. H. S., Troy. Technian. Classical. Art. Three Prizes. Oration, 1887.

William Eglin Carnochan,   Troy, Bradford Co., Pa.

Law Student. h. Troy, Pa., Oct. 17, 1867. f. Elmira, N. Y. Delta Kappa Epsilon. Logian. Seven Prizes and Prize for Prizes. Valedictory. Newburgh, N. Y., 1887.

Maxwell Warren Day,   Honeoye, Ontario Co., N. Y.

Electrical Engineer. h. Honeoye, N. Y., Mar. 20, 1865. f. Geneva. Zeta Psi. Logian. Art. L. N. H. Rice Prize. Y. M. C. A. Salutatory.

Frederick James Fessenden,   **Lockport, Niagara Co., N. Y.**

Teacher. b. Lunenburg, Mass., May 8, 1861. f. Lockport, N. Y. Zeta Psi. Pres. Classical. Five Prizes. Philosophical o., 1887.

Henry Knight Hyde,   **Honolulu, Hawaiian Islands.**

Student. b. Brimfield, Mass., June 17, 1847. son of Rev. Dr. Hyde, '52, and grandson of Hon. William Hyde, '00. f. Honolulu. Art. Pres. Logian. Classical. Y. M. C. A. Two Prizes. Oration, 1887.

Gardner Cotrell Leonard,   **131 Devonshire St., Boston, Mass.**

Insurance. b. West Springfield, Ms., Oct. 10, 1865. f. Acad., Albany. Delta Psi. L. N. H. Art. Three Prizes. Y. M. C. A. Philosophical o., 1887. N. Y. Life Ins. Co., Boston, since 1887.

Carroll Lewis Maxcy,   **89 Grand Division St., Troy, N. Y.**

Teacher. b. Norristown, Pa., May 27, 1863. f. H. S., Bridgeport, Ct. Delta Kappa Epsilon, Y. M. C. A. Four Prizes. Oration, 1887. Asst. Prin. Acad., Troy, N. Y.

James Ingraham Peck,   **Seneca Castle, Ontario Co., N. Y.**

Teacher. b. Seneca Castle, N. Y., Aug. 10, 1859. f. Acad., Canandaigua and Homer. Zeta Psi. Pres. L. N. H. Art. Oration, 1887. Morgan Scholarship, post graduate.

Philip Alexander Robinson,   **Delhi, Delaware Co., N. Y.**

Chemist. b. Newport, Vt., Mar. 11, 1865. f. Newport. Logian. L. N. H. Classical. Five Prizes. Cobden Club Medal, 1886. Philosophical o., 1887. Albany Law Sch., 1888-9.

1888.

Henry Warren Austin, Jr.,   **Oak Park, Ill.**

Student. b. Oak Park, Ill., Jan. 22, 1864. f. H. S., Oak Park and Chicago. Alpha Delta Phi. Technian. Orchestra. Five Prizes.

George Lynde Richardson,   **Troy, N. Y.**

Student. b. Troy, N. Y., May 8, 1867. f. H. S. Troy. Technian. Classical. Historical. Five Prizes.

George Benjamin Rogers,   **Albion, Orleans Co., N. Y.**

Student. b. Somerset, N. Y., July 14, 1866. f. H. S., Albion. Technian. Art. Two Prizes.

Ellis John Thomas,   **Utica, Oneida Co., N. Y.**

Student. b. Utica, N. Y., Nov 28, 1867. f. privately. Delta Upsilon. Logian. Classical. Art. Four Prizes.

Henry Daniel Wild,   **Charlotte, Chittenden Co., Vt.**

Student. b. Greensboro, Vt., Oct. 11, 1866. f. Acad., St. Johnsbury. Delta Upsilon. Logian. Classical. Seven Prizes. Thompson Scholarship.

Five other men of this class will probably be elected after their last senior examination in June, 1888.

Whole number, - - - 604.

Clergymen,	-	-	-	191	Lawyers, - - - -	105
Teachers,	-	-	-	118	Physicians, - - -	87
Journalists,	-	-	-	35	Business, etc., - -	37

Honorary Members.

William Earle Dodge.

Merchant. b. Hartford, Ct., Sep. 4, 1805. Clerk, New York City, 1819-27. Merchant, 1827-83. Firm, Phelps, Dodge & Co. 1833-83. M. C., 1865-7. Pres. Nat. Temperance Soc. Pres. Evangelical Alliance. Vice Pres. A. B. C. F. M. Director, U. T. S. Trustee, W. C., 1865-77. Donor, W. C. d. New York City, Feb. 9, 1883.

John Zaccheus Goodrich.

Manufacturer. b. Sheffield, Mass., Sep. 27, 1804. s. Law, Richmond and Lenox. p. Law, Lenox and Stockbridge. Editor Village Paper. Manufacturer. Mass. Senate, 1848-9. M. C., 1851-3. Lieut. Gov., Mass., 1860-1. Collector Port of Boston, 1861-5. Pres. Housatonic R. R. Co. Pres. Berk. Co. Bible Soc. Trustee, W. C., 1865-70. Donor, W. C. M. A. Williams, 1836. d. Stockbridge, Apr. 19, 1885.

Adam Reid.

Clergyman. b. Lanarkshire, Scotland, Jan. 4, 1804. Univ. Glasgow, 1827. U. S., since July, 1835. Pas. Amenia, N. Y., 1835; Salisbury, Ct., 1835-70. Trustee, W. C., 1847-69. d. 1876.

Charles Stoddard.

Merchant. b. Northampton, Mass., June 27, 1804. Resided, Boston, 1814-73. Treasurer Old South Church, thirty-four years. Deacon of same. Pres. Com. A. B. C. F. M., 1864-73. Trustee, W. C., 1869-73. Donor, W. C. m. Mary A. Porter, Aug. 6, 1836; two c., Phi Beta Kappa add. 1851. d. Boston, Apr. 21, 1873.

Sanborn Tenney.

Teacher. b. Stoddard, N. H., Jan. 13, 1827. Amherst, 1853. Tro Laboratory, Mass. Lect. Mass. Teachers' Institutes. Prof. Nat. His. Vassar. 1865-8. Prof. Nat. His., W. C., 1868-77. pub. "Zoology;" "Geology." m. Abby A. Gove, Milford, N. H., July 30, 1855; two c., Phi Beta Kappa soc. '76. d. Rocky Mt. Expedition, July 9, 1877.

Augustus Charles Thompson,   1 Linwood St., Boston, Mass.

Clergyman. b. Goshen, Ct., Apr. 30, 1812. s. Yale. grad H. T. S., 1838. Ord., Roxbury, Ms., July 27, 1842. Pas. Eliot Church, Roxbury, since 1842. D. D. Amherst, 1860. Lect. F. S. at A. T. S., at Boston Univ., and at H. T. S. pub. "Songs in the Night," 1845; "Young Martyrs," 1846; "Lambs Fed," 1849; "Last Hours," 1851; "Poor Widow," 1854; "The Better Land," 1854; "Yoke in Youth," 1856; "Gathered Lilies, 1858; "Morning Hours in Patmos," 1860; "The Mercy Seal," 1869; "Our Little Ones," 1867; "Seeds and Sheaves," 1858; "Moravian Missions," 1890; "Happy New Year," 1893; "Future Probation and Foreign Missions," 1896.

Abbreviations.

The plan followed in the early part of the catalogue of indicating all College Societies by their initial letters was found to be very confusing, and was continued in only a few cases.

The usual abbreviations are given to countries, months, points of the compass, honorary degrees and the names of well-known public bodies. Most of the abbreviations will be easily understood from the connection. When a State abbreviation is omitted, the one next preceding is understood.

It has not been found practicable to mark the distinctions of Pastor, Acting Pastor and Stated Supply, nor to discriminate between Editor and Journalist.

The last Philotechnian Catalogue was issued in 1873, and that of the Philologian Society in 1882. To the Technian list of this book should be added Nelson and Storrs of 1907, Bobo and Hall of 1908, Edwards of 1910, and Bryant of 1818.

Acad.—Academy.
Adel.—Adelphic.
Agr.—Agriculture, Agricultural.
Agt.—Agent.
Am.—American.
Anat.—Anatomy.
A. T. S.—Andover Theological Seminary.
Ass't.—Assistant.
Assoc.—Associate, Association.
Att.—Attorney.
Aub. T. S.—Auburn Theological Seminary.

b.—born.
Bapt.—Baptist.
Bd.—Board.
Berk.—Berkshire.
Bib.—Bible, Biblical.
B. and B.—Bar and Button.

c.—child, children.
Ch.—Church, Christian.
Chem.—Chemistry.
C. T. S.—Chicago Theological Seminary.
Col.—Colonel, Collector.
Coll.—College, Collegiate.
Cong.—Congregational.
Cor.—Corresponding.
Const.—Constitutional.
Conv.—Convention.

d.—died.
dau.—daughter.
Dea.—Deacon.
D. L. L.—Delaware Literary Institute.
Dep.—Deputy.
Dept.—Department.
Disp.—Disputant.
Dist.—District.
Div.—Divinity.

Ed.—Editor, Education.
Eld.—Elder.

Eng.—English, Engineer.
Epis.—Episcopal.
Ex.—Exhibition, Extemporary.

f.—fitted.
F. M.—Foreign Missionary.
Fr.—French.
Far.—Farmer.

grad.—graduated.
Ger.—German.
Gr.—Greek.
G. I.—Greylock Institute.

His.—History.
H. S.—High School.
H. of R.—House of Representatives.
H. M.—Home Missionary.
H. T. S.—Hartford Theological Seminary.

Ins.—Insurance.
Inst.—Institute, Instructor.
Int.—Internal.

Jud.—Judge, Judicial.
Jun.—Junior.
J. H.—Johns Hopkins.

K. A.—Kappa Alpha.

L.—Legion.
Lang.—Language.
Lat.—Latin.
L. N. H.—Lyceum of Natural History.
Lect.—Lecturer.
Lit.—Literature, Literary.

m.—married.
mem.—member.
Math.—Mathematical.
Med.—Medicine, Medical.
Mod.—Modern, Moderator.
Ms., Mass.—Massachusetts.

Nat.—Natural, National.

o.—oration.
Ord.—Ordained.

p.—practical.
pub.—published.
Pas.—Pastor.
P. A.—Phillips Academy.
P. T. S.—Princeton Theological Seminary.
Phil.—Philosophy, Philosophical.
Phys.—Physics, Physician.
Pres.—President.
Presb.—Presbyterian.
Prin.—Principal.
Prof.—Professor.

res.—residence.
Rev.—Revenue.
Rhet.—Rhetoric.

s.—studied.
S.—Seminary.
Sch.—School, Schools.
Sci.—Science, Scientific.

T.—Technian.
Tea.—Teacher.

U. T. S.—Union Theological Seminary.
Un.—Union.
Unit.—Unitarian.
Univ.—University.

W. C.—Williams College.
Wn.—Williamstown.
W. S.—Williston Seminary.

Y. T. S.—Yale Theological Seminary.

Index of Names.

Canning,
'74 Edward W. B.

Carnochan,
'76 William Egbs.

Carter,
'68 Franklin.
'77 Howard Williams.

Chadbourne,
'68 Paul Ansel.

Chamberlain,
'73 Robert Merch.

Chapin,
'59 John Bassett.
'88 William Wilberforce.
'89 Alfred Clark.

Cheney,
'59 William.

Childs,
'68 Henry Halsey.
'41 Timothy.

Chipperfield,
'78 George Frederick.

Claflin,
'38 Leet Fisk.

Clark,
'49 Josiah.
'43 Epaphras.
'94 Abram.
'44 Amariah Sylvester.
'96 James Dixon.
'54 James Alpheus.
'77 Hayford Parsons.
'94 Calvin Montague.
'63 Robert Anderson.

Clarke,
'54 George Ellery.

Cleveland,
'54 Samuel McCoskry.

Cobb,
'75 Charles Carroll.

Colten,
'76 Emanuel.

Cole,
'88 Edward Herman.

Collins,
'43 Charles Jewett.

Coll,
'74 James Dominick.

Colton,
'54 Wells.

Cooke,
'88 Parsons.
'80 Frederick Hale.

Cooley,
'60 James Seth.

Corning,
'81 Alfred Henry.

Crandall,
'69 Hiram Barr.

Curtis,
'66 Erben.

Cutler,
'97 Abel.

Cutting,
'91 Willard Starr.

Darling,
'98 Edwin Harris.
'94 Timothy Greville.

Davenport,
'68 John Gaylord.
'67 Charles Augustus.
'70 Frank Henry.

Davis,
'91 Emerson.
'94 Henry.

Durbson,
'45 Charles Augustus.

Day,
'76 Maxwell Warren.

Desmond,
'44 Charles.
'91 Charles Mason.

Denison,
'84 John Henry.

Denton,
'85 Jonas.

Dewey,
'06 Chester.
'11 Charles Augustus.
'14 Orville.
'40 Francis Henshaw.
'51 Charles Augustus.
'54 James Randolph.
'74 Justin.
'76 Francis Henshaw, Jr.

Dickinson,
'58 John Woodbridge.
'89 Hiram Madison.

Dike,
'61 Samuel Warren.

Dimmick,
'55 William Reynolds.

Dixon,
'54 James.
'76 Edward Luther.

Dodd,
'55 Cyrus Morris.

Dodge,
Hon. William Earle.

Downs,
'76 Edgar Balko.

Dudley,
'68 Myron Samuel.

Duenhaupt,
'74 Rudolph C. F.

Dunbar,
'71 James Robert.

Dunning,
'91 Charles Seely.
'85 William Arnette.

Durfee,
'84 Charles Stoddard.

Dutton,
'89 Thomas.

Dwight,
'60 Charles Chauncey.

Eastman,
'17 William.

Eaton,
'74 Francis Collins.
'78 James Francis.

Edmonds,
'74 Walter Dominguez.

Edwards,
'78 Justin.
'85 William Henry.

Egleston,
'70 Melville.

Eldridge,
'80 Orestes Gardner.

Ellis,
'86 James Homer.

Ely,
'90 Josiah.
'51 Samuel Partridge.

Emerson,
'63 Justin Edwards.
'64 Nathaniel Bright.

Erwin,
'94 Frank Alexander.

Everett,
'89 Charles Hall.

Fagan,
'84 Thomas Karsfield.

Fairbanks,
'87 Leland.

Farrington,
'81 Zenas Rogers.

Ferris,
'47 Jonathan Henry.

Fessenden,
'57 Frederick James.

Field,
'71 Lucian.
'85 David Dudley.
'28 Jonathan Edwards.
'26 Stephen Johnson.
'67 Samuel Tobey.
'50 Dudley.

Flske,
'78 Frederick William.
'79 Charles Albert.

Fitch,
'55 Charles Elliott.
'70 Robert Gresham.

Fletcher,
'79 Herbert Hervey.

Flint,
'90 George Henry.

Folger,
  '64 Charles Worth.
Forbes,
  '55 Samuel Baker.
Foster,
  '81 Addison Pinneo.
  '84 William James.
Fowler,
  '17 Henry.
Foxcroft,
  '71 Frank.
Freeman,
  '88 Charles March.
French,
  '32 Edward Warner.
  '53 Justus Clement.
  '87 John Abbott.
Garfield,
  '58 James Abram.
Gaylord,
  '16 Flavel Stebbins.
Geller,
  '81 Frederick.
Gest,
  '94 Nathan.
Gibbs,
  '78 George Clinton.
  '71 Herbert Russell.
Gilbert,
  '85 William Ball.
Gilson,
  '35 Charles Franklin.
Gladden,
  '39 Washington.
Gleason,
  '77 Herbert Wendell.
Goddard,
  '16 Joseph Bachellor.
Goodell,
  '31 William.
Goodhue,
  '84 John Howard.
Goodrich,
  '08 Elizur.
  '67 George Dickinson.
  '81 Chauncey.
Gosman,
  '43 Abraham.
Greenman,
  '91 Charles Edward.
Griffin,
  '84 Nathaniel Herrick.
  '85 Edward Herrick.
Gross,
  '78 Charles.
Guernster,
  '87 Frederick William.

Gulick,
  '85 Thomas Laton.
Gunn,
  '87 Franklin Fuller.
Haines,
  '70 John Charles.
Hale,
  '81 George.
  '70 Edward Danforth.
Hall,
  '08 Gordon.
  '34 John.
  '38 Thomas Amory.
  '42 Granville Stanley.
  '70 Robert Beales.
  '78 Charles Cuthbert.
Hallock,
  '79 Gerard.
  '18 William Allen.
  '80 Lowell Mason.
Halsey,
  '11 Herman.
  '58 Charles Storrs.
  '77 Rufus Henry.
Hand,
  '81 Aaron Hicks.
Harmon,
  '87 Rollin Eugene.
Haskell,
  '80 Henry Charles.
Hatch,
  '70 Lewis Clutenden.
Haven,
  '84 William LeRoy.
Hawkes,
  '44 Theron Holbrook.
Hawkins,
  '81 Walter Foxcroft.
Hawley,
  '81 Charles.
Hayden,
  '61 Warren Lake.
Hazeltine,
  '39 Henry Martyn.
Herrick,
  '71 William Hale.
  '81 Frederick Morris.
  '85 David Scudder.
Hervey,
  '34 William.
Hicks,
  '39 William.
Hill,
  '66 Clement Hugh.
  '79 Horace Greenwood.
Hitchcock,
  '73 Henry Beklen.
Holdington,
  '84 Henry Richard.

Hollister,
  '79 William Henry.
Holmes,
  '34 Charles Henry.
  '87 Samuel Van Vranken.
  '34 Thomas Samuel.
Holt,
  '74 Charles Sumner.
Hooker,
  '81 Edward Trumbull.
  '85 Thomas.
Hopkins,
  '24 Mark.
  '86 Albert.
  '38 Henry.
Horton,
  '84 Carlos S.
Hosford,
  '43 Henry Brown.
Howard,
  '70 Jacob Merrill.
Howes,
  '88 Rowland Sears.
Howk,
  '89 Charles Dewey.
Hubbard,
  '83 Fordyce Mitchell.
  '87 Ely Andrews.
  '79 Frank Gaylord.
Hudson,
  '34 Edward Payson.
Hunt,
  '88 Horace Junian.
Huntington,
  '78 Charles White.
Hutchins,
  '57 Alexander.
  '81 Charles Lewis.
Hyde,
  '81 Joseph.
  '88 William.
  '84 Alexander.
  '34 Charles McEwen.
  '81 Joseph William.
  '85 Henry Knight.
Ingalls,
  '04 Francis Theodore.
Ingersoll,
  '81 Edwards Piatt.
Isham,
  '38 John.
  '57 Edward Swift.
Jackson,
  '34 Robert.
Jennings,
  '78 Frederick Beach.
Jones,
  '75 Samuel Gowrie.
  '79 Robert Ellis.

Judd,
  'M Charles George.
  '77 Emerson Wadsworth.
Julson,
  '70 Harry Pratt.
Kellogg,
  '70 Daniel.
  '46 Allyn Stanley.
Kempshall,
  '81 Everard.
Kendall,
  '76 Francis Lockwood.
Kerr,
  '80 George.
Ketcham,
  '60 Henry.
Killam,
  '76 John Luther.
King,
  '76 Jones.
Kittredge,
  '71 William Cullen.
Kilns,
  '68 Virgil Polk.
Knowlton,
  '68 Dexter Ass.
Knox,
  '68 Samuel.
Laflin,
  '69 Addison Henry.
Lamberton,
  '66 John.
Langmuir,
  '61 Gavin.
Lasell,
  '84 Edward.
  '78 Nathaniel.
Lawton,
  '76 George Field.
  '76 George Perkins.
Leavitt,
  '51 George Roswell.
  '54 Burke Fay.
Lee,
  '72 Charles Alfred.
Lefavour,
  '78 Henry.
Leonard,
  '77 Gardner Cotrell.
Lewis,
  '68 Everett Edward.
Lincoln,
  '75 Isaac Newton.
  '55 Ephraim Livingston.
Locke,
  '73 Jeremiah Fuller.
Loomis,
  '69 Charles Wolcott.

Lord,
  '83 Willis.
Lund,
  '68 Oscar Frederick.
Lyman,
  '38 Henry Munson.
Lyons,
  '58 Curtis Jerre.
  '65 Albert Brown.
Mabie,
  '67 Hamilton Wright.
McClellan,
  '68 Samuel.
  '66 Josiah Griswold.
McClenon,
  '70 Rufus Burt.
Mack,
  '30 Eli Thornton.
McLean,
  '71 George Edwin.
McMynn,
  '84 John Gibson.
Magee,
  '57 Irving.
Mapes,
  '68 Walter Decker.
Marsh,
  '85 Charles.
Martin,
  '82 John Campbell.
Marvin,
  '84 William T. R.
Mats,
  '70 Herman Lewis.
  '72 Rudolph.
Maurice,
  '81 Charles Stewart.
Maxcy,
  '87 Carroll Lewis.
May,
  '73 Charles.
Mead,
  '80 Willis Waldo.
Mellen,
  '68 Seth Smith.
Merrimon,
  '70 William Edward.
  '83 Daniel.
Miller,
  '80 Jacob F.
  '84 Joel Drury.
  '87 Henry Clay.
Mills,
  '87 George Franklin.
  '78 Curtius Putnam.
Mitchell,
  '88 Arthur.

Monroe,
  '37 Francis LeBaron.
Montague,
  '41 Melzer.
Mooar,
  '81 George.
Morey,
  '79 George William.
Morgan,
  '85 John.
  '89 Horace Hills.
Morley,
  '69 Randis Brewster.
  '69 Edward Williams.
  '63 John Henry.
Murdock,
  '84 Hollis Read.
Myers,
  '68 Alfred Edwards.
Mynderse,
  '71 Wilhelmus.
Nelson,
  '67 John.
Newcomb,
  '36 George Benton.
Newman,
  '51 Charles.
Nichols,
  '39 Henry F. C.
Niles,
  '86 Ebenezer P.
Noble,
  '85 David Addison.
  '87 Mason.
North,
  '69 Theodore.
  '67 Thomas Mather.
Northrup,
  '84 George Washington.
Norton,
  '89 Jesse Olds.
Ogden,
  '89 Isaac Gray.
  '77 Rolls.
Olds,
  '78 Franklin Marcellus.
Olin,
  '85 Abraham Baldwin.
  '73 John Myers.
Olmsted,
  '80 John Crosby.
Orton,
  '85 James.
Paige,
  '78 Alonzo Christopher.
  '78 Howe.
Palmer,
  '84 William Pitt.

Parsons,
'57 Andrew.
'30 Eben Hart.
'61 Frederick Jennings.
Partridge
'04 Joseph Lyman.
Patterson,
'71 Robert Wilson.
Paul.
'84 John Marshall.
Peck,
'57 James Ingraham.
Peloubet,
'58 Francis Nathan.
Penrose,
'76 Stephen H. L.
Perkins,
'79 Charles Albert.
'70 Henry Poor.
Perry,
'58 Arthur Latham.
'80 Alfred Tyler.
'79 Ellis.
Phillips,
'76 John L. T.
Pierce,
'57 Charles Morgan.
'81 Frank.
Pike,
'80 Francis Vergnies.
Pixley,
'58 Stephen Clapp.
Place,
'73 William Francis.
Platt,
'76 William Alexander
'78 Charles Malcolm.
Pleasants,
'81 George Washington.
'75 Adair.
Pomeroy,
'75 Medad.
Pond,
'79 Milton Gomber.
Porter,
'54 William Augustus.
'58 Royal Loomis.
'59 William.
Powell,
'60 Elisha Barclay.
Pratt,
'58 Lewellyn.
'79 Waldo Selden.
'65 Davis Butler.
Prentice,
'56 William Packer.
Prince,
'59 Samuel Iranaeus.

Putney,
'62 William Brewster.
Ransom,
'78 Paul Carlton.
Read,
'61 Thomas Thornton.
Redd.
Hon. mem., Adam.
Rhoades,
'68 William C. P.
Rice,
'54 Caleb.
'51 James Lothrop.
'04 Edward Walker.
'68 Fred Martin.
Richards,
'19 William.
Richardson,
'88 George Lyman.
Rising,
'64 Franklin Almonol.
Robbins,
'68 Francis Le Baron.
Robinson,
'60 Charles Reynnour.
'70 Arthur.
'67 Philip Alexander.
Rockwell,
'54 Jarvis.
Roe,
'78 William Edgar.
'81 Walter Clark.
Rogers,
'68 Lewis Gould.
'86 George Benjamin.
Route,
'76 Clarence Burgess.
Rossiter,
'49 Newton Henry.
Rumsey,
'72 George Dole.
Sabin,
'81 Henry Lyman.
Safford,
'48 Daniel Ephraim.
Sanderson,
'67 Obed Hatch.
Saunders,
'78 Truman Wilcox.
Sawyer,
'51 Chem Josiah
Schauffler,
'59 Henry Albert.
Scholl,
'72 Henry Trunz.
Scott,
'79 Willard.

Scudder,
'57 Samuel Hubbard.
'59 Horace Elisha.
Seaver,
'54 Norman.
Newall,
'67 Albert Cole.
Seymour,
'71 Caleb Perkins.
Shaw,
'84 Charles Lyman.
Sheldon,
'81 Benjamin Robbins.
'20 David Newton.
'35 George.
'77 Charles Burt.
'47 Samuel Bridgm.
Sherrill,
'14 Franklin.
Skinner,
'85 Benjamin Day.
Smith,
'18 Royal Wells.
'34 Henry Augustus.
'86 Charles T. R.
'71 Claude Laurell.
'85 Fred DeLysle.
Snow,
'82 Francis Huntington.
Snyder,
'79 Peter Miles.
Spalding,
'60 James Field.
Spencer,
'82 Nelson Elwood.
'44 Charles Spafford.
Spear,
'83 Charles T. F.
Sprague,
'76 Norman Spencer.
Spring,
'68 Leverett Wilson.
Stark,
'60 William.
Stearns,
'70 Raymond Hoyt.
Stedman,
'77 Stephen.
Stetson,
'85 Francis Lynde.
Stevens,
'65 Homer Brom.
Stevenson,
'79 Halsey Bidwell.
Stoddard,
Hon. mem., Charles.
'61 Charles Augustus.
'71 John Lawson.

Stone.
'91 James Ferrar
'98 Charles Warren.

Storrs,
'65 Richard Baker.

Street,
'70 Alfred Erwin.

Strickland,
'34 William Phillips.

Strong,
'57 Stephen Chester.
'58 Theodore.

Stuart
'51 William.

Swan,
'61 William.

Swift,
'65 William Henry.

Sylvester,
'76 Charles Robbins.

Talcott.
'50 Samuel Austin.

Tatlock,
'81 John.
'56 John.
'57 William.
'71 Henry.

Taylor
'16 Stephen.
'50 John Ragg.
'76 Arthur Vincent.

Ten Eyck.
1752 Egbert.

Tenney.
Hon. mem. Sanborn.
'78 Sanborn Gove.

Thayer,
'50 Elijah.

Thomas,
'54 DeWitt Hurd.
'58 John Jenks.
'66 Ellis John.

Thompson,
Hon. mem., Augustus C.
'58 Lyman.
'76 George Hunter.

Tolman.
'77 Albert Harris.

Tomlinson,
'76 Joseph.

Tompkins,
'60 William Ripley.

Towner.
1787 Homer.

Townsend,
'68 Martin Ingham.

Tracy,
'64 Charles Chapin.

Trask,
'64 John L. B.

Treat
'83 Charles Bracut.

True.
'62 Albert.

Tucker,
'62 Gilbert Milligan.

Tupper,
'72 John Langdon.

Tuttle
'78 William N. H.

Tyng,
'56 Stephen Higginson.

Underwood,
'66 Rufus Scofield.
'63 Herbert Shadrigh.
'64 Arthur Waring.

Vanderpuel,
'50 Isaac.

Van Ingen,
'68 Henry Schmalia.

Van Vechten.
'50 Theodore F.

Washburn,
'75 Jonathan.

Walker.
'40 John Adam.

Walton,
'68 John Seymour.

Ward,
'50 Richard Halsted.
'63 Henry Baldwin.

Wardner.
'78 Morton Smith.

Warner,
'62 Oliver.
'63 Levi Francis.

Washburn,
'17 Emory.

Watson.
'74 Charles Henry.

Wells,
'54 John.
'60 David Ames.
'57 Horace Herman.
'64 Edward Phineas.

Wentworth,
'76 Henry Harding.

Werner,
'74 Julius Edward.

West,
'68 Emory Washburn.

Wheeler,
'30 Alvan.
'41 Samuel Greene.
'54 Thomas Macauley.

White,
'65 William Cosler.
'36 Bushnell.
'36 Joseph.
'51 James.

Whitney,
'43 William Dwight.
'46 Milton Burrall.

Whiton,
'18 John.

Wight,
'50 William Ward.

Wilcox,
'35 Samuel Corylus.
'44 Marshall.
'46 Nathaniel F.

Wild
'76 Henry Daniel.

Wiley,
'61 Edward Carroll.

Willett.
'75 Fernando Cortez.

Williams,
'05 Israel.
'59 George Ashley.
'75 Charles Ashley.
'50 William White.
'74 William Hill.

Wilson,
'56 Lavalette.

Window,
'59 William Page.

Wood,
'57 Samuel.

Woolbridge,
'18 Jonathan Edwards.
'78 Luther Dana.

Woodin,
'55 Simeon Foster.

Woods,
'18 John.

Woodward,
'59 George Franklin.

Woodworth,
'50 Westerlo.

Worthington,
'50 Charles.

Wright,
'36 Walter.
'41 Russell.
'60 Charles Eleazer.

Yale,
'11 Cyrus.

Youngman.
'48 Harry Vreeland.

Constitution

——OF THE——

PHI BETA KAPPA SOCIETY,

GAMMA OF MASSACHUSETTS.

PREAMBLE.

The object of the Society is the promotion of literature and friendly intercourse among scholars. Its name is Phi Beta Kappa; its motto is intended to indicate that Philosophy (which is understood to include Religion as well as Ethics), is worthy of cultivation as the guide of life.

ARTICLE I.—MEMBERSHIP.

The Society shall consist of Graduate and Honorary members, chosen at the annual meeting, or at a special meeting, by the Society-at-large; and of Undergraduates chosen in the manner hereafter described. No injunction of secrecy as to its proceedings shall be imposed and no ceremonies of initiation shall be required at the admission of members.

ARTICLE II.—AMENDMENTS.

No change shall be made in the Constitution and By-Laws of the Society except at the regular annual meeting, or at some meeting to which the annual meeting shall specially refer the subject.

ARTICLE III.—ELECTIONS.

In respect to the election of Graduate and of Honorary members by the Society-at-large, it is provided that:

First—Any member at any annual meeting may publicly nominate and recommend any Alumnus of Williams College for admission as a Graduate member, and any person for admission as an Honorary member, and the persons so nominated shall be balloted for at the same meeting in the order in which they are nominated. The person nominating shall state to the Society the scholarly achievement or attainment supposed to warrant the nomination.

Second—In balloting for Graduate or for Honorary members six negative votes shall be required to exclude a candidate, but no person shall be admitted on such ballot unless there are at least three affirmative votes to one negative vote.

Third—The result of the balloting for any person shall not be announced to the Society until all the ballotings for that day are concluded. Whenever any person who is not present at the meeting is elected, the Corresponding Secretary shall by letter inform him of the fact.

Fourth—No person who is a Graduate or Undergraduate of any other college or university, where there is a branch of this Society, shall be elected a member of this Chapter.

ARTICLE IV.—UNDERGRADUATES.

The Undergraduate Members shall be elected by the Immediate members (those at college already members.) It is the opinion of the Society-at-large that the elections should be conducted as follows :

First—Elections should not take place before the close of the third term of the Junior year of the persons to be chosen.

Second—Scholarship, with a generally good character, should be the ground of election into the Society. The eligibility of an individual should be left to the Immediate members, whose decision should be guided, but not governed by the Faculty's scale of rank.

Third—It is very desirable that the number of ten from each class should not be exceeded in choosing Immediate members; one-half of the number chosen at the end of Junior year and the remainder chosen on the morning after the last examination in the Senior year.

Fourth—The election of Undergraduates should be by ballot, and two negative votes should suffice to defeat an election.

ARTICLE V.—MEETINGS.

The annual meeting, until otherwise ordered by the Society, shall be held Tuesday noon of Commencement week in one of the College Halls at Williamstown. Special meetings may be called by the President, or in his absence by the Vice-President, whenever it shall be deemed necessary. Meetings of the Immediate members shall be held in the manner prescribed by the By-Laws.

ARTICLE VI.—OFFICERS.

At the annual meeting there shall be chosen by ballot from the members of the Society who are not Undergraduates, a President, a Vice-President, a Corresponding Secretary, and a Treasurer. A Recording Secretary and two Marshals shall be chosen by the Immediate members from their own number.

ARTICLE VII.—AUTHORITY.

The Society-at-large shall have the sole and exclusive authority to make all By-Laws, Rules and Regulations for the good government of the Society; but, subordinate thereto, they may delegate any authority to the Immediate members for the regulation of their own meetings.

ARTICLE VIII.--TRIENNIAL MEETING.

A Literary Committee* consisting of three persons, of whom the Corresponding Secretary shall be one, shall be appointed at every Triennial meeting of the Society, whose duty it shall be to secure an Orator, Poet and Chaplain for the ensuing Triennial Anniversary. The two Marshals and the Treasurer shall constitute a committee to make the other necessary arrangements for the Triennial Meeting and Dinner.

ARTICLE IX.—EXPENSES.

The expenses of the Triennial Meeting and Dinner shall be defrayed from the Treasury of the Society and, in case they do not prove sufficient, by an equal tax upon each of the Immediate members.

The President of the Society, or in his absence the presiding officer, may invite distinguished strangers, not members of the Society, to attend the Literary Exercises and Dinner.

Any member, with the previous approbation of the President and Vice President, may invite any one gentleman to dine with the Society at their Triennial Meeting, the ticket being at the expense of the member giving the invitation.

ARTICLE X.—NOTIFICATION, ETC.

It shall be the duty of the Corresponding Secretary to notify each member of the Society of the approaching Triennial Meeting at least eight weeks before its occurrence. The notification shall include the names of the Orator, Poet and Chaplain, and the place, time and cost of Dinner.

The Society shall never officially request a copy for the Press of the Literary Exercises.

BY-LAWS.

ARTICLE 1.—DISQUALIFICATION.

No election of this Society shall be given to a student who is known to have gained high standing by unfair means.

ARTICLE 2.—FEES.

Each person elected a member of this Society shall pay to the Treasurer the sum of five dollars as an admission fee, within three months from the date of his election.

ARTICLE 3.—BADGE AND KEY.

The badge of the Society shall consist of two ribbons, pink and blue. Every member shall wear the badge of the Society at all College and Society exhibitions and on the first four days of Commencement week. The purchase or wearing of the key shall be optional with each member.

*The present committee are Secretary H. H. Ballard, Prof. E. M. Griffin, and Prof. A. L. Perry, and the next Triennial Meeting will be in 1849.

ARTICLE 4.—MOURNING.

At the decease of an Immediate member, the Immediate members shall drape their keys for thirty days. At the decease of a Graduate or Honorary member the Immediate members may drape their keys for two weeks.

ARTICLE 5.—UNDERGRADUATE MEETINGS.

There shall be three regular meetings of the Immediate members during the collegiate year—on the fifth Tuesday of the Fall Term, on the sixth Thursday of the Winter Term, and on the fourth Tuesday of the Summer Term. The Recording Secretary shall, ex-officio, preside at all meetings. The order of exercises shall be as follows: Calling the roll; reading the records; reading essays, selections and criticisms; miscellaneous business; appointments for the next regular meeting and adjournment. Each Immediate member shall prepare for each regular meeting an essay or select reading, and any member failing to do this, unless excused by the presiding officer, shall be fined for the first failure fifty cents, for the second seventy-five cents, and for the third one dollar.

ARTICLE 6.—CATALOGUE.

The Society shall prepare every fifth year a corrected and revised Catalogue, and, if the way is clear, shall publish the same.

United Chapters
PHI BETA KAPPA SOCIETY.

ROLL.

Connecticut.—Alpha at Yale, Beta at Trinity, Gamma at Wesleyan.

Maine.—Alpha at Bowdoin.

Massachusetts.—Alpha at Harvard, Beta at Amherst, Gamma at Williams.

New Hampshire.—Alpha at Dartmouth.

New York.—Alpha at Union, Beta at University City of New York, Gamma at College City of New York, Delta at Columbia, Epsilon at Hamilton, Zeta at Hobart, Eta at Madison, Theta at Cornell, Iota at Rochester.

Ohio.—Beta at Kenyon.

Pennsylvania.—Alpha at Dickinson, Beta at Lehigh.

Vermont.—Alpha at University of Vermont, Beta at Middlebury.

Whole number 22.

The Alpha of New Jersey at Rutgers has voted to join, and will probably be received at the next meeting of the Council. The Alpha of Rhode Island at Brown has declined to join.

OFFICERS.

President.—Matthew Hale, of the University of Vermont.

Vice-President.—Thomas W. Higginson, of Harvard.

Secretary and Treasurer.—Adolph Werner, of the College of the City of New New York. (Address, 339 West 79th street, New York City.)

Senators whose terms expire September, 1889.—George W. Curtis of Brown, Theodore D. Dwight of Hamilton, Octavius B. Frothingham of Harvard, Daniel C. Gilman of Yale, Edward E. Hale of Harvard, Matthew Hale of Vermont University, Oliver W. Holmes, Jr., of Harvard, Francis P. Nash of Harvard, Adolph Werner of the College City of New York, Justin Winsor or Harvard.

Senators whose terms expire September, 1892.—James B. Angell of Vermont University, Joseph H. Choate of Harvard, John A. De Remer of Union, Thomas W. Higginson of Harvard, James R Lowell of Harvard, Henry C. Potter of Union, Richard S Storrs of Amherst, Francis A. Walker of Amherst, William D. Whitney of Williams, Stewart L. Woodford of Columbia.

Constitution

—OF THE—

UNITED CHAPTERS.

ARTICLE I.—NATIONAL COUNCIL.

The National Council of the Phi Beta Kappa Society shall consist of the Senators hereinafter spoken of, and of delegates from the several Chapters of the Society. Each Chapter shall be entitled to send three delegates, who shall be graduates of at least five years standing and members of the Phi Beta Kappa Society, but not necessarily of the Chapter by which they are chosen.

ARTICLE II.—SENATE.

The Senate shall originally consist of twenty Senators, chosen by the delegates at the first session of the National Council, from the Society-at-large. These shall be divided into two classes, whose terms of office shall expire at the adjournment of alternate regular sessions of the National Council. At every subsequent regular session the places of the outgoing class shall be filled by election as follows: On the day preceding the first day of each regular session of the National Council, the Senate shall meet, and shall nominate fifteen candidates in addition to the members of the outgoing class for the ten vacant seats, and also two candidates for the unexpired term of each Senator who may have died or resigned since the last regular session. Other persons not nominated by the Senate may be presented as candidates at the time of the election. Of every ten members whose term of office shall expire, one may be elected by the Council, Senator for life. In every election of Senators a majority of the votes cast shall be required to elect, and in such elections the outgoing Senators shall have no vote.

ARTICLE III.—OFFICERS

The officers of the National Council shall be a President, Vice-President, a Secretary and a Treasurer, and such others as shall be found necessary from time to time. The President shall be chosen from among the Senators.

ARTICLE IV.—SESSIONS AND FUNCTIONS.

The National Council shall meet on the first Wednesday of September in every third year, at such place as shall have been determined at its last regular session; and shall proceed at once to the election, first of its officers and next of the Senators. The National Council shall make such rules as may be found necessary for the carrying out of any provision of the Constitution.

ARTICLE V.—Functions of the Senate.

During the sessions of the National Council the Senate shall have no separate existence, but its members shall take their places with the delegates as members of the National Council, voting with the delegates, as well upon all other matters as upon the election of officers and Senators, except as provided in article II. When the National Council is not in session the Senate shall constitute an independent body, charged with the duty of representing the Phi Beta Kappa Society and speaking in its name, and exercising, in addition, the functions of a permanent Executive Committee of the National Council. It shall hold its meetings at such times and places as it shall determine, being first called together by that Senator who, at the original election of the Senate, shall have been elected by the largest number of votes. It shall recommend candidates for election as Senators. It shall also have power to call an extra session of the National Council. It shall furthermore prepare and recommend to the consideration of the National Council such matters as it may deem proper. It shall transmit its lists of candidates, and of matters recommended for discussion, by the hands of its Secretary, to the presiding officer of the National Council, immediately upon its organization being completed. It shall also transmit, in the same manner, to the National Council, a report of its doings between the sessions of the Council. Nothing herein shall be so construed as to derogate from the right of the National Council to appoint committees to sit between sessions, independently of the Senate, and to report at the next session.

ARTICLE VI.—New Charters

Applications for charters shall, in all cases, be made to the Senate, at least six months before the regular session of the National Council; the Senate shall at once notify all the chapters of such application, and such application shall be reported to the National Council with the recommendation of the Senate at the next meeting of the Council, and shall be passed upon by the Council, which shall have exclusive power to grant charters.

ARTICLE VII.—Quorum and Rules.

The National Council at any of its sessions, and the Senate at any time, may respectively make such by-laws and rules of order as may be thought expedient for their use, provided the same be not inconsistent with any of the provisions of this Constitution. A quorum of the National Council shall consist of delegates from a majority of the chapters and not fewer than three Senators; the Senate shall determine the number which shall constitute a quorum.

ARTICLE VIII —Rights of Chapters.

Nothing contained in this Constitution shall be construed as empowering the Senate or the National Council to restrict or abridge the rights or privileges now exercised by existing Chapters, except as expressly provided herein.

ARTICLE IX.—AMENDMENTS.

No change shall be made in this constitution unless the same shall have been first proposed at the session of the National Council next preceding the session at which the proposed change is voted for; and no vote shall be had upon any such proposed change except upon one day's notice, and at a stated hour previously ordered by the meeting, and no amendment shall be made without the concurrence of the delegations of two-thirds of the chapters represented in the Council.

ARTICLE X.—ADOPTION.

*This Constitution shall take effect when ratified by fourteen chapters.

These proposed amendments are to be considered by the National Council that meets in Saratoga the first Wednesday of September, 1840.

ART. II —Add, "The Senate may fill any vacancies in its own number until the next meeting of the Council   It may submit any proposition to all the Senators by correspondence, and they may vote thereon in the same way."

ART. VII.—Substitute the word "eight" for the words "a majority."

ART. IX —Strike out the words, "upon one day's notice and," or strike out the whole clause.

These resolutions were passed :

Resolved, That in the opinion of the National Council no charter should hereafter be granted unless the application be endorsed by at least one Chapter of the Society.

Resolved, That in the opinion of the National Council, there is nothing in the character of the Phi Beta Kappa Society making secrecy obligatory upon any Chapter.

*It was ratified by the Gamma Chapter of Massachusetts in 1863.

General Index.

www.ingramcontent.com/pod-product-compliance
Lightning Source LLC
Chambersburg PA
CBHW020315090426
42735CB00009B/1350